Echoes From the End Zone:
The Men We Became

Lisa Kelly

Lisa Kelly (Photographer: Lynne Gilbert)

Echoes From the End Zone:
The Men We Became

Lisa Kelly

Echoes From the End Zone
The Men We Became
Lisa Kelly
Kelly Creations, LLC

Kelly
CREATIONS

Published by Kelly Creations, LLC
Copyright ©2013 Lisa Kelly
All rights reserved.

No part of this publication may be reproduced, stored in a retrieval system, or transmitted in any form or by any means, electronic, mechanical, photocopying, recording, scanning, or otherwise, except as permitted under Section 107 or 108 of the 1976 United States Copyright Act, without the prior written permission of the Publisher. Requests to the Publisher for permission should be addressed to Permissions Department, Kelly Creations, LLC, LKND93@sbcglobal.net. Portions of some of these chapters appeared online as "Where Are They Now" player interviews on NoCoastBias.com, HerLoyalSons.com, UHND.com and IrishEyes.com under the byline of The Men We Became author Lisa Kelly.

Copyeditor: Mary Ann Falkenberg

Front Cover: Andrew Lamping

Front Cover Photo: Todd Burandt

Library of Congress Cataloging-in-Publication Data
Library of Congress Control Number: 2020912409
Lisa Kelly
Echoes From the End Zone: The Men We Became
ISBN: 978-1-7353488-0-3
Library of Congress subject headings:
1. SPO019000   SPORTS & RECREATION / History   2. SPO015000   SPORTS & RECREATION / Football   3. SPO000000   SPORTS & RECREATION / General

2013

ATTENTION CORPORATIONS, UNIVERSITIES, COLLEGES AND PROFESSIONAL ORGANIZATIONS: Quantity discounts are available on bulk purchases of this book for educational, gift purposes, or as premiums for increasing magazine subscriptions or renewals. Special books or book excerpts can also be created to fit specific needs. For information, please contact Kelly Creations, LLC, LKND93@sbcglobal.net.

For more information visit:
TheMenWeBecame.com, Facebook.com/EchoesFromNotreDame
and Twitter.com/echoesfromnd

Dedication

Dad …
You gave me my earliest memories of Notre Dame. Watching Notre Dame – USC games Thanksgiving weekends, learning my first colorful words and trips back to South Bend as a kid. Your continued love for Our Lady's University and your daily life as a true Notre Dame man have always left me with goals to strive for and achieve. I am so proud to be your daughter and I hope you are proud of me as well. I love you, Dad.

Mom …
You are a wonderful role model. You taught me that I could be whatever I wanted to be: mother, career woman or author. You always showed me that the possibilities were endless, yet ever attainable. Thanks, Mom. I love you.

Jim …
You supported me through all of the long hours of writing, research, phone meetings and travel. You let me follow my passion even when it made family life a little more challenging. Thank you for your love, your most important gift to me of all. I love you.

My Children …
You supported me in this crazy book writing endeavor and overlooked my shortcomings as I worked on this book. I love you both!

Acknowledgements

Oscar McBride
Thank you for helping me get this whole project started and for supporting me every step of the way.

Norm Sanders
Thank you for all of your writing instruction and editing help. This book would not have happened without your countless hours of guidance. I hope you don't cringe every time you see the words Notre Dame.

Tyler Moorehead
Thank you for your time, your valuable Notre Dame knowledge and your countless hours of editing. You never said no, even when you were busy.

Marv Russell
Thank you for always making me feel like anything is possible and for being the best writing coach ever. I have learned so much from you.

Catherine Russell
Thank you for always being able to see the big picture when I could not see the forest through the trees and for always helping me see there is more than one way to look at things.

Lynne Gilbert
Thank you for always being my loudest cheerleader, for always having my back, and for being the best Notre Dame photographer that I have ever known.

Susan Crosby
Thank you, lady, for talking me off the ledge when I didn't think I could go any farther, for being my sister in sports, and for always believing in the "Mayor of Notre Dame."

To my NoCoastBias family
Thank you for giving me my sports writing start and for always supporting me, no matter how crazy or far-fetched the idea.

To my HerLoyalSons family
Thank you for giving me the opportunity to be the only "daughter" at Her Loyal "Sons" and always believing that my writing belongs.

Matt Freeman and Andrew Lamping
Thank you, both, for your never ending support, your Notre Dame knowledge and your design expertise. You guys are on your way to greatness.

TNNDN and my Notre Dame family
Thank you for your never ending love and support and for continuing to amaze me on a daily basis. I love my Notre Dame family!

Table of Contents

Dedication v
Acknowledgments vi
Foreword
     Oscar McBride x
A Note From Coach Holtz xiii
Introduction 1
The Evolution of the Student-Athlete at Notre Dame 3

1.   The Linebacker in the Boardroom:
      Marv Russell 7
2.   The Marketer and Man of Character:
      Alvin Miller 15
3.   The International Waste Manager and Fashion Advisor:
      Allen Rossum 22
4.   The Sports Agent, Lawyer and Entertainer:
      Bobby Brown 30
5.   The Minister and Youth Director:
      Devon McDonald 39
6.   The Police Officer and Field Trainer:
      Joey Getherall 46
7.   The Oil Rig Leadership Consultant and Performance Coach:
      Germaine Holden 55
8.   The Forklift Executive:
      Marc Edwards 61
9.   The Stock Jock in Investment Banking:
      John Foley 68

10.	The Union Liaison and Youth Minister: Luther Bradley	76
11.	The Mentor, Author, Speaker, Coach: Oscar McBride	86
12.	The Motivational Speaker and Youth Empowerment: Mike McCoy	93
13.	The Football Coach: Pat Dolan	99
14.	The Color Man of the Viking Network: Pete Bercich	104
15.	The Smoothie King and Asset Manager: Irv Smith	111
16.	The Athlete Engager and Player Liaison: Reggie Brooks	117
17.	The Pilot and Commercial Construction Entrepreneur: Pat Terrell	124
18.	The Bond Manager and Finance Marketeer: Ryan Leahy	134
19.	The Vintner and Philanthropist: Rick Mirer	141
20.	The Athletic Director and Youth Engager: Vagas Ferguson	148
21.	The Enzyme Booster and Fund Raising Driver: Tim Brown	155
22.	The Influencer: Gerome Sapp	163
23.	The NASCAR Business Developer and Life Changer: Renaldo Wynn	170
24.	The Insurance Broker & Notre Dame Personality Tony Rice	181
25.	The Pharmaceutical Salesman: Mike Townsend	189

Epilogue	199
About the Author	200
Index	203

Foreword

Ahhhh Notre Dame … where do I begin? Some say it's majestic … some say it's indescribable … others say you have to experience it to appreciate it. Some people despise Notre Dame for being the pinnacle of intercollegiate student athletics while others worship the very ground where She stands so proudly. I would be inclined to agree with all those who have a love and respect for Notre Dame. After reading this account of our experiences as student-athletes and our journeys into the men we became I'm sure you will gain a greater appreciation for why we believe Notre Dame to be one of the most incredible places in the world.

Students attend the University of Notre Dame understanding that it's a special place, but still never fully grasp the concept of Her omnipotence until after departing for life "beyond the Golden Dome." Sometimes it takes distance or maybe even some time away from the peace and serenity of Notre Dame's campus to realize how much we took our short stay in Her presence for granted. I guess absence truly does make the heart grow fonder.

Of course, there are high academic standards and the pressure to consistently perform at the highest level comes as briskly as the fall breeze on a cool October evening… but there's even more to the Notre Dame experience than that. There's so much more to the experience than what is seen on television or maybe what can be surmised experiencing the electricity in the air at a football game in Notre Dame Stadium on a crisp Saturday afternoon.

Being a student at Notre Dame is tough enough – we all agreed. Now add an additional 20 hours of working out, lifting, film study, practice and games to that equation and you have the life of a *student-athlete*. Your life becomes consumed with the duality of sport and education … not to mention the challenge of leaving your own personal mark within the incredible depth of Notre Dame's Lore. As a football player at the University of Notre Dame, athletes are held to an even higher standard given the ever-present microscope they are placed under. *Nothing* is done without media scrutiny, public opinion or judgment by fellow students; which in itself, presents a completely different set of challenges.

There are no co-ed dorms, curfew is at midnight and there isn't even a Greek system on campus for those who might want to pledge a fraternity or sorority. Let's not forget to mention the weather, nicknamed "perma-cloud" which shows up around mid-October and lasts sometimes until the end of April bringing the worst cold and snow in the land.

For some of these very reasons, our football team became its own fraternity. A fraternity of brothers who would sweat, bleed and cry together ... a fraternity of brothers who helped each other get through the dark times and who learned to love each other more than the challenges they combated. A fraternity of brothers who, even today, are still bound by those experiences enshrouded by an unquenchable love for Notre Dame and everything She taught us.

From the classroom to the dorm and from the practice field to game day, our lives were consumed with Notre Dame Football and the tremendous expectations that fueled our quest for greatness. One of the things that made our time special was the leadership of the upperclassmen who showed us what it meant to be Notre Dame Men. We were taught how to be men of character, integrity and how to garner the most intent focus our young minds could muster. That said, leadership was passed down from class to class and team to team without fail.

All in all I wouldn't change my Notre Dame experience for the world ... and I'm sure that my brethren would say the same to you if such a conversation were to ever ensue. "Notre Dame is a special place," they would unanimously say; still taking into consideration the difficulty and challenges they all faced during their "Notre Dame Years" which shaped them into the men they are today.

The following is an account of some of those moments that only a select few know about. The author, Lisa Kelly, has given us the opportunity to share some of those moments with you and to be heard in our own words. She has captured some of our most vibrant memories and stories in this collection and we hope you enjoy reading them as much as we enjoyed the experience.

Thank you Lisa....
Go Irish...Forever!

Oscar B. McBride
Tight-End
University of Notre Dame du Lac '94

Notre Dame vs. Northwestern 1995. Football Coach Lou Holtz talking with players before running onto the field. (Photographer: Joe Raymond, photo courtesy of Notre Dame Archives.)

A Note From Coach Holtz

Students come to Notre Dame from all different walks of life and from all different parts of the country. They have different thoughts, different ideas, different values and different goals. However, they all have one thing in common, and that is, they were coming to Notre Dame and their lives would never be the same again.

It has been my honor to coach and watch so many young student-athletes develop into men who represent this great institution in so many impressive ways. From the moment I arrived at Notre Dame I realized that this University is not about football, it's about life. You should get two educations at Notre Dame. One is an education on how to make a living and the other one is how to make a life.

What we believe when we are young is predicated entirely on what our parents believe. I'm talking political, social and religious beliefs. As we get older, our thoughts, ideas and beliefs change, and we begin to make choices for ourselves and these choices influence our lives forever. That's why it's so important to be around good people in a very special environment so that when you make these choices you greatly increase your chance for success and happiness.

I had the privilege to coach many of the young men in this book and I have come to know many of the others of whom Lisa has told their stories. Men like Oscar McBride, Tim Brown, Mike Townsend, and Mike McCoy represent rare individuals who came to Notre Dame and had their lives changed forever.

While these individuals came from all different walks of life, they left Notre Dame with one parting thought that united them forever. They not only wanted to be successful, but they also wanted to be significant. Successful is when you make a lot of money, and when you die that ends. When you're significant, you help other people be successful, and that lasts many lifetimes.

    These men are significant and they strive each day to make an impact and difference in all things that they touch. These are Notre Dame student-athletes and I'm proud to have been a part of their lives. Lisa, thank you for your work and sharing with the Notre Dame Family what you so appropriately have named, "Echoes from the End Zone: The Men We Became."

Lou Holtz

Quarterback Tony Rice (#9) and Coach Lou Holtz walking on the sidelines, 1988. (Photo courtesy Notre Dame Archives.)

Introduction

On any level, it would seem hard to believe that I would have anything in common with a 6'5" African American football player who grew up in a single parent household in the south and battled on a daily basis to keep up with his peers at Notre Dame, who went on to play football in the NFL and then faced many struggles in making the transition from the fame and glitz of playing professional football to beginning a career and starting the next chapter of his life. But after listening to him tell his story, and the path which he has taken, I realized that my journey is not really that much different from his or the other 24 former student-athletes who allowed me to probe every aspect of their lives. From growing up, to playing football at Notre Dame, to starting new careers and families, I searched for the values and circumstances that drove these men to success both on and off the field. I sought to understand how family and faith played a role in who they became. And I sought to understand the significance and importance of the Notre Dame experience and the impact this experience continues to play in their growth and development as husbands, fathers, professionals and representatives of the Notre Dame experience.

As I completed each interview, I realized that we share similar journeys. We may have come from different backgrounds and had different goals, but the molding and shaping that we received at Notre Dame helped us grow into the men (and women) we are today. None of their paths are perfect. They are full of struggles and challenges, pitfalls and mistakes. They are full of derailments and redirection, yet full of success, celebration and moments of glory. But in every story, Notre Dame is at the heart of their life. A Value Stream that pulls them from every corner of the United States – that steers them to accept responsibility and accountability for their choices and decisions in life – that launched them into adulthood. They each discovered that Our Lady would provide strength to overcome adversity, perseverance to address the greatest challenges and empathy and humility to support them in the most difficult of circumstances.

The Notre Dame Value Stream is the core of this University. It demands integrity and the support of the community. It develops principles of leadership and rewards excellence in every endeavor. It is a constant search for spirituality, leading to discernment in decision-making in every aspect of life. This Value Stream is experienced by each student of this University and stays with them through their entire life. It's what draws and guides students to a small Midwestern community and charts their course during their time at the University. It's what sails them through the rest of their lives. It teaches them how to make it through the rough seas, and to celebrate the peaceful sunsets as well. Every story of these modern day gladiators brought me back to this calming force of the Notre Dame Value Stream, which gave these men the skills and strengths to make the right decisions, and to deal with the consequences when they made the wrong decisions. It's what keeps each Notre Dame man and woman grounded and looking forward to the future. It's what makes each one of us want to strive for greatness within ourselves, and to impart it to others as well. It's what connects the Notre Dame family, no matter our differences. It's what makes anyone who has stepped foot on the grounds of the Golden Dome, regardless of their connection to Our Lady's School, their faith or ethnic origin, to find love and respect for what Notre Dame represents.

As I have walked these men through their journeys, they have each (whether they realized it or not) passed along words of wisdom that I will share with you. The Notre Dame Value Stream has ever so carefully steered them along their respective paths, through rough waters and calm. Notre Dame did so much more for each of them than just prepare them for the football field. It prepared them for all of the adversities that they would face along life's stream. As you read each one of these stories, you gain a better understanding of what Our Lady's University means and has done for so many. And for those fellow Domers like myself, I hope it reconnects you to the Value Stream that drew you to Notre Dame and how She taught us to live our lives.

Lisa Kelly
University of Notre Dame '93
Author, Echoes From the End Zone: The Men We Became

The Evolution of the Student-Athlete at Notre Dame

"I didn't know what in the hell I was doing when I first took the job," said Mike DeCicco, a mechanical engineering professor at Notre Dame back in 1964 when he accepted Father Joyce's offer to become the Chief Academic Advisor of Student-Athletes, a newly created position. Notre Dame Executive Vice President Rev. Edmund P. Joyce C.S.C. and then President Father Theodore Hesburgh had a vision and felt a moral commitment that the University's excellence in athletics wasn't good enough. This was Notre Dame; and Our Lady of Victory was ready to create a new era in collegiate sports. No - these young men would become much more than mere "jocks" – instead now and forever known as "Notre Dame Student-Athletes".

In a 1988 interview with *Blue & Gold Illustrated*,[1] Mike recalled he had no idea what to do, but it was clear that Hesburgh and Joyce would know success when they saw it. "There was no template or benchmark for success. I'd sit down with a kid and ask how his school work was going. He'd say, 'Okay.' I'd say, 'Fine.' And that was that. Then when grades would be posted, I'd discover a lot were not doing as well as they said they were." Mike quickly learned he had to stay on top of each student-athlete's progress on a weekly basis, not once they were in academic trouble.

Mike created a methodology that would become the model for the best universities, and a standard to be adopted by the NCAA. During Mike's time as the ND Athletic Department's Chief Academic Advisor, ninety-nine percent who were enrolled and stayed in school for four years graduated. In 1988, Notre Dame became the first school ever to win a football national title while at the same time graduating one hundred percent of its players. Of the 59

---

[1] Mike DeCicco quotes taken from: http://notredame.247sports.com/Article/Notre-Dame-Mourns-Death-Of-Mike-DeCicco-123852.

other College Football Association member institutions who returned results that year, the graduation rate was 50.7 percent.

Mike always credited Father Joyce and Father Hesburgh for having the vision to create a position that many felt was unnecessary. "They recognized the constraints and time-factor difficulties student-athletes would eventually have with the increased emphasis on intercollegiate sports." Mike said. The three of them felt that if they were asking athletes to give their service and energy to the University, the University at the very least could assure them an equal chance to earn a degree along with the rest of their fellow classmates.

Mike's team set up tutorial services and a ten day orientation program which taught time management and proper study habits, and a summer school program; all of which have been a mandatory part of the academic year of a student-athlete for years. Luther Bradley and Marv Russell, two of the former student-athletes featured in this book, recalled Mike's role in their lives. "Two-months before we arrived on campus to start summer camp, we received a letter from this guy named Mike outlining academic expectations and what he and his team would do to insure our success in school."

Marv recalled, "I was a good student, studying theology which is a very tough major at a religious school like ND. Coach DeCicco (also the Notre Dame Fencing Coach) called me into his office and told me what it was going to take to be successful. He said 'Marv, this is how it's going to be. The minute I suspect you are not cutting it or you're having problems, we are going to reassess your major.' He said, 'I want you to meet with a graduate assistant every two weeks to assess your progress. Remember: you will get no breaks or special consideration.' I did what I was told and I was successful. Forty years later I saw Coach at a Notre Dame function and he still recalled that story. What made me feel great was when he said, 'I'm proud of you Marv and what you have accomplished.'"

Luther was focused on business as his major. He and Marv laughed at Luther's story of being called into Coach DeCicco's office for a chat, "You remember that fencing sword he had mounted over his desk? I walked into his office and sat down and all he said was, 'You see the sword behind me? If you don't get busy and study harder, you are going to find that sword up your ass.' Coach never minced words." Luther said, "I wasn't doing that bad in class, but he felt I wasn't working to my potential. He wanted our best just like Ara did on the field." Both Luther and Marv said what was even more important was if you weren't performing in the classroom you could bet Ara knew and it was likely Moose Krause the AD knew and you were going to hear from all of them.

The football players interviewed in this book all realize how they benefited from the evolution of the Notre Dame "student-athlete" concept.

Notre Dame is not an easy place for any student, let alone for those who have the additional demands of athletics. Without this visionary program, many athletes would be left by the wayside, as they are at so many other schools. Today, thanks to the leadership of Mike DeCicco, Father Hesburgh and Father Joyce, Notre Dame consistently leads NCAA schools in graduation rates and overall academic performance.

Coach DeCicco passed away in the spring of 2013. His impact on Notre Dame and the NCAA schools will be a legacy for decades to come. Notre Dame student-athletes owe a debt of thanks to this Loyal Son.

Mike DeCicco was Notre Dame at its finest – he was the Notre Dame Value Stream at work.

Marvin Russell, Notre Dame vs. Navy 1974.
(Photo courtesy of Notre Dame Archives.)

CHAPTER ONE

The Linebacker in the Boardroom
Marv Russell

"It had all the fiery passion from a Martin Luther King Jr. speech," wrote local reporter Dave Croyle about a July 4th anniversary celebration. "Only this man could cross the boundaries of races and nationalities, uniting each person into the common bond of community. His fervor conjured up the spirit of Ford City's past. His voice ignited patriotism of not only those who fought in our national wars, but also fought the wars of everyday life…" The voice this small town heard was that of Marv Russell, author, keynote speaker, global leadership expert and ordained Methodist minister.

Growing up in a Methodist family and wanting to become a minister, Marv's early path did not seem to include a later stop as a football player at Notre Dame. A young man who dealt with adversity many times and at one point was diagnosed with dyslexia, Marv put his strong work ethic and determination to good *use on the way to a successful collegiate football career and becoming a book author, consultant and nationally known leadership expert in the business world. His journey to Our Lady's University may not have been a direct one, but he knew what he wanted and was not afraid to go out and get it. How does a Methodist young man study theology at a Catholic University, one of the toughest and most analytical degrees at Notre Dame, and also become a starting middle linebacker and go on to enjoy a successful business career? It's not easy, so what was his journey?*

Notre Dame has never been a place where athletes lazily walk through courses designed as easy A's for jocks. Marv proved this point. When he got to Notre Dame and told them he wanted to study theology, they told him he was crazy, "Not only did I have a learning disability, but theology was a difficult degree to be undertaking while also playing football." Notre Dame did their best to try to talk him out of this major but he stuck to his guns. "It took a great deal of effort for me to succeed both academically and on the football field, but I feel that I gained so much from that experience. I met a Notre Dame professor and his wife at one of my speaking engagements recently. When they realized I majored in theology as a student-athlete, they were shocked. That still makes me feel good."

"My leadership framework and philosophy, and the behaviors of leadership that I practice, all come from and were exemplified by Ara Parseghian. He was not a philosophical leader, but his style of motivation, engagement and inspiration took our performance to the next level. That was a unique skill that Coach possessed. He has told me that he thinks I give him more credit than he deserves, but I disagree. He was not a coach who demanded that you follow him, but rather you wanted to follow him because he inspired you, and gave you more strength and confidence than you ever thought you had."

But the day Marv opened a letter from the Notre Dame football office he was devastated, "I went into shock, my mother cried and my dad dropped his head. This was a letter from Ara and it said simply, '*We regret to inform you that our offer for you to play for the Fighting Irish must be rescinded.*'" Ara's message was clear: this was a great player, a solid person who had great values, but Marv's academic scores did not meet Notre Dame's standards, and that academics were an integral part of the University. "I was humiliated and hurt, everything that I dreamed of was gone." Yes, his life had changed, but quickly he would discover a new chapter had just begun.

With his parents each working two jobs, the most important decisions of his life were being made. These decisions were about committing to what was important to your life. It was about growing and beginning to mature as a young man. "I went to college prep school for a year after high school, took the college boards again, and got in to Notre Dame. While I was at Wyoming Seminary College Preparatory School, they diagnosed me with a slight case of dyslexia. They also taught me how to study, which made a big difference in my studying habits and in my academic success." Just a few adjustments made such a huge difference for Marv. After you've been told you're not ready, you're not good enough, most 17 year olds would give up. Not this family, not Marv, you make it anyway, "Notre Dame became even more special to me. I wanted it. I wanted to prove myself."

Like any western Pennsylvania kid, Marv grew up following such schools as Pitt, Penn State and West Virginia, but then he got hooked on Notre Dame by listening to their Sunday morning broadcasts with Lindsey Nelson. (In the pre-cable TV era, edited replays of Notre Dame football games were aired on Sunday mornings.) He thought the school was interesting and very intriguing, and the Notre Dame mystique really drew him. Marv grew up in a very staunch Catholic community. These were blue-collar workers who worked in the plate glass plant and steel mills. "Once I started to experience some success playing football, everyone wanted to know if I wanted to go to Notre Dame. I really wanted to be a Methodist minister, but the idea of studying theology at Notre Dame was very inspiring to me, even though I am not Catholic."

Even with his academic challenges Pitt, Michigan State, West Virginia and Ohio State chomped at the bit to get their hands on this recruit. That letter from Ara was a new beginning, "I wasn't even a student, yet the Notre Dame Value Stream was changing my life. I had taken a different path. Going to college preparatory school was great for me but it was still a gamble as to whether or not I would actually get into Notre Dame, but it worked. It helped me mature and begin to realize my potential. When I got the final acceptance into Notre Dame, other academic institutions such as Bucknell and Colgate also offered me scholarship opportunities. Things really changed for me in that year. I went from being a great athlete to being a great student-athlete and Notre Dame was definitely where I wanted to be."

For every man who has donned the blue and gold, there is at least one moment that truly summarizes what it means to be a part of Notre Dame and to play football for Our Lady. "You never forget those moments when all things in life are perfect. We were sitting on the bus, late on December 31, 1973 (or early on January 1), on the way back to the hotel. We were celebrating that we had just won the National Championship an hour before. Unbelievable. Everyone else in the world was celebrating New Year's Eve, but we had something extra special to celebrate."

Marv describes another one of those great moments in life that he will never forget, "You never forget the first moment when you run out of the tunnel as a Notre Dame football player, it is quite remarkable. The first home game my freshman year, running out of the tunnel on that beautiful fall day was incredible. I can remember being so choked up, tears in my eyes. It was pure. When you go from the concrete and your spikes hit that grass cushion: that is why you go to Notre Dame – a Saturday afternoon doing battle on that field is one of the most perfect places in the world. You think about all the students who have gone to ND or will go in the future – when you think about all of the people in this country who love college and professional football, you suddenly realize how blessed you are and that very few will have that experience."

Being a football player at Notre Dame has a certain amount of camaraderie, tradition and lore that comes along with it. But being a part of a national championship team has a spirit all its own. "As a freshman, and being one of the few freshmen who was able to play that year, it was a pretty special experience for me. I had never been on a winning team the whole time I played football. As we kept winning games I was thinking, 'Wow ... is this what it's really like?'" Marv was a freshman when Notre Dame played Southern Cal at home in 1973. "Winning that game was when we started to believe. We looked at the rest of the schedule, and how up to that point we were just dominating teams, and we just knew we could continue to roll. Our last game of the regular season was against Miami; we played them in the old Orange Bowl. Coach (Ara) Parseghian reminded us that we still had one more game to go, and that we had better not forget this team because we were in their house and were ripe for the picking. We had no problem beating Miami, but those are the games that tend to upset apple carts."

At the end of the 1973 season Notre Dame was ranked third, and headed to the Sugar Bowl to play No. 1 ranked Alabama. Oklahoma was No. 2, but was ineligible to play in a bowl game. "There were three undefeated teams that year, and yet the championship game ended up being No. 1 playing No. 3. How fortunate were we? And we proved to the nation that we deserved to be there, narrowly defeating them in a tremendous game, 24-23."

Each coach who has ever coached at Notre Dame has his own style of leadership and vision of how to translate his Xs and Os onto the field. The success of any one team often depends on how well the coaching staff and players work together in executing said plan. But having to transition from one head coach to a new head coach during your brief collegiate career can be challenging even for the most successful of players.

"A good coach will make his players see what they can be rather than what they are." -Ara Parseghian

Marv spoke of his teammate and friend, both in their freshman season, "Luther Bradley was so nervous before he started his first game. Coach Parseghian taps him on the back and tells him, 'I would not put you in a circumstance if I didn't think you could succeed. We are going to be there for you. Just be Luther Bradley and do what you do best.' He had several interceptions that day. Ara did what Ara did best: Engagement ... motivation ... inspiration.

You can motivate people in many ways, but when you motivate them through inspiration, that's the difference. Your mind, body and soul all want to succeed."

Marv reflected on the departure of Coach Parseghian and arrival of Dan Devine. Times were different in the mid-70s. When a coach left the team everyone was upset but that was life, another learning experience, "We all knew Coach Devine was not going to inspire in the same way that Coach Parseghian had. Coach Devine was a strategic, philosophical kind of leader. He sat back and let his lieutenants do the engagement, while he was the leader who was successfully pulling it all together, molding the talent and creating an environment that led to that success. Those were Devine's gifts."

Marv would not be one of the very few that would go to a career in the NFL. The wear and tear on his knees had taken its toll, "When I graduated there were two football leagues, the NFL and the World Football league. I had a chance to try-out with the Denver Broncos, but I turned it down due to the fact that I had just come off knee surgery, was recently married and had a child on the way."

"The Chicago Blitz, from the World Football League, was very persistent in pursuing me to come for a tryout. I went to their fall camp, but my heart just was not in it. I was not that big of a guy compared to the other linebackers. Mostly I went to camp to have the opportunity to experience it, but I realized that my priorities had changed. I knew the odds of having a successful professional football career were long. I did, however, run the 40-yard dash in 4.9 seconds … pretty impressive for a 5'11, 240-pound linebacker in those days. I wrote about the experience in a local newspaper article."

"My goal post-college was to save the world. I wanted to be the next Martin Luther King, Jr. I became a Methodist minister the summer after my junior year at Notre Dame, and was doing some work in a local church. My first job out of college was at South Bend Youth Services Bureau. Then I was a probation officer for the St Joseph County Probation Department in Indiana. I was promoted from there to be the chief probation officer in Elkhart County Probation Department, and then the State Deputy Director for Indiana Civil Rights Commission. I loved working in social services, and I loved my job until a new governor got voted in and I lost my job."

"At that point I landed a job as a Human Resources manager for a local company, Carrier Corporation, and I ended up seeing more success than I ever imagined. After working my way up the corporate ladder at several companies, including assignments living in Europe, I ended up as the Senior Vice President of Human Resources for Ascension Healthcare (www.ascensionhealth.org), which is the largest Catholic healthcare organization and largest not-for-profit healthcare company in America with over 100,000 employees."

The transition from social services to human resources was not difficult for this former linebacker. After all this is a man whose entire life has been focused on people, "In the early days I pastored two churches, but when I took the human resources job, I found that my new career took up too much of my time and travel. I was not able to dedicate myself the way I wanted to, to my churches. But no matter what career I was in, I always was a speaker. I went to law school for one year and ended up hating it because it not only took so much time away from my family but we were young and getting started, I needed to work to provide for my family. But I finished my Master's Degree from Indiana University while our kids were still little, which helped me move up the corporate ladder."

"After many years in corporate human resources and living and working as an expat nearly 10 years in Paris, France, and Copenhagen, Denmark, and traveling and working in nearly 30 countries, I decided to start my own company. I wanted to be that person who develops and motivates and inspires people. I knew that I was good in front of a crowd, so it seemed like a logical transition to me."

"In 2011 I wrote my book, 'Linebacker in the Boardroom: Lessons in Life and Leadership,' (www.marvrussell.com), and began my leadership consulting business. I'm a keynote speaker for corporations, associations and academic environments to inspire and teach them to be better leaders. Being on stage is almost like running out on that field the first day. I am inspired and driven and feel myself at full capacity. Motivational speaking is a gift, and I love my gift. I try to do six to eight speeches a month, inspiring people of all walks of life: leaders, young people, preaching on Sundays in a church, student-athletes, Notre Dame campus events and Alumni Club events ... any chance I can get to inspire others."

"I had been talking about writing a book for years, when suddenly I felt it. I knew exactly what I was going to write. It just all started coming together. I wanted to write a book that really talked about leadership and ethical behavior, but I also wanted it to be about my story of leadership and to introduce my leadership philosophy. I explain in the book how that leadership philosophy molds and shapes a person. I watch our politicians, how so many of them totally and completely are letting us down as leaders, and how integrity and trust matter in leadership. I challenge the leaders of the world to build their foundations on integrity and trust. This foundation consists of the 3 E's – Essential (performance), Exceptional (performance), and Ethical (performance). You need to figure out what it is that you do as a leader that is essential to others, do it exceptionally and ethically, and then use it as a sustainable ability to lead others. Essential Exceptional Ethical Leadership™ has become my trademarked theme and philosophy around my consultant and keynote activities."

"The most important thing for me is not necessarily the fact that I overcame the odds, but that I can use my experiences to inspire, mold and shape other people. Being successful as a student-athlete is one of the most difficult things you can do, especially at Notre Dame, and it is a big part of how I came to be the person I am today."

Marv recently finished writing his second book, 'Finding Your Internship: What Employers Want You To Know,' designed to teach students how to find the ideal internship and how to be successful in the business world. Marv and his wife Catherine live between Chicago and South Florida. They've been married nearly four decades and were the first undergraduate couple married while at Notre Dame. They have two adult children, Angela and Marvin Charles who live and work in the Chicago area.

Marvin Russell

Lessons from Marv's Notre Dame Value Stream of Life:

- The time that athletes should be getting advice is when they come to Notre Dame, not when they are leaving. They should be looking at the Notre Dame experience as one that is going to last for the rest of their lives. Every day when I sit at Starbucks and write, someone comes up to me and says, 'You played football at Notre Dame, right? You wrote that book, right?' There is something special about who you are when you are a product of Notre Dame.
- Many of the players that played the 10 years before (current Irish coach) Brian Kelly don't understand what they got from the Notre Dame Value Stream. They don't get that even though they didn't win many games, they still won a way of life. They won integrity, which is something many players leave behind.
- What I would say to those college athletes who receive the gift of playing in the NFL is the Lord giveth and He taketh away - just like that. NFL careers, they come and go so quickly but your Notre Dame education, relationships and values last a lifetime.
- In the face of adversity, we must find renewed inspiration.
- Each of us will face derailment at some point in our lives. This derailment must be viewed as a learning opportunity.

Notre Dame vs. Army, 1985. Allen Pinkett (#20) running with the ball while Alvin Miller (#17) blocks. (Photographer: Joe Raymond, photo courtesy of Notre Dame Archives.)

CHAPTER TWO

The Marketer and Man of Character
Alvin Miller

Life in St. Louis, Missouri, is a unique one. When you are introduced to a native St. Louis resident, the first question they ask you will have nothing to do with what you do for a living or where you went to college, it will be, "Where did you go to high school?" The answer to this question has become more important to Alvin Miller than he ever might have guessed. Alvin was not only a high school football standout at St. Louis' Kirkwood High School, named Parade Magazine's All-American Player of the Year his senior year of high school, but he was also a track star. He almost single-handedly won the state track meet for Kirkwood High School in 1983, when he captured four individual events: the 100 Meters, 110 Hurdles, 300 Hurdles and 200 Meters. He was named a National High School Track and Field All-American in 1983 and Hertz No. 1 Performing Athlete of Missouri that same year. Alvin still holds Kirkwood High School track records in the 100 Meters, 200 Meters and 110 Hurdles and the track at Kirkwood High bears his name. The reason his name is on Kirkwood's track is not due to the records he holds, it is because of his character and how he gave back to others and his school. Today he coaches the 8th grade football team that feeds into the Kirkwood High squad. "Do unto others as you wish to have them do unto you. If you want people to be a good citizen to you, be a good citizen to them. What I did off the track is more what I am remembered for, than what I did on the track."

Alvin earned four varsity letters in basketball, three in football and two in track and field. After a visit from head coach Gerry Faust, Alvin decided to commit to playing football at the University of Notre Dame. After a somewhat turbulent collegiate career and a knee injury that would prevent Alvin from playing in the NFL, he went on to construct a successful career for himself, first in the travel industry and later in sales and marketing, which he continues to this day. Alvin currently resides in St. Louis with his wife Romona and their three children Scottie, Ariel and Lauryn.

Like so many of his peers, the importance of receiving his Notre Dame degree is never so clear as it is when it comes time to put it to use. "After I graduated from Notre Dame I went to training camp with the Buffalo Bills (1988). I had so many lingering problems from my knee injuries that I knew I would not last long in the NFL so my career ended with training camp. Never was I so thankful to have a degree from Notre Dame. I started my career as a travel director with Maritz Travel Company (www.maritztravel.com). My job was to take top sales leaders from various companies on business trips and to sales meetings. I got to take them to such events as the Super Bowl, the US Open, and destinations such as France and Hawaii. I was with them for 14 years and it was an amazing experience. After 14 years of traveling though, I was at a point where I wanted to settle down and start a family, and it was time to find something that didn't have me away so much."

"After my 14 years at Maritz, I took a position as a territory sales manager for Altria, the parent company for Phillip Morris USA (http://www.altria.com). I currently work in their sales and marketing division and have been there for 15 years now. It's the perfect fit for me as it allows me to use my people skills and be able to be an integral part in raising my family."

When Alvin was growing up, Notre Dame football was not aired on NBC every Saturday like it is today. On Sunday mornings, however, you could watch the replay of the game from the day before. It was run without commercials and they cut out the unnecessary parts of the game so you could enjoy it without interruptions. "When they would get to the part where the commercials would have been, the narrator would say, 'and we move to further action.' They just gave you the good stuff. I would watch these replays every Sunday before church. This was my first exposure to ND football."

When Alvin was looking at colleges he narrowed his choices down to five schools: Illinois, Iowa, Missouri, UCLA and Notre Dame. He took official visits to each one of those schools with the exception of Missouri. "I had great experiences at each of the schools in different ways. Illinois was probably the most fun, and UCLA was cool because it was my first visit to California. Those two stood out to me. The best combination of football and academics, though, was Notre Dame. My host during my official visit to ND was strong safety Joe Johnson." Alvin's trip to Notre Dame was the first of the official trips that he took and he traveled to South Bend in December. "I'll never forget it. They came to St. Louis and picked me up in a private plane so that I could play in my basketball game that Friday night, and when we got to South Bend the plane flew around the Dome. It was my first flight ever and it was this tiny little plane and all I remember was that my ears were killing me! I was so glad when we finally landed."

"Notre Dame is just special. People ask me to describe it. I say if you've been here, no explanation is necessary. If you haven't been, no explanation will suffice." ~Lou Holtz

When it came time for Alvin to make his final decision, he sat down and made a list. What did he want to get out of college? During this process the Notre Dame Value Stream stood out to Alvin and it quickly became apparent that this was where his path was headed. "If I wanted to play pro football, to stay healthy, get a good education, Notre Dame seemed like a good fit for me. There were a lot of guys there (at ND) who were similar to me and not only did you have the opportunity to get a good education at Notre Dame, they stressed to the student-athletes how important it was to actually finish your degree before you left. When it came right down to it, Notre Dame was the only school that left me with the feeling that if I chose another school ... would I always be wondering 'what if?' That pretty much sealed the deal for me."

Playing one sport at Notre Dame is a challenge, let alone two, but Alvin was not afraid of the challenge. In fact, he embraced it. "It was kind of an interesting situation for me. In high school I played three sports, and by only playing two sports at ND I felt like I should have been doing more. The busier I was, the better I was able to manage my time. When I was not playing any sports, I always felt like I had plenty of time to get things done and then never got anything done."

When asked about the highlights of his Notre Dame career, there were moments, teams and people that definitely stood out for Alvin. "USC was definitely the game that I most looked forward to each season, because that was the game that was most talked about. USC was such a popular team at the time and getting to put on the green jersey was incredible." The best player he played with? Without hesitation he answered, "Without a doubt, wide receiver

Tim Brown." The best player he played against? "The best player I played against had to be quarterback Bernie Kosar (University of Miami)."

And then, of course, there is that one shining moment. "In 1983, my freshman year, we went down to Memphis to play in the Liberty Bowl. It was my first bowl game, it was absolutely freezing, and I caught a touchdown pass. Not only did I catch a touchdown pass, but that was the only touchdown pass that I caught my entire career at Notre Dame. We beat Doug Flutie and Boston College, 19-18. I also remember meeting Miss America, Vanessa Williams, in the lobby of our hotel. She had spoken to our team earlier, but then I bumped into her in the lobby. Quite memorable!"

Alvin had the opportunity to play under two different head coaches during his time at Notre Dame: Gerry Faust and Lou Holtz. The two could not have been any more different, but each brought their strengths to the table. "Compare it to this. A young man graduates high school and goes to college to play football. A lot of freshmen never get to play their first year. Coach Faust left a high school coaching position and went straight to a head coaching position at Notre Dame, and so in a sense he was a freshman. It was tough for him to have consistent success early on."

"Coach Holtz, on the other hand, had already been coaching at other colleges. He came in to Notre Dame as a seasoned veteran, and so, in a sense, he came in as a senior and was completely ready for the job. Faust still beat some big time teams, who were really upset, even though overall he had little success during his time at Notre Dame."

Alvin's path at Notre Dame had some ups and downs the same as anyone else. I asked him to talk about his situation with the NFL agents and whether or not he would have done anything differently.

(Notre Dame wide receiver Alvin Miller has been declared ineligible for his (fifth year) senior season because he signed with New York agent Norby Walters, the Atlanta Journal-Constitution reported. The newspaper claimed Notre Dame Athletic Director Gene Corrigan admitted that the University and Miller made up a story last month that the senior would not return for the 1987 season because of a knee injury. But Corrigan, who is leaving Notre Dame to become commissioner of the Atlantic Coast Conference, refuted the charge in a prepared statement.)[2]

"Quite honestly, if you would have asked me this question in my early to mid-twenties, I probably would not have answered you. It was such a traumatic event in my life and it really felt like the end of the world to me. But as a forty-something man, with some time and perspective on the situation, I realize that it was just part of the journey and it has made me who I am today." The Notre Dame Value Stream kept Alvin standing tall during some of his

---

[2] Excerpt from the Los Angeles Times. Read more: http://articles.latimes.com/1987-07-19/sports/sp-4984_1_notre-dame

most difficult moments and supported him as he moved forward through his life's journey. "I really appreciated the tough love and support I received from Coach Holtz and Mr. Corrigan. Father Hesburgh meeting with me in a private court room was a spiritual-like moment. I was very hurt that the NCAA never spoke to me about this and never has. They declared me ineligible (to return for a fifth year) but I was gone after my fourth year of playing."

Today, Alvin spends a great deal of his time working with youth. He shares his views on life and his experiences hopefully to help prevent them from making the same mistakes he made. "Here is my advice to young people who are embarking on their journey: be aware that everyone is going to try to entice you and manipulate you to do something that is not the right thing to do. Sometimes you do the wrong thing for the right reason. But the one thing that comes along with making that wrong decision is that once it happens, you can never take it back. Before you do something that you think might possibly be questionable or wrong, ask a few people for advice. Talk to others first. Don't just listen to one person and do something that you may possibly regret in the future."

"Things that looked so devastating, so bad to a 20 or 22 year-old, look much different to me now. Now I want to share my experiences with others to teach them how to make better decisions. Once you sign your name to something, you can't take that back five hours later when you realize that you've made a mistake. You're in too deep — signed, sealed and delivered — it's too late. Make good decisions and then you will never have to live with that regret."

Living and working in his hometown of St. Louis, Missouri, allows Alvin to remain active at his former high school in Kirkwood and to be able to pursue his passion of working with area youth. "It's pretty great. I am still very active at the high school and with their athletic programs. Currently, I coach the 8th grade football team that feeds into the Kirkwood High School football team. I make the kids look at my name on the track and talk to them about it. The records that I hold at Kirkwood High School in track and field are just a small part of why that track is named after me. When I was in high school, I interacted with everybody. So many people remember me because I did not keep to myself; I had friends in all walks of life. They may not have played sports with me but they may remember a time in which I helped them out in school. The reason my name is on that track is because of my character and how I gave back to others and my school. Do unto others as you wish to have them do unto you. If you want people to be a good citizen to you, be a good citizen to them. What I did off the track is more what I am remembered for than what I did on the track."

During his journey through Notre Dame, head coach Lou Holtz was an integral part of Alvin's successes. Coach Holtz made sure that his young men had the support network they needed to become the best young men possible. He prepared them for what they experienced on the field as well as life after football. His words of wisdom, however, often came with a little Holtz humor. "During Coach Holtz's first year at Notre Dame, we were in a 4th down situation with two yards to go and Coach Holtz called a time out. He was trying to figure out whether or not we could get these two yards. The offensive line was already pretty pumped up and so first Coach Holtz asks the right tackle, 'Can you beat your man?' And he responds with a resounding, 'Yes!' Then he asks the guard, 'Can you push your guy back?' And he answers with a resounding 'Yes!' He asks the entire line, 'Can you do it?' And in unison they say, 'Yes!' And then Holtz says, 'Okay, let's punt.'"

Alvin is currently about four or five chapters away from coming out with his book. The book is a narrative of his high school and collegiate athletic careers along with his life thoughts mixed into it. "The timing of this book could not be better. The Kirkwood High School football team just won the Missouri State Football Championships and Notre Dame just played in the national title game against Alabama, this is my year for sure. I have been working on the book for two years with my writer. I had been talking about writing it for about seven or eight years, and two years ago I finally decided to do it. I want my book to pay tribute to the guys that I looked up to when I was in high school and college. I want to give credit to the outstanding athletic things that they did along with the incredible character that they had — guys like Tim Brown and Michael Jordan. I want to show people that, while your son is trying to be like Tim Brown when he grows up, you had better prepare him just in case he ends up being like Alvin Miller. To play pro football was my dream, but to get an education was my goal."

In addition to working with youth through his high school, Alvin is currently involved in a not-for-profit Christian group called Hope Unlimited (www.hopeunlimitedkirkwood.org). They are dedicated to building relationships that change lives through one-on-one tutoring and mentoring, Bible study and discipleship, summer camp, sports, work training/placement and exciting field trips. They work primarily with at-risk youth in the metropolitan St. Louis area and introduce them to Jesus Christ. "All kids today are at risk and need positive role models and uplifting relationships to steer them in the right direction. Our goal is to equip them with the skills they need to become productive members of society in their families, schools and places of employment."

Alvin and Romona Miller and their three children Scottie, Ariel and Lauryn.

Lessons from Alvin's Notre Dame Value Stream of Life:

- Make good careful decisions and then you will never have to live with regret.
- Look to multiple people for advice and not just one person. The more information that you can gather to prepare yourself will allow you to make the best decision possible.
- Do unto others as you wish to have them do unto you. If you want people to be a good citizen to you, be a good citizen to them.

Player Allen Rossum (#15) on the field in between plays. 1996.
(Notre Dame University Photograph, photo courtesy of Notre Dame Archives.)

CHAPTER THREE

The International Waste Manager and Fashion Advisor Allen Rossum

What do careers in waste management, high end apparel and fashion, and facilitating sales to first-time home buyers have in common? They are all careers presently being juggled by former NFL standout Allen Rossum. A determined entrepreneur who does not know how to sit still, Allen has his hands in multiple pots these days; he also runs a children's foundation and is raising four daughters (12-year old twins Avian and Alexa, 10-year old Trinity and 7-year old Talia) with his wife Angela (a Temple University graduate he met in Philadelphia) in Atlanta, Georgia. Allen, the only player in NFL history to return a kickoff for a touchdown with five different teams, developed his blazing speed in his home state of Texas and unleashed its fury at Notre Dame and later in the NFL.

Allen was big man on campus at Skyline High School in Dallas, Texas, where he lettered in football, and track and field. In high school he played option quarterback, receiver and tailback in addition to playing defensive back. He totaled 580 tackles, 13 interceptions during his career and rushed for 1,634 yards and 12 touchdowns as a senior. He was also the captain of his track team all four years and set the 1993 high school record in the 100-meter dash at 10.02 seconds. While the state of Texas begged for his services, Allen left his home state and instead chose to play for The Fighting Irish of Notre Dame. Allen had a remarkable career with the Irish, setting an NCAA career record with nine touchdown returns (three interceptions, three punts and three kickoffs). He also was a two-time All-American in track in the 55-meter dash and he graduated college early with a dual degree in business and computer applications. His NFL career was also special. He was a third-round draft pick of the Philadelphia Eagles in the 1998 draft and his 12-year pro career included a Pro Bowl selection in 2004. Allen played for the Eagles, Green Bay Packers, Atlanta Falcons, Pittsburgh Steelers, San Francisco 49ers and Dallas Cowboys during his NFL days and was voted the MVP four different times on those teams.

Allen started his transition from the NFL to post-football life long before he was ready to retire from playing football, "When I was still playing in the NFL, I began getting involved in different business opportunities by investing or internships. One of my internships turned into a job with The Masada Resource Group. At Masada (www.masada.com/scalability), we take solid waste/trash and turn it into ethanol. My territory is from Miami to the southern tip of South America and we are affiliated in over 30 countries. My job is to develop relationships in 12 South American and Caribbean countries with the governing entities or companies that control the trash/waste management within the country. We then explain how they can significantly reduce their landfills and turn their waste into six or seven different byproducts by building one of our plants."

One would think that one global job would be enough, but not for Allen. He is also involved in two consulting jobs. "The first is in the apparel business with a company called Robert Talbott (www.roberttalbott.com). I am the head of their Made-to-Measure division for professional athletes. It gives me a great opportunity to be in the locker room and attend games. Finally, I am a principle partner of a private equity firm in Atlanta called Cocke Finkelstein (www.cockefinkelstein.com). We purchase mutli-family homes, mobile parks and condo units. We also have a non-profit, CFCares (www.CFCaresInc.org), that helps people purchase homes who normally would not qualify for traditional loans."

For a guy whose NFL specialties included kickoffs and punt returns, Allen is the last person that you'd expect to see being schooled by head coach Lou Holtz. But that's exactly what happened early on in his career at Notre Dame and is one of Allen's favorite memories. "I would have to begin with my memories of him teaching me to catch punts. Hilarious! Even though I never returned a punt or a kickoff before, Coach Holtz asked me if I could return one kickoff per game for him. The funny part was, him attempting to catch them. He swore he also taught Rocket Ismail and Tim Brown the same thing." His next favorite Lou Holtz memory came prior to the first game of the 1996 season. "Coach Holtz had us all in the indoor facility, lying down on the field, all the lights were out and he's talking us through the game that would occur the next day. 'Sophomore Allen Rossum is going to take the opening kickoff. You guys are going to block for him and he's going to score.' Thanks for the pressure coach, I thought. Well, as it so happened, Purdue kicked the opening kickoff to me and I ran 99 yards and scored a touchdown. I was so excited that I was just jumping up and down in the end zone. After that I would return one kickoff per game and scored twice more that year."

"Another favorite Coach Holtz memory occurred during my sophomore season while we were in Washington playing the Huskies. Toward the end of the game Derrick Mayes scored the go-ahead touchdown and we led by 2, I think. All we needed to do was hold them for the win. They were putting together a big drive to win the game when I intercepted the ball with only the need to take a knee for the win. Well, I had other thoughts as I raced up the sideline. Lou was screaming at me, 'Get down, get down!' He was saying other things that are rated R but after I crossed the 50-yard line he changed his tune (and said) 'Run, Run, RUN!' I wound up scoring the touchdown that sealed the game. He went from cursing me out to cheering me on to score."

The restructuring of college athletic conferences is nothing new. When Allen was looking at colleges, several conferences in the NCAA were restructuring. "At the time that I was looking at universities, the Southwest Conference was breaking up. Some of the schools were joining the Pac 10 and others the Big 12. I didn't really want to be a part of that transition and the feeling of not knowing their next step, so those schools were off my radar. Besides I needed a change and a chance to find out about myself as a man."

During his sophomore year of high school Allen was highly recruited by schools such as Duke, Stanford, Vanderbilt and Princeton but none of those schools had the kind of football team that he was looking for. His junior year he started receiving interest from other schools such as USC, Notre Dame, Michigan and Penn State. They were all good academic schools, but the latter group had better football programs than the list from the year before. "I began taking official visits beginning with Penn State, Tennessee and Notre Dame. On every trip, players were attempting to team up and go to school together and used crazy criteria to eliminate schools for the slightest of reasons. For instance, I took a couple trips with Peyton Manning with the thought we would both attend school together but one problem developed. He didn't want to go to Notre Dame with Ron Powlus potentially starting for the next 4 years, and I didn't want to go to Tennessee because some of my friends committed the weekend of our visit."

Allen eliminated California schools because of a recent earthquake and the University of Michigan because of a blizzard covering the state. Penn State had only one person from Texas on their team so that was another easy decision. That is where the Notre Dame Value Stream took hold of Allen and guided him towards his decision. "And that left me with Notre Dame. I was told of the great experience and the chance at a priceless education. I visited the locker room and took pictures standing in front of the library, aka 'Touchdown Jesus.' I chose Notre Dame hoping it would be a place where I could be surrounded by like-minded people, and looked forward to moving from Dallas to a new place to broaden my horizons."

Coming out of high school, Coach Bob Davie was originally recruiting Allen to play for Texas A&M. "He kept telling me, 'It's cold in South Bend. Your friends and family can see you play if you come to A&M.'" Then he ended up getting the defensive coordinator job at Notre Dame. Davie became Allen's new best friend and ND was the greatest institution in the land. "When Lou Holtz arrived at my house to recruit me and talk to my family it was such an amazing experience. He knew from my grades that getting a good education was important to me. He said, 'It's not a party school. The weather gets pretty cold. But once you get your degree it stays with you forever. It's four years and a possible career in the NFL.' He told me about the impressive Alumni Association network and that was one thing that stood out more than anything. Going to class and getting good grades were ultimately more important than playing football.'" The Notre Dame Value Stream and the concept of the student-athlete. This was Allen's kind of place.

Allen ended his career at Notre Dame playing under head coach Bob Davie. "When Coach Holtz left, it was such an interesting transition from him to Coach Davie because I had different relationships with them both. Coach Holtz and I had a father-son relationship, and Coach Davie and I were more like brothers. We viewed each other more like good friends than a coach–player relationship. We engaged in so much small talk over the years and then all of the sudden he was the head coach. It was tough to know when we could joke around and when we had to be serious at times, but they both were good coaches who taught me a lot about football and life."

Allen not only played football at Notre Dame but he ran track as well. "It was actually pretty cool to play two sports because as soon as football season was over I was in semi-good shape for track. That was a benefit to me because I could qualify for nationals quickly. Once I qualified I could concentrate on getting in better shape. Indoor track was fun but it proved to be a challenge leaving my warm cozy dorm room on Saturday mornings in January and

February to go compete at Loftus Athletic Complex when everyone else was snug in their beds, but it was worth it. Besides I got to travel and meet a lot of people I would have never met otherwise. To add, track is my second love behind football and I ended up a two-time All-American both seasons I ran."

Coach Holtz and Coach Davie did an excellent job preparing Allen for his future both on and off the field. "Looking back, I think I had a great career. I got to play with some great players, hang around some good people and break a couple of records in the process. With the help of my teammates, I got the credit for setting a NCAA career record for touchdown returns (three interceptions, three punts and three kickoffs). When I tied the record, during the Boston College game in 1997, everyone had pretty much stopped kicking the ball to me. They would punt the ball sky-high or kick it short on kick offs, trying to lessen the chance I would return it. On the record-tying touchdown, Boston College decided to kick it to the 20-yard line to one of our backs that normally blocked, but I went over and got the ball. The very next weekend, and our last game, we played at the University of Hawaii and I intercepted the ball and ran it all the way back for a touchdown. It was the first defensive play that I made that game and it broke the record. I was so excited that I removed my helmet, which got me in a little trouble with the referees. Besides the bowl games, that was my greatest collegiate athletic moment. Being a two-time All-American in track and field was great, but breaking the NCAA record was even better."

If you had the opportunity to see Allen play football, you probably heard the crowd cheering 'Awesome Rossum' at some point. "Crazy enough, I got the nickname in the fifth grade. For some reason no one could pronounce my name correctly being a new transfer to the school. During one of my first days there, they had a field day and I won every single event I participated in. After that day, one of the kids started calling me "Awesome" and the rest is history. While at ND during my sophomore year I went back to return a kick off, and heard the crowd chanting, 'Awe-some Ros-sum!!!!' ... the nickname had followed me to college. After that, every time I would go back to return the ball or if I made a play I would hear the chant. Hearing them chant gave me energy and I fed off the crowd and their cheering. But it didn't die there. Even into the pros, friends of mine would come up and recall the chants and in a couple of games I heard the chant."

After the Notre Dame Value Stream had prepared Allen for his future whether it was on or off the football field, it was time for the NFL draft. "My family was in town and we were having a barbecue enjoying our time and hanging out with friends. I actually missed my first draft day phone call from the Eagles. Then my phone started ringing a bit later and it was the Eagles informing me that they had taken me in the 3rd round. I was so excited for the opportunity and swore to make the most of it. The transition to the

NFL was easier than I thought it would be because one my ND teammates, Bobby Taylor, played for the Eagles as well."

Going to the Pro Bowl in 2004 was a huge accomplishment in Allen's NFL career. He was able to take some of his family to see the game in Hawaii and it was a special moment for him. Along with the Pro Bowl, Allen was MVP four different times, twice with the Atlanta Falcons, once with the Green Bay Packers, and once for the Eagles. "I was also very fortunate during my NFL career to break numerous records, including franchise and one NFL record. During the 2004 season I set a NFL playoff record in a win against the St. Louis Rams with 152 punt return yards on just three returns, an average of 50.7 yards. I scored a touchdown on the first punt and almost on the second one as well, but got tackled at the 5-yard line. Ultimately, I had really good blockers and coaches and without them I couldn't have achieved anything." Even with all of that great fortune, Allen also experienced the lows of the NFL as well. "Losing was always tough. Having to switch teams every few years was tough. Just as soon as you get to know a group of guys you have to leave and start all over again. When I left the Falcons and moved to Pittsburgh, my wife and kids decided to stay in Atlanta. That was really tough. I missed taking the kids to school. I missed date nights with my wife. Although she came up every weekend it still wasn't the same as having her and the kids there all the time."

Even with all of the business ventures that Allen is involved in today, that is not the end of what Allen does to fill his days. He also runs a youth foundation called the Allen Rossum Healthy Kids Foundation. "It's an organization I started in 2003 shortly after arriving in Atlanta called the Healthy Kids Klub (HKK). I wanted to leave a legacy that would last long after I retired from football. No one was talking about childhood obesity at the time and I thought it was an important issue that needed to be addressed. I started out by trying to get recess back in schools with a state representative. We went to the legislature in Georgia and to the Atlanta public schools and started getting the word out that way. By 2005, Jerry Stackhouse of the Dallas Mavericks with his Triple Threat Foundation, and I merged our programs and formed a nationwide foundation called Athletes Helping Youth."

"The program was run on the premise of athletes setting the trend to combat youth obesity. We launched programs in New York City and LA and hit every major media outlet. We were joined by such big names as Usher, Dwight Howard, Jason Kidd and 32 different athletes from all of the major sports including NASCAR. All of the athletes and entertainment personalities donated their time for the cause. We all teamed up for this one cause: to get athletics back in schools, kids to be active and to eat healthy. Then The Home Depot, The Atlanta Falcons and Kaiser Permanente partnered with us and helped us get the program into schools and the rest is history. Now we also do backpack giveaways, filled with school supplies and a DVD, which talks to the kids about getting active and eating healthy. At every backpack giveaway or camp weekend, the kids would get to meet some of their favorite athletes and entertainers, but it's never a sports camp feel. It is more of an educational forum where the kids get to have fun while they learn. So many kids have poor diets and do not eat well at school or play sports. To date, we feel like we've done a great job getting the word out and changing kid's lives for the better."

"Play the game of life like its fourth and goal."
-Jack Snow

The preparation that Allen received both on and off the field at Notre Dame set him up for a life of success. His 'never sit still, never quit' mentality rubs off on everyone around him and motivates others to give back as he does. The Notre Dame Value Stream taught him what a little hard work and determination could produce: a lifetime of success. "Sacrifice four years or so for the rest of your life, both on the field and in the classroom. It could take you to Chicago for a consulting job; it could take you to the NFL. It can take you to the 'Biggest Fan of the Big East' contest (laughs) ... it's all up to you. When the clock strikes zero at the end of the game only you, your coach and maybe your teammates know if you gave 100% during that game. You want to be able to say that you left it all out on the field. I left it on the field every single time I played and who would have known that I, of all people, would have played in the NFL for 12 years because of that mentality."

Lessons from Allen's Notre Dame Value Stream of Life:

- Make sure that going to class and getting good grades is your priority, with playing sports being a close second. Sacrifice four years for the rest of your life, both on the field and in the classroom.
- Start preparing for your future long before you get there.
- Give 100% of yourself all of the time. You never want to look back and think that you didn't leave it all out there ... whether on the field or in life.

Allen Rossum and his wife Angela.

Notre Dame vs. Georgia Tech, Stadium Rededication Game, 1997. Bobby Brown (#88) running with the ball. (Photographer: Joe Raymond, photo courtesy of Notre Dame Archives.)

CHAPTER FOUR

The Sports Agent, Lawyer and Entertainer Bobby Brown

Life today for Bobby Brown is very much a balancing act. One day you will find him in court practicing law with his law firm in New York City. Next you'll find him jetting off to Chicago or Miami to host a glamorous party with his entertainment company so appropriately named 'Excessive Celebration.' And then you'll find him at home, a family man, with his wife and two small children. There is no such thing as an ordinary day in the life of Bobby Brown. Extraordinary is more the rule than the exception.

Inspired by his mother and brother's dedication and persistence, former Notre Dame receiver Braynard "Bobby" Brown did not let adversity slow his eventual path to success. He is perhaps best known for a controversial penalty he got for excessive celebration – a penalty he still insists was a simple misunderstanding of his actions. Despite this, Bobby was able to look beyond football and graduated college with a triple major in government, sociology and computer application along with a minor in African-American studies. He later had stints in the NFL with the Green Bay Packers and the Cleveland Browns before embarking on his post-football career. Today he has turned his excessive celebration moment into a positive as he owns an entertainment company which shares the same name. He met his wife, Emily, at Notre Dame and they currently reside in the New York City area with their 2-year-old son, Bray, whose nickname is "Deuce" and their 5 month old son, Thatcher Annson.

One thing that Notre Dame did, and did well, for each one of us was prepare us for our future. Whether that future was to involve a professional football career or a law career you knew when you walked out of Notre Dame that you had all the skills you needed to be successful wherever life took you. "That transition was interesting for me. After I played for the Green Bay Packers and then the Cleveland Browns, the Browns wanted to send me to NFL Europe going into what would have been my third year. I told Coach Butch Davis thank you but no thank you, much to some of my family member's dismay, because at that point I was ready to move on and pursue other things. Coach Davis looked at me like I had eight heads! The odds were really not in my favor that going to NFL Europe would result in making the team. It would have been an additional mini-season right before starting training camp, the most grueling physical and psychological experience imaginable. I reasoned that the NFL is a short window of opportunity, whether you want to believe that or not. It wasn't a very popular decision with some of my family and friends, but my brother understood it and gave me his blessing. (He was my agent.) I turned the page and went to law school at Notre Dame, and then business school at Yale. I was going to do them both at Notre Dame, but my mother got sick and I ended up taking some time off to work full-time at a law firm between the two degrees."

"While I was working at MF Global, which was my first job out of Yale Business School, the company ended up going bankrupt, so once again I was back to the drawing board. Shortly after MF Global went bankrupt, my mother passed away after a long battle with cancer. I look at those few months as the absolute low point of my life. Losing a job to an unexpected bankruptcy was one thing, but losing my hero and my best friend (my mother) was an entirely new level of disappointment. To make the situation even more hectic, my second son was born in a New Jersey hospital the day before my mom passed away in a Florida hospital. Flying back and forth, I got to witness both life-changing moments. (We named our newborn Thatcher Annson because my mom's middle name was Ann). Ironically, I think my roller coaster experience in the NFL prepared me for this roller coaster period in my life and so I quickly got back on my feet."

"During my time at MF Global I started doing public speaking, got my NFL agent license and was representing two guys in the NFL draft. I started the agent business with my older brother. Before my mom passed away, she got to see us start the business together. I can recall one night my brother and I were about to drive up to Jacksonville, Florida, to present to a potential client. We left the printed materials on the kitchen table before we left and my mom picked it up and started reading it. When we walked into the room she was smiling from ear to ear as she was beaming with pride. She was so pleased that her two boys had joined forces to build something from the ground up. After she read the materials from cover to cover, she told us that she was just as pleased to see our business model consisted of helping, educating and providing off-the-field opportunities for clients. I will never forget her smile when we walked into the room and that memory has helped my brother and me fight through some tough, early stage days in the business."

Getting a quality education was a priority in Bobby's college search and Lou Holtz made it very clear during the recruiting process that you were a student first and an athlete second. "I took visits to Michigan, Boston College and Notre Dame, and also had 'unofficial visits' to Miami, Florida State and Florida because they were right in my backyard. Coach (Lou) Holtz was very instrumental in my decision to attend Notre Dame along with Notre Dame's exceptional graduation rate. I was very interested in a school that could give me opportunities in both athletics and academics, and Notre Dame was the perfect combination. The guys that hosted me during my visit to Notre Dame were Allen Rossum and Ivory Covington. The three of us hit it off right from the beginning. The other person that had a big role in my decision to go to Notre Dame was Shawn Wooden. He made me feel so comfortable that weekend. He was going to be a fifth-year senior, yet he was hanging out with the freshmen and the recruits. That left a big impression on me."

"Being that I was from Florida, I had no idea how cold it would get at Notre Dame. I lived under the impression that everywhere was warm and sunny like Florida. Before I made my official visit, they advised me that I needed to pack a warm jacket. On that trip I was cold the entire time, but everything else that I experienced that weekend outweighed the cold. I knew it was exactly where I needed to be. I called my mom my first night and told her that I changed my mind, I'm going to Notre Dame."

"Irv Smith always says that he was the recruiting guru of his class ... well I was that guy in my class. Every big recruit that they gave me to entertain on their recruiting weekend I got, all but one (Laveranues Coles). That was what we did, we sold Notre Dame football."

Every journey, however, comes with its bumps in the road. Bobby's redirection on the Notre Dame Value Stream came during his fifth year at Notre Dame. "In the final minutes of the 1999 Notre Dame-Michigan game I made what could have been the game-winning catch, only to be flagged for 'excessive celebration' after the play. The referee said that I had taunted the fans by making 'Mickey Mouse' ears- imitating a moose. The fifteen yard penalty was enforced on the kickoff so it changed field position and put the defense in a tough situation to stop a shorter drive."

What the referee and fans saw and what really happened are quite different. "What really happened? The 1999 football season was my fifth year of eligibility. One of the reasons that I was originally considering NOT attending Notre Dame was because they did not have any fraternities and I really wanted to join this national black fraternity (Omega Psi Phi). But once I found out there were other avenues to join the fraternity while still attending Notre Dame, then it was an easy decision for me to go to Notre Dame. During the spring of my fourth year at Notre Dame, I started a process that would eventually lead to me being a member of Omega Psi Phi Fraternity, Inc. During this Notre Dame – Michigan game my big brother happened to be in the end zone where I caught that pass, and not only is he also a member of the same fraternity, he has always been my role model. After making what I thought was a game-winning catch, right in front of my brother, I did what was natural to me. I threw up a sign that is closely associated with my fraternity. I had only planned on doing it once that year, the first time I got into the end zone, and this was it. It was a salute to my fraternity brothers around the country. It was quick and I thought it was harmless. Unfortunately, it happened to be mistaken as me imitating a moose or making Mickey Mouse ears to the fans, and it was considered taunting, and he threw the flag."

"It was tough having to come back to the sideline to watch Michigan's David Terrell on the go-ahead drive, making taunts at the fans and not getting called. My excessive celebration penalty was definitely a home official call. Only in the Big House. Getting blamed for a loss at 21 years (old) really messes with your sleep at night. No matter how passionate the fans are, the players are still human beings. God only gives you as much as you can handle and as a fifth-year senior, I was definitely able to handle this. If it would have happened to a freshman, it could have destroyed their confidence and their collegiate career. I am happy that it happened to me instead of one of the younger players. I have, over the years, used that experience to push myself to be a better person. Making light of what was once a very tense situation, I even named my entertainment company 'Excessive Celebration.' I have been able to take the negative and make it into a positive."

"The head official wrote me a letter a few weeks later that same season apologizing to me. He had no idea that what I was doing was connected to a historic and positive black fraternal organization. I'm sure lots of people had no idea what I was doing. So by bringing it to people's attention what I was really doing, it opened up a dialogue that might not have otherwise happened. That fact is another silver lining that I have come to appreciate over the years."

As a football player at a prominent school such as Notre Dame, where winning is expected, you fall under harsh criticism by those who supposedly love and support you. "There was one fan who kept writing me letters about my moose sign. Another one who claimed it was a gang sign. The Omega Psi Phi fraternity was founded in 1911. It has many prestigious members including Bill Cosby, Michael Jordan, Ronald McNair and Jesse Jackson among many others, but so many people are unaware of it. I took this situation as an opportunity to promote the values of the fraternity. I grew up in a household where my father was not around for a period of time and several 'Omega men' were instrumental in making sure that did not turn me into a negative statistic. It was important for me to support and represent my fraternity in a positive way whenever the opportunity presented itself."

Bobby is now taking his experiences and using them to help guide and educate others. "I'm now writing a book and the foundation of the book is the excessive celebration penalty, but it discusses the ways that sport allows cultures to collide that would not otherwise cross paths. The occasions that I remember first interacting with diverse groups of people outside my neighborhood were all sports-related: at a track meet, football game or a basketball tournament."

One of the experiences that Bobby discusses in his upcoming book is the 'black table' in the dining hall. "In the book I talk about a bunch of interesting things like the 'black table' in the lunch room at Notre Dame. It was not an intentional thing that we did; it was just something that happened without us even realizing it. There were so few minorities at Notre Dame, and so naturally you just all kind of ended up at a table together in the dining hall. My roommate freshman year asked me one day, 'Why do you always sit at the black table in the dining hall? We always walk in together and then you go sit at that table instead of eating with us (the roommates). Why?' Before he said that, I had never really thought about it like that. But that is exactly what I did. After he said that to me, I really took notice of things like that."

The excessive celebration penalty may stand out in Bobby's mind as a time when he struggled on the Notre Dame Value Stream but there are plenty of positive memories from his undergraduate career. "Coach Holtz's last game is something I'll never forget. During my time at Notre Dame I was a part of many monumental games. We beat LSU on the road. We beat Michigan right after they had won the national championship. Of course, every game at Notre Dame is a big game. I also had some huge and memorable catches like the game-winner against West Virginia. But being a part of Coach Holtz's last game at Notre Dame Stadium was very special to me. To be able to share that with him, to be able to contribute to such a big win, is something I will never forget."

"I will say our road win over LSU was pretty memorable as well. When we got off the bus at LSU, they made a human gauntlet. There were 90-year-old women with no teeth throwing up their middle finger and calling us Tiger bait. Very aggressive fans. It was a pretty intimidating experience, but we knew we could win."

Notre Dame has a way of pushing you to your limits and helping you develop into the best possible version of yourself. Bobby's time at Notre Dame was no different. "My fifth year at Notre Dame was remarkable in my overall growth and development. I had a significant leadership role and I was respected by my peers. But when you are 5-6 going into the last game of the season, things start to snowball and people start to point fingers. There was this skeleton in the locker room that the trainers used for demonstrations. Joey Getherall, a younger wide receiver who was only a sophomore at the time, dressed the skeleton up in my practice uniform and my shades. When I walked in and saw it, I was just crying in laughter. At the end of the day none of us wanted to lose, none of us wanted to quit, it was just one of those things. You learn from it and move on. A big part of personal growth is how you perceive yourself and how you respond to challenges. It was an important year for me despite the win-loss record."

"During my last year at Notre Dame the 'experts' said I should have left after the previous year. Notre Dame's record during my fifth year was 5-7. Six of our seven losses came down to the last possession of the game; we were plagued with time mismanagement, penalties, turnovers and other mishaps. Unfortunately, NFL teams are not very creative. They scout people in very traditional ways and tend to favor players from teams that are winning. To a certain extent, I felt teams never really took a meaningful look at me because I was not a workout warrior and our team had a bad record. As a result, teams just passed me by in the draft. Jarious Jackson was the only one who got drafted from Notre Dame that year, and he didn't get picked until the seventh round."

"After the NFL draft ended I started getting a lot of phone calls from various teams. I ended up getting picked up by Green Bay as a free agent and had my chance to show what I could do. It was definitely tough. How you get into the NFL, either via the draft or free agency, determines the opportunities that you receive. It determines how many reps you get, whether or not you get to start ... how many chances you get. It's a business. When I look back at it now, I went into their camp and they had about 17 receivers and three of those were rookies they had drafted. But those odds never crossed my mind. All I could think of was: where am I going to live because I am going to make this team."

Bobby's time in the NFL helped him see what he wanted to pass on to other student-athletes and the kind of legacy he wants to leave behind. Though the positive experiences of the NFL were present for him, the negative ones showed him how many young men need solid trusted guidance during such high profile life journeys. "The highs definitely included meeting some great people. The coaches trusted me right away. I came from nowhere according to the scouts and the rankings, but they knew I could play. It's the internal reporting that's far more important. When you get the nod of approval from veterans that have been there for a while, that is what you want. It was a huge accomplishment for me to be able to make it at that level and overcome odds that were so huge as an undrafted free agent."

"Post football, I see that very few guys actually get to do productive things with their careers. In order to make it at the NFL level you have to be able to overcome not only physical challenges, but psychological and emotional ones as well. So many guys don't take the determination they have on the field and apply it to the business side of the NFL. So many players got chewed up and spit out like meat. So many talented guys never achieve their potential off-the-field and post-football. That sad reality is one of the lows of the NFL."

During his time at Notre Dame, Bobby had the opportunity to play under two very different head coaches. Each brought their strengths and weaknesses to the table and each provided a very different experience for all those involved. "It is difficult for me to compare the two coaches because as far as I am concerned Coach Holtz was the best of the best. He was the main reason I chose Notre Dame. He is a legend. I think if Coach Davie had the chance to do it over, he would probably take a few more pages from Coach Holtz's playbook in terms of how to be a head coach. He was young and ambitious and wanted to do it his own way, and you have to respect that, but I really liked Coach Holtz's style of coaching and playing under Coach Davie was a big challenge for me."

"People always ask me, was Coach Holtz really that mean? He demanded the absolute best out of everyone, and that can come across as mean, but he asked more of you than you could ever have asked of yourself. In doing that, he was changing the level of expectation you had for yourself. He knew how to build you up as well as break you down. He had a special way of treating each player because he took the time to get to know what made you tick. He knew who to push and how hard to push, but he also knew when you needed a hug and to be built up. It was a constant roller coaster, but he was great at what he did."

Coach Holtz wasted no time in setting his expectations when Bobby's class arrived on campus in 1995. "When Lou Holtz had his first meeting with my freshman class, we thought we were pretty hot (stuff). We were the consensus No. 1 recruiting class that year. The freshmen and the coaches who recruited us were all sitting in this big meeting room waiting for Coach Holtz. As we are sitting there waiting we are all talking, bragging about all of the things that we accomplished in high school, and the buzz is getting louder and louder. When Coach Holtz walks in, the noise quiets down some, but apparently not as much as he had expected. Coach Holtz says, "I'm going to walk out of this room, and when I walk back in, you're going to be sitting quietly with your shoulders back, heads up tall, and your hands on your knees." I didn't even know I possessed that kind of posture. But he said it with such conviction that we all knew that we had to be sitting perfectly and quietly when he came back in. When the upperclassmen came in a few days later, he walked into the room and they did it automatically. We were all in awe at the respect that he demanded … and received. Just like that."

"Every year there is one player who has the classic Coach Holtz accent, who is the token Coach Holtz impersonator. That was me. At the end of the season the freshman put on the skits at the bowl game. I got to do the Holtz impersonation at the Orange Bowl and I was so nervous that Holtz would see it. In my best Lou Holtz accent, talking about me: 'When I recruited you from Florida, they said you were fast. Your film must have been in fast forward, I don't see speed. Can you hit fast forward please!'"

"I think he practices his pep talks at night. There is no way someone can say the witty things that he does without practicing. He is a brilliant man. Even when he's being condescending and making you feel like a gnat he does it in a brilliantly witty way."

Bobby has taken it upon himself to help others find their way based on what he has learned from the Notre Dame Value Stream. He feels that if he can help just one person along their journey, it is all worth it. "I like helping NFL players, sharing with them the pitfalls of the NFL and helping them to avoid them. Some agents only focus on the here and now, but we try to help them start from day one preparing for their eventual transition from the NFL to the next chapter of their life. It's disappointing to me that so many guys don't have a successful life after football. Because I had Mrs. Bettye Brown, my mother, in my ear always telling me 'use the game, don't let it use you,' I was always prepared for the transition. We try to share our mother's philosophy with each client."

"My mother was an educator for over 40 years in the Broward County School System. With the help of all my siblings, we started the Bettye W. Brown Scholarship Fund to provide financial assistance for a select Broward County public school graduate pursuing their dream of higher education. Continuing my mother's legacy through the scholarship fund means more to me than any athletic, academic or professional accomplishment that I have ever had. Eventually I will probably try to get back onto Wall Street again. But for now my law practice, speaking engagements and agent duties are all keeping me busy. I know my mother is looking down on us with that same beaming, proud smile because she likes seeing us working together and helping other people."

"Find your passion and the rest will come."
~ Bobby Brown

Bobby's time at Notre Dame left an indelible mark on his life and he continues to give back to his Alma Mater. "I am still very involved with Notre Dame. While I was in law school, I served on the NCAA Faculty Board and the University's Council on Diversity. I was also a two-term president of the Black Law Students Association and an active member of the Business Law Society. I am currently on the Notre Dame Law Advisory Council, Black Alumni board and Diversity Council."

Bobby Brown

Lessons from Bobby's Notre Dame Value Stream of Life:

- Prepare yourself for the future. If you prepare early for your future, no matter what detours you face in life, you will always be able to find your way.
- Miscommunications will happen in life. Be ready to explain, clarify and stand up for what you believe in.
- Whenever you can, give back. It is so important to share your experiences with others to help set them up for their most successful futures possible.

Notre Dame vs. Michigan, 1992. Devon McDonald (#15) looks to tackle Michigan's Tyrone Wheatley (#6), who is running with the ball. (Photo courtesy of Notre Dame Archives.)

CHAPTER FIVE

The Minister and Youth Director
Devon McDonald

After a successful NFL career Devon McDonald decided there has got to be more to life than this. Following an introduction by his brother, Devon met Steve Grant of Sports World Ministries and his entire life changed. Today he is blessed with the opportunity to make a difference in young people's lives on a daily basis. Born in Kingston, the capital city of Jamaica, in the shadows of the Blue Mountains, American football was not a sport Devon or other Jamaican kids played. When Devon was eleven years old, his family left the crystal blue waters of the Caribbean and moved to Paterson, New Jersey, where both he and his twin brother Ricardo got involved playing football. Both boys displayed considerable talents, and there was no question football was in their futures. However, Devon and Ricardo ended up taking different football paths both during and after graduating high school. Devon decided to play football at Kennedy High School and then for the

University of Notre Dame while Ricardo opted to play football at Eastside High School and then for the University of Pittsburgh.

An American Studies major at Notre Dame, Devon's successes on the field included being the team captain as a senior, receiving Honorable Mention All-American in 1992, being a member of the 1988 national title team and he was named co-MVP in the 1993 Cotton Bowl game. While in the NFL he played linebacker for four seasons; three of them for the Indianapolis Colts and one for the Arizona Cardinals. He is now an ordained minister (since 1998) who is active with Sports World Ministries, an organization that speaks to students about life choices. He practices his ministry in Indianapolis along with his wife Shereasher, and their two daughters Jazzmine and Rachel.

Often times, the journey from point A to point B is less than clear. "When I was released by the Colts and got picked up by the Cardinals I was at a point in my life where I made a spiritual conversion. I had a spiritual moment in my life out in Arizona that completely changed me and I began to follow Christ. I decided that there has to be more to my life than football. I took a personal training job and looked into buying the club or being a part owner but at the same time I was still trying to get back into the NFL. I went to the NFL combine and I ran the 40 in 4.58 and that was the fastest time I'd ever run. What I didn't realize was that my pushing myself so hard was weakening my hamstrings. I went to another combine and ran the worst time I'd ever run in my life. I had never felt like I did that moment, as if my hamstring was about to pop at any moment. In 16 years of playing ball I'd never felt that way. I was just devastated. There's got to be more to life than this."

Devon looked to his brother for guidance to help him transition into the next phase of his life. "My brother Ricardo knew this player Steve Grant (West Virginia alum) that I played with at the Colts and that he played against when he was at Pitt. He had just retired from the NFL himself and they had reconnected at a Pro Athletes Organization conference. Grant told my brother for me to give him a call because he had a job opportunity that he wanted to run by me. As soon as Steve and I met, I just knew we were a good fit. He was also interviewing two other Colts players for this organization he was involved with, Sports World Ministries (www.sportsworld.org), but he knew right away I was the guy."

"During the two years that I played Arena Ball in Tampa Bay, I was a Deacon during the year and then I played football during the Arena season. When the Arena league moved their season from March to January I had to make a decision. Did I want to continue playing football, or was my calling to speak at schools through Sports World Ministries, something I believed in more. While I had this need for the limelight, and wanted to prove to the world that I was still a good player, I took a look around at all of the young people that I had a chance to positively impact. That was something I wanted to be a part of, so I gave up football."

Devon, along with many other professional athletes, is making a difference with today's youth every day. "Our mission at Sports World Ministries is 'to send professional athletes to share personal life experiences with students, helping them to recognize the consequences of their choices while challenging them with the message of hope.' As an ordained minister, the best part of my job is knowing we are making an impact; that we're encouraging positive choices."

Devon's life took a huge turn at the age of eleven when his parents relocated his family from Kingston, Jamaica to Patterson, New Jersey. When you think of culture shocks, I can't think of a bigger one than such a move. This move, however, was what introduced him to American football. "When I was eleven we moved to New Jersey and I saw the game of American football for the first time. There was something about all of the hitting that really drew my brother and me into the game. Ricardo and I both started out playing high school football at Eastside High School (the school featured in the 1989 movie *Lean On Me*), but during our sophomore year our football coach told us that if we really wanted to play Division I football that we should think about transferring to a different high school. My brother Ricardo stayed at Eastside High, and I transferred to the rival high school, Kennedy High School. During my sophomore year at Eastside High School they went 0-8-1. During my senior year at Kennedy High School we went 10-0-1 and were State Champions. So I think I made a good choice."

"You're going to have haters in your life, and you're going to have people who think you can do no wrong, but here's the difference…what are you saying?"
~ Devon McDonald

It quickly became apparent to Devon that football was something he excelled at and doors started to open up before him. "Then the colleges came knocking from about every college out there. My mother's prayer was that first and foremost we get a good education, and then secondly that we'd get to play football. I took four official visits. My first visit was to Iowa. I got there and it was a big drunken party weekend and I thought, this is it, this is my school. My coach said, 'let's look at a few more schools.' Next we went to Illinois, and then after Illinois we went to Notre Dame. When I got on (Notre Dame's) campus in December it was 65F. I had heard that the west was warmer, and this was the mid-west, so this was great! This is how God works." Little did he know 65 degrees in December in South Bend is not the norm.

"As soon as I got on campus I saw the Golden Dome, I said to myself, 'This is it. This is where I want to come.' I enjoyed the weekend, but it was love at first sight. Rod West was my host on campus that weekend. And then after ND, my final visit was to the University of Miami (Florida). Jimmy Johnson was the coach at Miami and they had very heavily recruited me. During my recruiting trip to Miami they took my mom out, wined and dined her, showed her a good time and she said this is where you are going to school. She didn't cook for me for a week when I told her I wanted to go to Notre Dame. The recruiter from Miami told me, 'Next year we're gonna kick your butt.' And in my mind I'm thinking, wow. So for us to beat them 31-30 (the next year) at home, that was big. My twin brother, he chose the University of Pittsburgh, and we beat them every year. Life was good."

When you are the first person to do something, being a pioneer comes with certain challenges. "I didn't have educated parents so they could not help me with many nuances of college life. They didn't go to college so I didn't have anybody to reference – 'Look out for this.' They did the best that they could but they couldn't provide me great direction. My pops loved the sport, but never really got engaged. I called home one day and said 'I'm hurt' and his response was, 'Quit.' I said, 'No, I don't want to quit. I want your advice.' There was a great deal of pressure put on us both academically and athletically. You had to do well in class, and you had to win."

"As they say in the NFL ... you don't get paid to play, you get paid to win."
~ Devon McDonald

Devon did not closely follow Notre Dame football before attending the University. "The first ND game I saw from beginning to end was actually the first game of my freshman year. It was at home versus Michigan under the lights. Prior to that, I had watched five minutes of a Notre Dame game during my senior year in high school just so that I could tell the coaches that I watched Notre Dame football games."

His most memorable shining moment on the field came during the Michigan game in 1991. "My biggest game at Notre Dame was a Michigan game, I think it was in 1991, when I had 18 tackles against the Wolverines. I hated Michigan. I hated those helmets. Those are some ugly helmets. My last game at ND was pretty great as well. I was the defensive MVP at the Cotton Bowl on January 1, 1993 vs. Texas A&M."

One thing Coach Lou Holtz taught Devon was that you can never be too prepared. "My freshman year we were down at the Fiesta Bowl playing for the national title, and as we were wrapping up our last practice Coach Holtz said, 'We're going to practice how to celebrate after we win the national title.' We all look around at each other, he can't possibly be serious. Yep, he was serious. We practiced celebrating after the win. Talk about attention to detail. And then, to see it all come true and we all knew exactly what to do after we won. Classic Coach Holtz."

Devon also learned at Notre Dame that perception and reality are often quite different. "I didn't think I looked mean, but I was told time and time again in college and in the pros that I looked mean. No one would mess with me. What they didn't know was that I had (painful) hammer toes and that's why I had that look on my face (laughs)."

When you are feeling sure of what your future has in store for you, it is often at these times life throws you a curve ball. When it came time for Devon to move on from his collegiate career at Notre Dame and try his hand at professional football, his path didn't go exactly where he thought it was headed. "I watched the NFL draft at home, expecting that I'd be picked in the second or third round. The Giants had been calling me and asking me questions and that is where I thought I'd end up. When the Giants came up to make their selection, they picked a linebacker from Texas A&M who I had outplayed during the Cotton Bowl game. That made absolutely no sense to me. I had been the MVP and he got drafted before I did? He was a bit smaller than I was and maybe that's what they wanted. So then the Colts started calling me and I was thinking to myself, 'The Colts?' My brother (who entered the NFL with the Cincinnati Bengals the year before me) had told me, 'the team who's going to pick you won't show any interest until the very last second because they don't want to show their hand'."

"I remember going to see my brother, driving through Indianapolis on my way to Cincinnati, and there was something about Indianapolis that had piqued my interest even then. I just couldn't put my finger on what, but that's where I ended up so it worked out. The Colts wound up drafting me as the 107th pick of the fourth round."

Devon feels that a big part of his successes had to do with being surrounded by good people and having his priorities in order. Being able to surround yourself with trustworthy people is an important step in keeping afloat on the Notre Dame Value Stream. "Student-athletes need to get their priorities in order and know their purpose. When you know your purpose it's easy to get your priorities straight. It helps you know who you are and what you're supposed to be doing. It is also important to surround yourself with good people. As you go through your journey, you will need to weed out the people who you don't need to be around. You're going to lose some people along the way but that's okay because they are not going where you are going. Be comfortable in your own skin. That's 90% of the battle of life. I'm fine being me. That's when you can make more money than you'll ever hope for. What is the most natural act? Being you. Things become work when you are acting or performing, but be yourself and what comes out will be from the heart."

Devon's NFL experience was a good one. The positive experiences were great and the negative ones were manageable. "To be completely honest, the money was definitely one of the highs of playing in the NFL. Money gives you the ability to afford a lot of freedoms that you couldn't otherwise have. The lows include what comes along with the money ... the gold diggers. Not just females, men just as much as women. People come out of the woodwork with business propositions for you. More players get taken than you'd ever know because they will never tell you that they got taken. Some of the guys that I played with on the Colts, they lost millions of dollars being taken by people whom they thought were trustworthy. It's a business; it is not just a game like college is. You have to learn very quickly who you can trust and who you can't. You have to make sure to surround yourself with good people."

"I played in the NFL for four years. Three years with Indianapolis and one year with Arizona and then got cut by the Cardinals. I tried to get picked up by another team but it just didn't work out. I got picked up by an Arena Football team down in Tampa Bay and played there for two years. It was exciting to still be in the game, but then my next opportunity came and I decided it was time to move on."

> *"This life is hard ... this life is you ... you can't blame anyone else. The more you take responsibilities the better you will do in life."*
> *~ Devon McDonald*

Today Devon has made it his life's work to make a difference in the lives of the youth in his community and across the nation. Fulfilling the mission at Sports World Ministries, "to send professional athletes to share personal life experiences with students, helping them to recognize the consequences of their choices while challenging them with the message of hope," allows him to pass along what the Notre Dame Value Stream taught him so many years ago. As an ordained minister, the best part of Devon's job is knowing that he is making an immediate impact on the lives of these young people; showing them how to make positive choices every day.

Lessons from Devon's Notre Dame Value Stream of Life:

- You're going to have people tell you that what you're doing is wrong, or that you can't do something. The difference is what you believe. If you believe in yourself, you can do anything. Push the nay-sayers away and follow your heart.
- This life is hard ... this life is you ... you can't blame anyone else. The more you take responsibilities the better you will do in life.
- Be a difference in the world. Encouraging others to make positive choices in life not only helps their lives but it also makes your life better as well.

Devon McDonald spending time with his canine friend.

Notre Dame vs. Nebraska, 2000. Joey Getherall (#18) running with the ball. (Notre Dame University photograph, photo courtesy of Notre Dame Archives.)

CHAPTER SIX

The Police Officer and Field Trainer Joey Getherall

For most people a typical day on the job does not include seeing multiple people getting shot by an AK-47 rifle. But for Joey Getherall, now a Field Training Officer for the Los Angeles Police Department (LAPD), this is just another day at the office. Joey, the product of a father who was a detective for the LAPD for 30 years, and a sister and two brother-in-laws who are also involved in law enforcement, knew there was a place for him in the high-action world of crime fighting. Part of what makes Joey so good at what he does is his personal tenacity. Joey is not the kind of person who takes no for an answer. He was once told that there was no way he could play football at Notre Dame — he only became more determined that he would make it there and succeed — and he did just that. Named a third-team All-American as a punt returner by College Football News, Joey was Notre Dame's top receiver in 2000 based on receiving yards and was also the ninth-ranked punt returner in the country, returning two punts for touchdowns. His various contributions that year personified the Irish team effort and he went on to be selected to play in the 2001 East-West Shrine Senior all-star game. Today Joey lives with his wife Jennifer and their two toddler boys, Joseph Aiden Tsuyoshi and Jacob Hunter Isamu, and continues to push himself towards new endeavors.

At the end of his Notre Dame career Joey signed with the Pittsburgh Steelers as a free agent. "I remember watching the NFL draft. Mel Kiper had me going either in the end of the fourth round or early in the fifth round. I had talked to Kiper on his radio show a couple of days before the draft, and he had me going to the Eagles. I had done workouts with many different NFL teams, including workouts with the Eagles and special teams coach John Harbaugh. When I went undrafted, I was then listed as one of the top guys who was still available in free agency. It was kind of crushing to know you didn't go in the draft, but being signed as a free agent (with the Pittsburgh Steelers) made it better; however, I got injured during training camp and was released."

"Then the Miami Dolphins picked me up and sent me to play in NFL Europe for the Amsterdam Admirals. During my time in Amsterdam I seriously injured my foot which then required several surgeries and screws in my foot. After my surgeries I was still being retained by the Miami Dolphins and was on their injured reserve list because I had done so well in NFL Europe, but eventually got released when my foot was not healing fast enough. After my release from the Miami Dolphins I signed with the Indianapolis Colts and passed my physical, but injured my foot again, and was then released by the Colts. I had an offer to go play in the Canadian Football League but by then I knew my foot would never be the same again and I had pretty much lost my drive to pursue it any further. I had my one credited year in the NFL and that was good enough for me."

The next phase of Joey's journey may seem an unusual one to you and me, but it was a completely expected destination for him. "I come from a family that is heavily involved in law enforcement. My father was a detective for the Los Angeles Police Department (LAPD) for 30 years. My sister and two of my brother-in-laws were also involved in law enforcement and so I knew there was a place there for me. When you grow up around law enforcement it just seems to come naturally. I don't feel like working for the LAPD is a stressful job. I saw my dad go to work every day and he was never stressed out."

When you are a Police Officer, you see things that other people don't see. Joey's first day on the job he saw multiple people get shot, including three people who got shot by an AK-47 rifle. "It's one of those jobs where you become callous to a lot of things. That's your survival instinct. Currently, I am a training officer. I train the brand new guys who have just graduated from the academy. One of the first things I tell them is that this job is not for everyone. You have to have a lot of integrity and intestinal fortitude for all that you will see on this job. You need to be able to bite your tongue and take a step back. You need to make sure you can control yourself and watch the things that you do. It is my job to make sure that they are safe and that I lead by example, so that they are doing their job the right way. If they do their jobs incorrectly they could lose their livelihood or even their life. We are here to protect and serve, not only others, but ourselves as well. We go from call to call, helping people solve their problems, very similar to a psychologist. You never know when the people you are helping are going to fight or run, though."

Growing up under a heavy "left coast bias" in the shadows of USC and having a father who was a Trojan alum, it seemed doubtful that a kid like that could be convinced to leave southern California and play football in the frozen tundra of South Bend, Indiana. "The funny thing is, I'm a southern California kid and I grew up watching USC and UCLA sports and was pretty stuck on that, that is until I saw the rivalry between ND and USC. As a kid you gravitate towards going against your parents' wishes and with my dad being a USC grad and wanting me to go there, I naturally went the opposite direction and became interested in Notre Dame. During my junior year of high school I started getting really serious in my interest to play football at Notre Dame, and started to actively look into what ND was all about — at the same time they started getting interested in me. The Notre Dame recruiters (including Urban Meyer) came out to visit me the summer before my senior year and I think I knew at that point that if they offered me a scholarship that I would take it in a heartbeat."

When Urban Meyer initially came out to southern California to recruit Joey he asked Joey's high school head coach, 'Where is Joey Getherall?' and his coach pointed him out to Coach Meyer. Meyer said, 'That kid can't go to Notre Dame. No way in hell can I recruit *that* kid.' "After hearing that, anyone else in their right mind would probably say to themselves 'I guess I should look for another college to go to,' but instead it lit a fire under me and only pushed me to work harder, to be an even better player and prove people wrong. People see my size and stature (Joey was listed at 5' 7" and 175-pounds) and say, 'He can't do it,' but those people never deterred me from chasing my goals. A lot of coaches in the athletic world, or bosses in the business world, give you the eye test and sometimes you don't pass. They automatically assume by your appearance or first impression that you can't do something, but all too often there is much more than what meets the eye."

Joey's first official visit was to the University of Wisconsin when Barry Alvarez was the head coach. At the end of any recruiting weekend the recruit meets with the head coach in his office. He lets the recruit know what he thinks about him and at that point the recruit is often offered a scholarship. So as Joey sat there in Coach Alvarez's office he told him what he liked about his play and finished their meeting by offering Joey a scholarship to Wisconsin with the following disclosure. "He said, 'I know you are taking your visit to Notre Dame next weekend. You know that I used to be a coach there and coached during the national championship season in 1988. If Notre Dame offers you a scholarship next weekend, you can't pass it up.' So here is Alvarez, recruiting me to play at his school, Wisconsin, and offering me a scholarship ... yet in the same breath telling me that if I get an offer from Notre Dame that I can't refuse it. Who is this guy? I'm thinking to myself, wow, if the head coach at Wisconsin is telling me that I can't pass up an offer to ND, then I guess I can't."

Prior to taking his visit to Notre Dame, the Irish played USC, and the week after the game Lou Holtz resigned and they decided not to play in a bowl game. At that point all recruiting contact from ND to Joey stopped and he started getting nervous. USC was no longer interested in him at that point as they had their sights on two other wide receivers, and now no contact from Notre Dame. "I started thinking great, now I'm going to get lost in the shuffle with the new coaching staff. Then I got a call from Tom McMahon. He said they were still very interested in me but it all depended on who the new coach was and whether or not McMahon was retained on the coaching staff. A few days after that Bob Davie was hired as the new head coach and both Tom McMahon and Urban Meyer were retained and the recruiting process resumed with a fever pitch. When I took my visit to Notre Dame I could not get what Coach Alvarez said out of my head. It was snowy and cold, just like it was the weekend before at Wisconsin and as a California boy I kept thinking I was out of my mind to want to come to a school with weather like that. At the end of the weekend, Coach Bob Davie had my dad and me in his office and he offered me a scholarship. I said yes right then and there."

Joey's two hosts during his official visit to ND were Kory Minor (from Bishop Amat High School) and Brad Williams (from Mater Dei High School). They were both California boys and did their best to convince him that the weather in South Bend really wasn't all that bad. They also took him to some well-known places in South Bend and made sure he had a fun trip! But in reality, he already had his mind made up that ND was his school even before he got there. "Unofficially I looked at some other west coast schools (UCLA, USC, San Diego State) before I took my trips to Wisconsin and Notre Dame, but after I committed to ND I cancelled the rest of my recruiting trips. (Although, it was tempting to take a fun trip to Hawaii just for the heck of it, but I resisted.) I felt like I was wasting their time and mine because I had already decided that ND was where I wanted to be. The coach from Washington was in town and was being quite persistent in coming to see me but I told him no thank you. I'm sure he thought if he could get a face-to-face meeting with me that he could change my mind, but I knew I was set in my decision."

A key element of the Notre Dame Value Stream is the concept of the student-athlete. Since its creation by Father Hesburgh, Father Joyce and Mike DeCicco, Notre Dame has stressed the importance of Her students being able to focus on academics first and foremost and athletics secondly. That's not to say that performance on the field is not important, but what is learned in the classroom has to be given first billing as it will sustain them beyond football and throughout their lives. "Being a student-athlete means just that, being a student comes first. If you don't get it done in the classroom then you don't belong on the football field. Notre Dame has the number one graduation rate right now in football, and being a part of an institution with such a record is a great honor. Some people don't care about the classroom part of the college experience, but there is more to college than football. Greg Bryant's dad (Bryant committed to ND in the 2013 class) said it's not about a four-year career, it's about a forty-year career, and he's right on. You have all of these Fortune 500 companies who can't wait to get their hands on Notre Dame student-athletes when they graduate because they have all the qualities these companies want in an employee. They know how to work hard, have great character and perseverance. I do remember having a moment freshman year, though, when I thought I couldn't do it. Classes were hard, I had gotten injured, and I called home and told my dad I wanted to go home. My mom got on the phone and said, 'you are staying there.' Starting as a true freshman and getting injured was tough."

Many people don't realize what it takes to be a successful student-athlete at a school such as Notre Dame. The days are never ending, both physically and mentally, and often times there are not enough hours in the day. "As a Notre Dame football player, your days are long. You get up at 4 am for your morning workout. Then you're off to breakfast at training table, a visit with the trainer, class at 8 am, lunch and then more classes. After class you may stop by to watch some film if you have time. Then practice, more film, dinner at training table, maybe back to have another visit with the trainer, and then of course you still have to study. Your day may not end until 11 pm. That kind of schedule is incredible for a kid who is 18 or 19 years old. And during finals your days are even longer. To be able to keep these 15-18 hour days you have to have a great work ethic, and this translates very well into the business world and into life."

Again, this is what makes ND unique, and what makes the Notre Dame Value Stream such a critical influence on each of its student's lives. "You *are* a student first. You are in the same classes with everyone else who is a student there. I can guarantee you that the guys at USC are not taking these kinds of classes. But what is even more impressive than a school like Notre Dame is the military academies. I was recruited pretty hard by West Point, and those students are the epitome of a true student-athlete. Not only do they have the academic and athletic rigors, they also have their military responsibilities. I admire them tremendously. But what I am most thankful about Notre Dame is that they looked at us as a whole person. They made sure that when you left Notre Dame you were well rounded with experiences both in the classroom, on the field and in extracurricular activities. They put you in a position to be the most successful moving forward. *That is Notre Dame."*

"Successful people push other successful people to do even better."
~Joey Getherall

"My freshman year I took full advantage of the opportunities that I had. The freshmen football players get there a few days before the upperclassmen do to get started on drills and plays. By the time the upperclassmen got there Coach Davie had already moved me into the first and second team offense, and I was the first player to get the "freshman stripe" taken off my helmet. Here I was a true freshman, not a redshirt freshman with a year of practice under my belt, already practicing plays with juniors and seniors. I had to get it really quick. I was going up against All-Americans like Allen Rossum, and looking back it was a huge honor to have my stripe taken off so quickly. When you are practicing with such quality players, it becomes a trickle-down effect. Successful people push other successful people to do even better. The upperclassmen just pushed us to work even harder. This has continued as we move forward with our lives. We watched the guys ahead of us graduate, move on, and get involved in their careers and charity work, and we all followed suit."

Everyone asks Joey if the Oklahoma game in 1999 or the Nebraska punt return in 2000 are his favorite ND football memories. While these are, without a doubt, great memories and big plays, they are not what is most memorable to him from his time at Notre Dame. His most cherished memory as a member of the Fighting Irish football team is that very first moment he donned the Blue and Gold and stepped foot on the sacred ground that is Notre Dame stadium. "My favorite Notre Dame memories would have to be running through the tunnel for the first and last time. The feeling that you get running through the tunnel for that first time is amazing, unexplainable, unfathomable — you get chills."

Joey never expected to start the first game of his freshman year. True, he had made it this far, but very few true freshmen earn the privilege of getting to start their freshman year. "Two weeks before the start of the season my freshman year I had screwed up a play in practice and my position coach Urban Meyer sprinted 40 yards downfield, punched me right in the shoulder pads, got in my face and screamed at me, 'You are never going to step out on the field at Notre Dame. Ever.' During the recruiting process they tell you how great you are, and then when you get to ND they tell you how terrible you are and try to break you down. This is an effective motivational tool for some guys, and for others it makes them crawl back into their shell. For me, it just pushed me to work harder. After he screamed at me I did everything I could to get better. The day before the Georgia Tech game, when Coach Meyer told me that I was going to start the next day (as a true freshman) I was completely blown away. The emotion that you feel as you are standing in the tunnel waiting to run out onto the field for the first time, seeing 80,000 fans cheering for you; it really got the best of me. And as emotional as that moment was, the last time I ran out of the tunnel my senior year was equally as emotional for me. You take for granted that you're going to run out of that tunnel every week, but sooner or later it comes to an end. I wish every fan had that opportunity to run out of that tunnel, touch the *Play Like a Champion Today* sign. It's an unexplainable feeling."

Urban Meyer was Joey's position and special teams coach during all four of his years at Notre Dame. "He was such a unique guy. He is still an inspiration to me to this day. He is a super intense guy. He puts everything he has into coaching, puts it all out onto the field. He makes sure his guys are prepared to play the game, and if they are not he feels like he's a failure to himself and his players. He puts his heart and soul into making sure his team is ready to go, which is probably why he had the health problems that he did. When he was coaching at Utah I stayed with him for a week and tagged along to see if coaching was something that I'd be interested in pursuing. It was during spring ball and so for a week I watched film with him, went to practice, went to meetings; it was only spring ball and Meyer and his staff were putting in 18 hour days. It was quite intense and I didn't think I could see myself doing that full time. My heart was still in the game, and I thought I could be successful as a college football coach, but I was not ready for that kind of schedule. I had the opportunity to be an assistant coach, but declined it and I have no regrets at all. I knew that kind of lifestyle would make it difficult to have a family and that was something that I wanted even more than to stay involved in football. Coach Meyer definitely taught me a lot about hard work, dedication, giving something your all and never giving up."

Intense is an understatement when it comes to describing Coach Meyer. "He used to love to slam the remote down when watching game film. He was the coach that would get right in someone's face and scream at them. He was a Bobby Knight type of guy — super intense. He defines the word intense. What he learned, though, was that he needed to find a balance in his life. If he had continued on coaching like that he'd probably be dead right now. When he got to Ohio State he set what the tone was going to be like and that's why they went 12-0 in 2012. When Meyer was at Florida, he sold his soul for the game of football. In the past few years he's backed off significantly. He took some time off between leaving Florida and taking the job at Ohio State to spend time with his family. He had lost sight of being a whole person and making sure that his family was part of his life. Sometimes, when you're in a head coaching job like that, you forget about everything else. You have to have a strong wife and kids to hold a family together when you have a job like that."

When you work for the LAPD there is no such thing as a normal day on the job. In January of 2007, Joey was involved in an incident that he will never forget. "It was an unfortunate thing. My partner and I, we went to a house, and it seemed like a pretty customary thing. We would get a lot of calls where it's a battery call, assault with a deadly weapon, and there were multiple suspects in the house. During the altercation one guy decided to try and shoot a police officer (my partner) and he shot the officer multiple times. One shot went through and through, in his chest and out his back. One shot hit his badge. At this point I made the split second decision to shoot the suspect. He was trying to take my partner's life, I had no other choice. My partner survived his gunshot wounds, but the suspect did not. You've got to take action. There is no time to hesitate. You have to have the mindset to make that quick decision, to step in and take the appropriate action."

Joey's years of playing football actually helped him to handle moments just like this one. "Athletics helps you to be always prepared. In athletics, you have to visualize success. Visualize yourself making the big play. It's the same thing in law enforcement. You are trained to visualize what your reaction will be in different situations. You have to be able to go from zero-to-sixty in that moment, without taking a second thought."

Besides his career as a LAPD Field Training Officer in South Central Los Angeles, Joey also helps his wife out in her business endeavors. She runs a group home for adults with developmental disabilities such as Autism, Down's Syndrome and Epilepsy called Monte Vista Family Home. Right now she's also in the process of opening a second home. "My aspirations for the future not only include helping her reach her dreams, but I think I'd like to head back to school and get my law degree and become a lawyer that defends Police Officers. When a citizen files a complaint against a Police Officer, they need someone to defend them who understands not only the law but also being in the line of duty as well. A lot of my friends are getting their graduate degrees which has just pushed me to go ahead and further my education. I want to set an example for my kids and show them how important it is to get a good education (and I would be honored if they decided to someday follow in my footsteps and attend Notre Dame)."

Besides getting his law degree he'd also like to start a not-for-profit organization that would give disabled individuals the chance to do things they wouldn't otherwise be able to — an organization that would give them the opportunity to do such things as go to Disneyland or a major league baseball game. "I believe it's our job to educate others that even though they may suffer from a disability they are still functioning adults and that they should be treated with respect. Everyone has their issues or problems, if you think you don't, then you are fooling yourself. My dad is a veteran of the Vietnam War and helps veterans who suffer from Post-Traumatic Stress Disorder. I've also talked about doing a not-for-profit organization to help veterans out as well. I want to help others. If you aren't giving back then you aren't getting your fulfillment out of life. We need to help each other out."

Joey Getherall together with his wife Jennifer and their two boys Joseph and Jacob.

Lessons from Joey's Notre Dame Value Stream of Life:

- Never give up. Never let anyone tell you what you can or cannot do. And never take no for an answer.
- Take full advantage of all opportunities put in front of you.
- Do your best to help others out. If you aren't giving back then you aren't getting your fulfillment out of life.

Portrait of football player Germaine Holden, 1991. (University of Notre Dame photograph. Photo courtesy of Notre Dame Archives.)

CHAPTER SEVEN

The Oil Rig Leadership Consultant and Performance Coach Germaine Holden

Australia is a vast mass of land that lies between the Indian and Pacific Oceans. Its massive territory is occupied by a multicultural and multiracial blend of people who mostly inhabit its coastal cities. Off the shores of this great continent stand hundreds of man-made erector sets of steel, drilling the depth of these blue seas in search of the liquid gold called oil. Working on these oil rigs is a special breed of men including a 6'4" 250-pound former ND linebacker/defensive end. Roughneck Leadership Consultant Germaine Holden is at home in this world which is quite a change from the scenery growing up in South Carolina or playing football in South Bend, Indiana. Germaine took quite a leap of faith in taking this opportunity in the middle of the ocean just like he took a leap of faith when he decided to leave the warm South Carolina days behind and enroll at the University of Notre Dame.

"In May of 2011 I left GMT and joined RLG International (www.rlginternational.com), based in Vancouver, Canada. They are predominately a consulting company that trains executives to become more effective and productive leaders, and my role is that of a performance coach. We work with companies throughout the world to create an alignment between the corporate expectations and the realities of the front line. What is expected from upper management and what is heard by the employees on the front line is often quite different. We connect the front line employees with the bottom line results. Transocean is my current client. They are the largest owner of off-shore drilling rigs." Germaine works on these rigs teaching each day, "I'm not a traditional rough-neck, but even as a leadership trainer on a rig, it's tough work and a tough environment. I teach them how to express their technical goals to their employees. Often times these managers excel at the technical aspects of the job but need help with the managerial side. It's my role to bridge that gap." What a job and career for a man who did not know where Notre Dame was located when the recruiting process began.

Even though football did not become a big part of Germaine's post Notre Dame career, the preparation he received from his academic rigors set him up for success in life. "My first job (after football) was for an independent living facility for at risk youth in Anderson, South Carolina. Then I got hired at Notre Dame as an academic counselor in their academic services department, which was very enjoyable, but the money was not great. At the time I was married and had two children and needed something that would better take care of my family. One of my teammates, Tracy Graham, who was like a brother to me, had started a business right out of college (Internet Services Management Group) and was looking to start a second one (GramTel). He asked me if I would be interested in partnering with him and I accepted. That was my introduction to business. I worked for Tracy from 2000 to 2004 and then was offered a job in Denver, Colorado, for Republic Financial Corporation (2004 to 2007). Then in May of 2007 I was offered a job with GMT Global Republic Aviation and worked there from 2007-2011. While I was at GMT I also earned my MBA from the University of Denver."

When it came time for Germaine to start looking at colleges, Notre Dame was not even on his list let alone near the top, but then again neither was a rough-neck career in the middle of the ocean, 10,000 miles away from his hometown. Germaine didn't even know where ND was located. He had heard of Notre Dame and had seen the football team play on television but was by no means a lifelong fan. "My first real exposure to the University came when Tony Rice went there, as he is from a town that is about 30 minutes away from me (Greenwood, South Carolina). Then when Jeff Burris (Rock

Hill, South Carolina) committed to Notre Dame I decided I should take a closer look. During my school search, I took five official visits. I was at Miami during Thanksgiving weekend of 1990. I was at Notre Dame the following weekend. Then in mid-January I went to UCLA, Nebraska, and then finally to South Carolina. I saved my trip to South Carolina until the end because when you live in South Carolina that is the last chance for your parents to get courted and doted on from the local school. I had no intention of going to South Carolina, though, unless they completely blew my mind."

Part of the magic of Notre Dame recruiting is how the current players get involved in selling the school and the program. One of the most dynamic recruiters in the Holtz tenure was tight end Irv Smith. "Irv Smith and Nick Smith were my hosts during my official visit to Notre Dame. I had made an unofficial visit to ND the summer before, so I already had met a bunch of the guys which made my official visit seem very natural, very comfortable."

When it came time to narrow down his choices and decide where he was going to attend college, Germaine's parents put the decision solidly in his hands. It was time for him to choose where his future was going to begin. "My parents did a great job in raising me, and they trusted me to make the right choice so they left the decision 100 percent up to me. They supported me and would give me advice if I asked, but they wanted me to be the decision-maker. I had the good fortune of having a brother who was four years ahead of me in school, who had been recruited to play college football, and I had already gone through the process with him. I got to tag along on his trips and had a chance to observe his journey, which helped me a lot with mine. My brother ended up playing football at Furman University in Greenville, South Carolina. I saw the benefits and the burdens that came with going to school so close to home. With him being so close, we could invade his life whenever we wanted to. Geographically it was impossible for him to gain his independence. He didn't have to cut the cord and my parents didn't have to either. He could come home on weekends and do his laundry and have Sunday dinner and I saw how that was not a beneficial thing for him. From his experience I realized that I did not want to be close to home. I wanted people to have to plan to come visit me and not just drop in. Four of the five schools that I took official visits to were not close to where I am from."

At some point during the recruiting process each player must come up with some sort of criteria to base their decision, and again the Notre Dame Value Stream comes alive and Our Lady draws another young man to Her world. "One, I did not want to be close to home. Two, I did not want to play on turf. Three, I did not want to be redshirted my freshman year. Four, I did not want to go to a school that was in a big city because I was not from a big city and they intimidated me. Five, I didn't want to go to a big school. I wanted to go to a small school in a small town where I could get a good education and play football for a good program."

> *"So in the end what I wanted was a little school
> with a big name, and that was Notre Dame."*
> *~Germaine Holden*

"The big drawback was the weather. It was by far my worst visit. There was this awful ethanol smell in the air all weekend. It was the least 'fun' of any of my recruiting trips, but the guys were very cool." But leave it to one of Our Lady's sons to make the decision perfectly clear. "Derek Brown, a tight end at Notre Dame, sat me down and said to me, 'Look, listen man. Here's the deal. You can go to Miami if you want to, and if you do you'll probably have a blast, and when we play you we will beat you. You can go to Miami and you can kick it for four years. Or, you can come to school here, win a lot, be a part of a great program, graduate with a degree from Notre Dame and kick it for the rest of your life.'" And once again the Notre Dame Value Stream shows why the decision to attend Notre Dame extends far beyond the four years that you are in school.

The four-year journey through the hallowed halls of Notre Dame is not always an easy one. Many students who excelled in high school had a rude awakening to the rigors of Notre Dame academics freshman year. Germaine's experience was no different. "Honestly I don't think I was quite prepared from an academic perspective with how tough it was. I was thrown for a loop. Just being around so many extremely smart people who had been at the top of their classes in their respective high schools across the nation and now I'm sitting next to them in classes. I might have been in class with them before, but I was not peers with them before. Academically, I felt a tad bit overwhelmed. The characteristics that athletes have which make them successful in sports also make them successful in school and life. Academic life at Notre Dame was a microcosm of the business culture of the United States. If you can make it through your studies at Notre Dame, you can make it anywhere. You just learn to adapt. That's what all of us did at ND. We got through it. I wasn't an All-American or a first round draft pick. I had many frustrating moments when I wanted to pack up my stuff and go home, but I would not change one moment of my time at Notre Dame. It made me who I am today." The Notre Dame Value Stream always seems to give you just what you need in order for you to be successful both in the present moment and as your journey continues. It was what prepared each and every one of us for the challenges that were ahead of us.

Lou Holtz was also a big part in preparing the young men he coached for their future life journeys. He not only prepared them for success on the field, but he made sure they were ready to face whatever was ahead of them. "I had the luxury of starting six games my freshman year because one of my teammates got hurt. We were in practice one day and I blew my assignment and Coach Holtz stopped practice. He called everybody around ... coaches, players, trainers, in a circle around me and had me in the middle with him. He called me to task (something that he did to his players early and often, especially if he believed that you had potential. He wanted to build a bridge between your potential and your future.) He told me to tell everyone around me why I was so damn special. 'We've got ten other guys out here doing what they are supposed to be doing and here you are doing what you wanted to do and not what you were supposed to do. Why is that?' He kicked me out of practice and I had to sit there on the sidelines and watch the rest of practice."

"He called me back out on the field to run sprints at the end of practice and then at the end as I was walking off the field he called me over to him. He said, 'You understand why I did what I did, right?' And I said, 'I think so.' And he said, 'Look, I cannot emphasize to you enough to do the little things the right way. Not some of the time but all of the time.' He reached up and patted my head ... and then patted me on the butt and said, 'You're doing a great job, keep up the good work. We love you and we need you.' If I could turn my children over to Lou when they turn 17 or 18 years old I would. There is no one I'd rather turn them over to than someone like him."

Of course, being a student-athlete at Notre Dame is full of many wonderful memories as well. Germaine talks about the key moments during his time at ND. "One of my best moments at ND was when I set the bench press record, and then went on to hold it for 15 years. I believe I pressed 520 or 530 pounds." But his favorite football memory does not consist of a winning game or a big play, it revolves around the incredible people who surrounded him. "Having my teammates around me is what I enjoyed most about my time at Notre Dame. It was a fraternity, a brotherhood, at a school that does not have fraternities or sororities. The collective experience of being around such a great group of guys and to know that I was not going through it by myself was such a huge benefit. We were in it together and that is what it was all about. One team. One mission. That is really what I hold so dear of my time at ND."

When you walk out of Notre Dame with a degree in your hand you have high hopes for what your future holds and what you will become. Sometimes dreams are achieved and sometimes they are not. But either way, the Notre Dame Value Stream equips you with the skills you need to handle what lies ahead and carries you on to the next part of your journey. "I played for the Pittsburgh Steelers for a short time. They paid me, I was on their roster, but I did not enjoy it. The camaraderie was gone. And that was the door that closed on my athletic career. The experience just soured me on the game that I had loved for so long. I am a great fan of the NFL and am thankful that some of my teammates went on and were successful. It was a big part of many of my teammates' lives, but it didn't play a big part in mine. Today I love the challenges in my life and Notre Dame is at the core of who I am today." The man Germaine has become is one who teaches and influences others in the middle of the ocean off the coast of Australia – He is a true product of the best of Our Lady's Value Stream. Germaine currently splits his time between Denver, Colorado, and Australia and has three sons: Baer, Tyger and Wulf.

Germaine Holden

Lessons from Germaine's Notre Dame Value Stream of Life:

- Take advantage of the platform that you have available to you when you are in college. The world is literally at your fingertips. It is limitless what you have access to, if only you reach out for it.
- Learn how to ask for help and accept it. We, as athletes, are used to people coming to us to ask for things, but we never learn how to reach out to others for help. Being able to reach out and really take advantage of what the world has to offer us is very important. Many athletes never learn how to do that until they are out of school and on their own. They should learn that skill while they are still in school and have available resources. Learn to humble yourself and reach out and ask others for help.

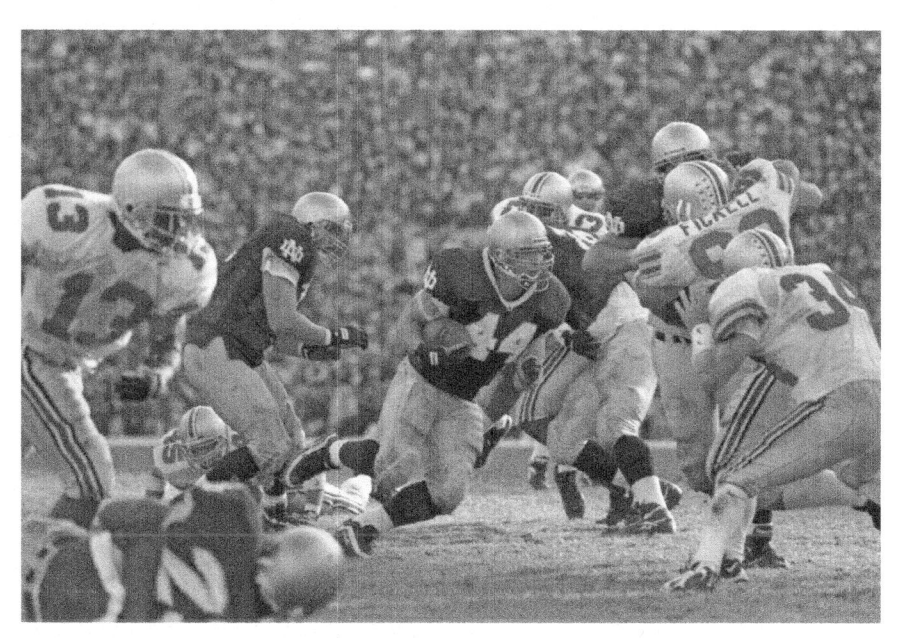

Notre Dame vs. Ohio State, 1996. Marc Edwards (#44) running with the ball. (Photographer: Joe Raymond, photo courtesy of Notre Dame Archives.)

CHAPTER EIGHT

The Forklift Executive
Marc Edwards

Marc Edwards was known as a dangerous fullback who could deliver punishing blows as he carried a football into the end zone during his days at Notre Dame and in the NFL. It seems appropriate and ironic that today this piece of human machinery from a blue-collar Ohio community is committed to protecting workers from the potentially grave dangers that accompany forklift operations in the workplace. "Through a Notre Dame connection, I was introduced to the forklift business, which really caught my eye. It was something that I could not only get into the technical side of, but could also get my hands dirty. I ended up buying into the company, called Speedshield Fleet Solutions (www.speedshield.com), and became a partner. What the software does is allow the end-user to monitor their entire fleet online. It allows them to pick and choose who has access to each piece of equipment. It alerts them to speeding, accidents, and keeps track of OSHA regulations; it can even shut the forklift off.

It is a great way for a company to monitor safety and product efficiency. It was the perfect opportunity for me. I can get my hands dirty, I am out in the field rewiring forklifts, and I am also in the office teaching people how to install the software and operate it. I found something that was challenging to me both mentally and physically and protects workers. It really was the best of all worlds."

You'd recognize him anywhere. His signature crew cut, thick neck, stocky build, his massive 2002 Super Bowl championship ring; the perfect example of a fullback. Marc was named Ohio's "Mr. Football" in 1992 as the state's top football player. Then he donned the Blue and Gold of the Fighting Irish from 1993-1997. Like many NFL players Marc experienced life in the NFL with several teams including the 49ers, Browns, Super Bowl champion Patriots and finally, stints with the Jaguars and Bears. His book, "Odyssey: From Blue Collar, Ohio To Super Bowl Champion", is a story of Marc's winding road from blue-collar Norwood, Ohio, to the NFL and ultimately a Super Bowl winning season with the New England Patriots. Marc is married and has four children ranging from toddlers to teenagers.

Today as Marc looks back into a box from his high school days he stumbles upon a folder that has written on it in bold letters "Notre Dame sucks." Notre Dame was the very last place Marc thought he would end up playing football. But with some maturity under his belt, he came to realize the long-term benefits of attending Notre Dame and it was at this point that the Notre Dame Value Stream started to pull him and found a way into his heart. "During the late 1980s I hated Notre Dame. When Notre Dame was in the run for the 1988 National Championship I was not a Notre Dame fan at all. I was rooting for Miami to beat Notre Dame. But by the time I got into high school, I started to change my mind. I knew that I would get a great education from Notre Dame. I knew that I would graduate, and would have skills to fall back on if I did not end up playing football. I knew that the fullback position was a key position in the Notre Dame offense. Had I gone to Ohio State, I would have been nothing more than a blocking mule for Eddie George. I knew that Notre Dame was always in the hunt for a national title. Notre Dame was only four hours from home, which also was a plus. So when Notre Dame started to recruit me and show interest in me, it really was a no-brainer. What they had to offer me truly was the entire package." Not to mention Notre Dame had head coach Lou Holtz, who made every day at practice a new adventure. "The things he said were funny as hell as long as he was not yelling at you! We were getting ready to play Air Force and Holtz was yelling at one of the players. He's yelling at the guy and says, 'You're so dumb, you don't even know what state you are in. Son, what state are you in?' And the guy says, 'Indiana?' 'No, your butt is in the state of confusion.'"

Marc excelled at a position that has all but disappeared from college football. He explained that football is an evolving game even today. In order to be successful you need to be able to adapt your skills to the current needs. "The sad part is that it has not just disappeared at Notre Dame, but it's disappeared from football in general. The fullback position right now is a dying breed, both in college and in the pros. Football is cyclical to a certain degree. New offenses come along every so often because the defenses have figured out the old offenses. Eventually they have to go back to the bread and butter plays."

"I was at Notre Dame several years ago when Ron Powlus was the quarterbacks coach, and was telling Ron that I'm not sure if today, in today's game, that I would be a Division I athlete. Fullbacks are just not used any more. Using a fullback may not be as exciting as throwing the ball, but when you have to knock it in from the one yard line, having an elite fullback is definitely a bonus. Even when the use of the fullback position was prevalent, not every team used it. It will probably never return like that again, but who knows."

Marc's time at Notre Dame was full of successes under head coach Lou Holtz. He experienced a huge high in his collegiate career during the Notre Dame-USC game his junior year (1995) when Notre Dame was an underdog headed into the match up. "At that point, we had beaten USC for 10 straight years. In the 11th year we tied them, and here we were the underdogs of this meeting. It was Keyshawn Johnson's senior year, USC was undefeated going into the game and we were coming in 3-2. It was being hyped that this was the year that USC was going to come in to our house and beat us. And what happened? We came out and put a major beating on them. Physically, mentally, we beat them in all aspects of the game. I probably had the best game of my life. I ran like crazy that game, scored three touchdowns, threw for a two-point pass and ran for a two-point conversion and ended up being carried off the field. I was the NBC Player of the Game. It was a surreal experience. We beat USC 38-10. It was the first time I was an integral part of a big time victory as a starter."

As a student-athlete, when your time in college is drawing to a close your hope and dream is to be given the opportunity to play at the next level. As a college football player, so much pressure is put on where you are chosen in the NFL draft, when more times than not it's not where you are selected, but what you do with the opportunity you are given. Marc shares this sentiment. "If I had draft day to do over, I probably would have played golf all day and not obsessed over it. I thought I would go either mid-second round or mid-third round. We had a draft day party at a local restaurant in Cincinnati. The draft party started at noon, which is when the draft coverage started on ESPN. They showed the first three rounds on Day 1, as each team got 15 minutes to make each pick. I was the 55th pick on Day 1 of the draft and I didn't get picked until 8:30 pm. People at the party kept asking me when I thought I was going to get picked, and I kept telling them, 'I have no idea!!' Cell phones were just starting to be prevalent at that time, and a few people started to call me on my cell phone and I kept telling them, 'quit calling me I need to keep this line open!'"

"When I finally got drafted, the TV coverage had moved from ESPN to ESPN2, and the restaurant that we were at only had ESPN. The main draft on ESPN went from noon to 7:30 pm, and then it switched over to ESPN2. At this point, the owner of the restaurant is frantically calling the cable company and trying to get them to activate ESPN2, but they were not able to do that before I got the call."

"So I finally got a phone call on the restaurant's phone. They called me over and I picked up the phone. All anyone heard me say was, 'yes sir, great news, thank you very much;' and then I hung up. At this point no one knew what team I was going to. I had three boxes of hats. I had to dig through all three before I finally found the hat that I'm looking for in the third box. I paused for a second, picked it up and put it on (San Francisco 49ers), and the whole place when nuts. I still have never seen the footage of my name being called. I didn't sleep at all that night. I was the designated driver that night for my friends to celebrate. Then I went home, packed, and caught a 6 am flight the next morning. I finally caught a few hours of sleep on the plane."

Even though Marc's draft day seemed to be an anticlimactic experience for him, he certainly made the best of the opportunity he was given to play football at the next level. He did learn that playing football in the NFL did not have quite the family feel of his time at Notre Dame. "The best thing about playing football in the NFL is that you are still competing and you are still playing the game. Sundays are great, paydays are great, but it is a job. It's much different from playing during your college years at a place like Notre Dame. There is not the camaraderie that you had in college. I keep in touch with 8 or 10 guys that I played with in college. I have also met guys from different generations of Notre Dame teams, some from the 1988 championship team and some who played after me, with whom I have since become friends."

"When you get done playing in the NFL, it is a business, and you don't necessarily keep in touch with anyone with whom you played. It is a very cut-throat industry. They are always looking for someone bigger, better and cheaper than you. The older you get, the more you see and realize that. You are a commodity and you are not a brother. When I go back to Notre Dame, I am always welcomed with open arms and I have an instant connection with anyone who is a Notre Dame alum, regardless of whether or not they played football. The NFL is not a family. Once you are done, they are done with you. It's a different mentality when you reach that level, not the same warm feeling as at Notre Dame." The Notre Dame Value Stream is much more than just preparing us for life after college. It is a feeling of family and belonging that you carry with you everywhere you go. It's that bond that holds us together and drives us to take care of each other no matter what.

"The high point of my NFL career has got to be winning a Super Bowl with the New England Patriots. It was a storybook season for sure. The year before the Patriots went 5-11. They gave up two first-round draft picks and hired Bill Belichick, and even before they recruited me as a free agent I thought they were crazy. When New England started to show some interest in me, they ended up signing me and nine other free agents. None of us were big name players, but we all had several years of experience under our belt. This was Belichick's strategy to build a winning team. Drew Bledsoe was the team's franchise guy, and the season before quarterback Tom Brady was the fourth-string guy. The only reason he was still on the team was because New England, unlike most other teams, kept four quarterbacks. After Brady's performance during the 2001 summer camp, he was moved up to second string."

"After the first game of the season, 9/11 happened, and then there were no games the following week. Our first game after 9/11 was against the New York Jets, which was a very emotional game. We lost that game, and Mo Lewis hit Bledsoe during that game, which caused him to be out for the rest of the season. Tom Brady came in with the team already 0-2, and we really thought we were in big trouble. We faced Indianapolis the next week and the whole team rallied together and we beat the Colts. It seemed more like a college atmosphere than a NFL atmosphere, and we played as a team, not as a bunch of guys relying on our franchise quarterback to bring home the win."

"We lost to Miami next week. We were 1-3 at that point and started fighting back. We got to 5-5 after a loss to the St. Louis (Greatest Show On Turf) Rams. After that game, we started on a magical run. We went on to win the division, had the number two seed going into the playoffs, beat the Raiders in the 'snow bowl' game, and went into Pittsburgh to win the AFC Championship game. We traveled to the Superdome in New Orleans to face the Rams in the Super Bowl, and beat St. Louis on a last-second Adam Vinatieri kick. It was quite a season. A good looking kid from Michigan takes over as quarterback and ends up taking the team to the Super Bowl."

"That year was unlike any other year that I played in the NFL. There was camaraderie on that team that I never saw on any other NFL team. After practice was over we would stick around the locker room and play Dominos and Backgammon. About twelve or so of us would hang out every Thursday night at this local BBQ joint. Then on Friday nights we would all go out to dinner and have some drinks and relax. We threw our own team Christmas party. The chemistry of that team really felt like a family."

When it came time to move on to the next stage in his career, Marc was not exactly sure what the next destination on his journey would be. He had thought about going into coaching, but by that time he already had three daughters who were all getting involved in sports and coaching requires an immense time commitment. "When you are a coach there is no time off. You have to make a decision between being a full-time coach and being a family man. Being a good coach is more than a 9-to-5 job, it's a 24/7 job and your family takes second place. There is no job security. You end up moving every few years. I decided to veer away from that and put my kids and family first."

"Like many guys who move on from the NFL, I was a little bit lost. Towards the end of my NFL career, I had some ownership in an insurance company. After I retired from the NFL, I went and got my insurance license and my series seven, tried to get involved in the insurance business, and found out that it made me bored out of my mind. As an NFL player, you rarely were told no. All of the sudden I am making insurance sales calls, my phone calls were not being returned and people were telling me no."

"In 2007-2008 when the market was crashing, it was a very bad time for me. I was trying to break into the insurance business and one of the other challenges I faced was that I was 31 years old with an established family, and all of my peers in the insurance industry already had 10 years under their belt. I felt like a college graduate just trying to learn a new career. At this point I realized I need to try to find something enjoyable and challenging all at the same time. Insurance was not it." This is when the Notre Dame Value Stream guided him exactly where he needed to be: to his forklift safety operations business. "I'm really happy and content where this business is headed and I look forward to the challenges my business offers me each day."

Looking back on his time at Notre Dame, Marc, like so many of his peers, credits head coach Lou Holtz as being an integral part in preparing him for life after football. "Coach Holtz's philosophy was to put all the pressure on you during practice so that game time was easy. I used to dread going to practice as a freshman because I knew he was going to get on me about something. If I took a crossover step instead of a lead step, he was running down the field yelling and screaming at me. The offensive and defensive squads practiced on different fields. And then if you messed up, they sent you down to the scout team's field to get better and then maybe if you were lucky you could come back and practice with the main squad. The worst part about being sent down to the scout team's field is that everybody could see you heading down there, and they all knew you had screwed up. It was so embarrassing. But come game time, he rarely yelled at all. The older you got, the less he got on you. You had already been through the battles and proven yourself. He didn't have to break you down any more. But he'd still chew you up from time to time to let you know he was the boss."

Marc Edwards

Lessons from Marc's Notre Dame Value Stream of Life:

- In order to be successful you need to be able to adapt your skills to the current needs. Life is dynamic and changing and the ability to be flexible is so important.
- Make sure you take advantage of and use to the fullest potential every opportunity you are given.
- In life, just as in football, the more you prepare in advance for the big game (or big meeting) the more successful you will be. The ability to ready yourself beforehand is just as important as the main event.

Notre Dame vs. Alabama, 1987. John Foley (#49) at the bottom of the pile. (Photographer: Joe Raymond, Photo courtesy of Notre Dame Archives.)

CHAPTER NINE

The Stock Jock in Investment Banking
John Foley

The Chicago Southside will ever be known as a tough blend of cultures that includes a multitude of ethnic origins and it is the home of an American President. If you've ever known a Chicago Southsider, they take pride in their world that houses Chicago's Chinatown and McCormick Place, and they love the Chicago White Sox, abhor the Cubs and die for the Monsters of the Midway – the Chicago Bears. What does Investment Banking and the Chicago Southside have in common? The answer is simple: survival has become a way of life and your name has to be John Foley. If you've known a Chicago Southsider, you know John Foley - an avid White Sox fan, a tough, hard-nosed, 6'3" linebacker with a Chicago Bears mentality. Today an investment banker successfully negotiating the world of global finance.

John is simply a Proposition 48 Notre Dame Value Stream Investment, with an ROI of Global Financial Investment success. "In January of 2004, I took a job with Oppenheimer (OPY) (www.opco.com), and worked in the new business division until December of 2008. Currently, I work for Barrington Research Associates (www.brai.com). It's a family run full-service investment bank, providing investment research, institutional sales and trading, corporate and executive services, investment banking and asset management services and was started in 1983 in Barrington, Illinois by the Paris family. I have never been happier. I work long hours, but I love what I do and it does not seem like work at all." John, the student who struggled with dyslexia and only took one accounting class at Notre Dame, is now in investment banking and making deals every day. The Notre Dame Value Stream did a great job of teaching John how to look life straight in the eyes of a challenge and turn that challenge into a successful career. "Success is most definitely a state of mind. If you think you can do something, you most always will."

"I'm what you would call a 'stock jock'. I work with institutions, advising them as to which companies they should invest their money in. I work with some of the smartest people on the planet, and even though I don't have a degree in finance or accounting, they recognize me as being a smart person as well as a result of the well-rounded education that I received from Notre Dame. When I tell people that I was a linebacker at Notre Dame they always laugh in disbelief, 'No way, you must have been a kicker!' They laugh and then I smile and say, let me explain what I can do and how I can help you in your wealth management".

"The thing about Notre Dame is, when you spend four years around bright, ethical, moral people, you learn a great deal about what it takes to succeed. You not only want to succeed on the field, but you want to succeed off the field as well. We're competitive people, not just in athletics, but in life as well. Why would I go to work every day unless I wanted to be number one at what I am doing? Why not treat everything in life with that approach? Never tell me I can't do something — that just makes me even more motivated to succeed."

"In 1997 I got into the finance industry. My first job in the finance industry was with Robby Stevens. I went in to this job interview, with only a degree from Notre Dame, a B- student and no MBA, interviewing for a job in which an MBA was required. I went into the interview and told him to just give me a chance. 'I will outwork anyone in your company.' The interviewer's name was Tom Sheddy. Then I told him, 'how about I get Lou Holtz on the phone and he can tell you?' and the guy says, 'Sure.' So I get Lou on the phone to speak with him and he asks me to leave his office so that he can talk to Lou. I am finally asked to come back into his office a half an hour later and he says, 'You're hired.'"

"I said to Tom, 'I thought you didn't hire people who didn't have MBA's?' and Tom replied, 'I asked Lou one question. I asked him, if I was going to hire John Foley, what would be the best thing to hire him for? And Lou's answer was: Sales. John is the best sales person in the world.' And that was the job that I was interviewing for, my job was selling stocks. I ended up being one of the top brokers there. We did deals with eBay, ESPN, and all of the major internet IPOs."

John always found a way to see the silver lining. Though he admittedly struggled in his academics, he shined on the football field at St. Ritas high school and was one of the top linebackers, not just in Chicago, but in the nation. He was fortunate enough to get accepted to Notre Dame in the first class of Proposition 48 students, and was able to continue playing the sport he loved at a high level. John is a shining example of why it is so important to finish your college degree. His football career was tragically cut short, but that did not stop John from pursing his dreams and proving to others that quitting is not an option.

For a young man that struggled with academics, Notre Dame didn't really seem like a realistic goal, let alone a Wall Street career that has him traveling all over the country, but that never stopped John from following his heart. "I decided that I was going to attend Notre Dame when I was in second grade (laughs). Let me explain. Growing up, my dad was an Irish Catholic beer truck driver on the south side of Chicago. Father Griffin would come to our house quite frequently to hang out with us. Actually, we used to have priests to our house all the time for family meals. I told one of the priests, 'I'm going to go to Notre Dame and play football one day.' And he said, 'yeah, right.'"

"In 1986, when I was looking at colleges, you would not believe the things I was being offered. One school offered me $100,000. Another school offered to buy my parents a house. When Lou Holtz came to recruit me, he explained to me that Notre Dame was more than just football; it was an excellent education as well. He told me, 'Son, one day you are going to get hurt, and then what are you going to do?'" Little did John know that this very situation would become his reality during his career at Notre Dame. No one ever expects to be the guy who sustains the career ending injury, but when you are at an institution like Notre Dame, you have a built in backup plan. "I was a top rated player coming out of high school. I could have gone where ever I wanted, but what Coach Holtz told me is why I chose Notre Dame."

John took official visits to Boston College, Iowa, and then his third stop was Notre Dame. He had two more visits scheduled (USC and Texas) but after his visit to Notre Dame he cancelled them. He was already sold and apparently he left quite an impression on head coach Lou Holtz as well. "During my visit at Notre Dame I told Coach Holtz that I loved this coach that I met at Iowa named Barry Alvarez and how much of an impression he left on me during my visit at Iowa. About three weeks later he was hired at Notre Dame."

Any student-athlete at Notre Dame or any other Division I football school faces adversity during their collegiate careers, but John's situation was quite unique. "Tony Rice and I were among the first student-athletes admitted to Notre Dame under Prop 48, and it was horrible." John realized that no university is perfect and neither are the students no matter how smart they are, "My fellow students taunted me and treated me poorly because they thought Notre Dame had gone beneath its standards to let me in." These are the moments that make you stop and question your decisions. "I walked away from money, cars, and houses to come to Notre Dame and get an education and this was how I was treated by my peers. Part of the stipulations of Prop 48 was that I had to sit out my freshman year. The good thing about that was it helped me get caught up academically. It allowed me to focus. The bad thing was having football taken away from me." But it didn't take Foley long to win over his peers.

"Coach Holtz used to walk in on Sunday, when it was time to go over game film, and look at me and say, 'John, the psychiatrist is here to see you. Jesus, you're nuts.' When I finally earned my starting position on defense, he told me that I no longer needed to play special teams. 'We don't need you to play special teams any more. We need you 100 percent on defense.' But I told him that I wanted to continue to play on special teams. The students loved my big hits on special teams, and they expected it from me. When I'd take the field to defend a kick off, you could hear them cheering, 'John Foley!'"

"We played for those students. They would follow you so closely every week, they'd know every step that you made in the game and they'd tell you about it when they saw you in class on Monday. They were so excited. We took a lot of pride in playing for the students. When I first got on campus I was so tortured by my peers, but eventually they came to love me, and I loved them back."

The adjustment to college is often a big one, even for students who aren't on athletic scholarship. Being away from home and having to be responsible for managing your time is a huge challenge for students, even the most organized student. But the student-athletes had even more restrictions on their time. "My biggest challenge as a student-athlete was managing my time and being able to get my homework done. Most days we didn't get out of football practice until 9 pm, which didn't give a whole lot of time for studying. Football was your full-time job, but then you still had to find time for your school work. I don't think I would have survived without my tutors."

Over 15 percent of the world's population has some form of dyslexia and John is not ashamed to say he is one of those millions. Throughout his primary education, John always thought he was not a bright student. It was not until he was a student at Notre Dame that he was diagnosed with dyslexia. It had nothing to do with his intelligence level, it was a matter of being taught how to study. "I was not diagnosed with dyslexia until I was a freshman at Notre Dame. Once they figured that out, I was finally taught how to study and learn. Growing up in the inner city of Chicago, my parents didn't have any resources to help me. Finally at Notre Dame I got the help I needed."

Even though John's football career at Notre Dame was short, he made the absolute best of his time there. And when asked what his best football memory at Notre Dame was, it was an off the field experience that first came to his mind. For so many guys, the Notre Dame football experience was much more than the playing time on the field. "Absolutely positively for me it was the national title game. It was surreal. I didn't even get to play in the game but because of the work I did with the coaching staff I was on the field during the game. That's also how I got my national title ring."

"The National Championship game was special. The guys treated me like I was part of a team, and I really thank them for that. I was supposed to start. I was the Sporting News preseason All-American. They could have treated me like an outsider, but they didn't. It's amazing how close the bond is of the Notre Dame family. It's an instant connection. Today, when I do work on Wall Street, I work with a lot of Notre Dame graduates. They trust me, because we have that bond." Because of the connection we have and similar experiences we shared as Notre Dame students the Notre Dame Value Stream continues to connect us and guide as even in our careers and throughout our lives.

"I was nice to everyone when I was a student at Notre Dame. Some of my clients, who are among the top leaders and most successful individuals on Wall Street: Bob Takazawa (CastleArk Management), Tom Eck (Cortina Asset Management), Larry Playford (JP Morgan), Frank Latuda and Tim Hasara (Kennedy Capital Management); are peers of mine from Notre Dame who remember me from college. These gentlemen have not only been clients of mine, but have also been positive attributes to my successes throughout my career over the years. At Notre Dame, you're taught three things: TRUST, LOVE and COMMITMENT. These men are a prime example of all three. I always try to make a connection with someone, but at soon as you say Notre Dame, it's already done."

> *"Life is ten percent what happens to you*
> *and ninety percent how you respond to it."*
> *–Lou Holtz*

During the tail end of John's sophomore year John suffered a career ending injury during the 1987 Cotton Bowl which matched up Notre Dame and Texas A&M. "It was the third kickoff of the second quarter and I was on the kickoff return team. The Aggie who tackled me ended up hitting me in the side of the head. The pain was crazy. I could not feel one whole side of my body. I couldn't feel my arms. It happened right about the time that Tim Brown's fight over the towel started."

"I played the rest of the game with a spinal injury. Back then, if you could walk, you could play. You never gave up on your guys. My injury ended up being much worse than anyone had realized. I had no feeling in my arm for almost two years. That's the Notre Dame spirit. You never give up. In retrospect, I kind of wish I would have though, because playing the rest of the game made my injury much worse."

"Four hours after the game I started having convulsions. I was at a relative's house in Texas and they ended up flying me to Chicago. They put needles in me to shoot in electricity and I could not feel a thing." If there ever was a time for the Notre Dame Value Stream to help someone carry on, this was it for John. He could have easily given up and dropped out of school. In fact, his father was ready to bring him home but John knew he would get the support he needed from the University and wanted to achieve his dream and graduate from Notre Dame. "After my injury, my football career was over. Of course there was always a hope that I'd be able to return, but that did not happen. When you sustain an injury such as I did, you get transitioned from an athletic scholarship to a 'Sorin Scholarship.' My dad did not want me to return to Notre Dame after my injury. He felt like if I returned to ND on a scholarship and was not playing football that I was freeloading. I went to Coach Holtz and explained my situation to him and Coach Holtz ended up hiring me to work with the football staff in recruiting. When that happened my dad let me return to ND to finish my degree. That is also how I got my national title ring, because I was on staff with the football team."

Lou Holtz may have been a big supporter of John during his time of need, but their relationship was not always rosy. "In college, I was a hot head. When I was on the field I was a completely different person than I was off the field. Off the field I was pretty mellow, and definitely not aggressive. On the field, I was a man possessed. My teammates knew that as long as there were no cheap shots in practice everything would be fine, but watch your back if you deliver me a cheap shot."

John learned many lessons at Notre Dame that enabled him to manage the tough days when things were not going well, "One day in practice this guy takes a cheap shot on me and I lose it. And we all know how these things work, it's not the first guy who gets caught, it's the guy who retaliates. So Coach Holtz catches me retaliating against this guy and kicks me out of practice. As I am walking out of practice, furious, I start giving away my equipment to kids/fans standing on the sideline watching practice — mouth guard, pads, I'm taking it all off and handing it out. I was kind of sarcastic back then, and I really didn't care. You kick me off the team screw you."

"The next day, Coach Holtz watches the film, sees that it was a cheap shot, and invites me back to practice. 'That was a really bad hit. We saw it on film. Come back to practice tomorrow.' Coach Holtz's policy was to immediately discipline you, watch film later, and THEN if you weren't at fault you'd get asked to come back to practice."

"A few weeks later, another guy takes a cheap shot at me. It's like déjà vous. I retaliate, I get caught, and I get kicked out of practice. And once again, I'm walking out of practice, furious, and giving away my equipment. Holtz watches the film the next day, sees it's not my fault, and invites me back to practice."

"A few weeks later the same thing occurs, except this time as I'm walking out of practice Coach Holtz yells at me, 'And this time don't give away anything! I'm tired of reissuing you equipment.'" (howling with laughter).

Through all the adversity that John endured at Notre Dame he was more than prepared to head out into the world and accept the new challenges in front of him. He didn't just accept the new challenges, he attacked them head on. "My first job out of college was working for Frank Eck. I worked under Frank at Advanced Drainage Systems, Inc (ADS) selling pipes. During my first year I won Rookie of the Year, and within three years I was the top salesman in the division. At 24 years of age they told me that I was at the top and that there really wasn't anywhere further for me to go. It's pretty crazy to be 24 years old and be told that you've done all that you can do at a company. Then I took a job with Al Dunlap at Scott Paper and helped turn around its distribution in Chicago."

Our successes contribute a lot to who we are as individuals, but our struggles and how we respond to them contribute just as much. One of the best things that happened to John's career was when the book "The Tarnished Dome" was published in 1993. "They really criticized me in this book, absolutely ripped me apart. I took the cover of the book, laminated it and have carried it with me every day in my brief case. It's still there to this day. In 2005 I had the best year of my career. I sent a letter and a copy of the cover of the book to the two authors who said that I was an idiot, along with a copy of my W-2's and said, 'Who is the idiot now?'"

"One other thing that I think makes me good at what I do is that I'm always asking people for help. People love being asked questions. They love to help others, it makes them feel valued. We all have that sense of excellence. To be the best we can be. That we are capable of doing anything. Notre Dame just made us believe that we are unstoppable." Today John and his wife Rebecca live and raise their family in Chicago, the city where it all began.

John Foley and his wife Rebecca.

Lessons from John's Notre Dame Value Stream of Life:

- What you are today is only a stepping-stone to what you are going to become tomorrow. I've come from a Southside beginning to a prominent career in investment banking and who knows what tomorrow has in store. Always keep striving towards the future.
- When it comes to pursuing your dreams, follow your heart, never give up, and never let anyone tell you that you can't. Anything is possible if you put your mind to it.
- Do your best to turn the negatives in your life into positives. Our struggles define us as much as our successes, and push us forward to continue to excel.

Luther Bradley (#20) on the field, c1973-1977. (Photo courtesy of Notre Dame Archives.)

CHAPTER TEN

The Union Liaison and Youth Minister
Luther Bradley

Teammates called him The Old Man. He had an aged look about his face and was prematurely grey so he shaved his head. The grey hair was a stark contrast to his very dark skin and perfectly chiseled face. Underneath this aged appearance, was the perfect specimen of a man. At the age of 18 Luther Bradley already had a fair amount of grey hair, but he was and is at age 56 still the perfectly built defensive back who started on the 1973 Notre Dame National Championship team as a freshman and went on to earn consensus All-American in 1977 for the National Champion Fighting Irish. Today he uses the intellectual skills that were developed at Notre Dame to sit down with union workers and attempt to bring resolution to the conflicts that occur in everyday work life. He works in the heart of Detroit where the economy has not been kind to anyone and tries to solve problems just like the 18 year old kid who walked into Notre Dame Stadium on game day to stop the opposition.

"I was blessed to be a first round draft choice of the Detroit Lions. But right out of college I took a job at Merrill Lynch." Luther is the product of parents who were educators and who emphasized while the NFL is great opportunity, that world would end one day, "I played football during the football season and then during the offseason I worked at Merrill Lynch. Following my time at Merrill Lynch I took a job with Prudential as a stockbroker. These jobs were both held during my time playing football. After I retired from football I decided that I wanted to move into the field of marketing and sales. I took a job selling office furniture for Herman Miller which I enjoyed tremendously. When the office furniture market began to decline I decided to quit and put all of my efforts into finding a new job. It did not happen quite as quickly as I had anticipated but after eight months I landed a job with Blue Cross Blue Shield. I had a friend who worked there who introduced me to one of the vice-presidents and that is how I got on with Blue Cross, and I have been there ever since. I started out at Blue Cross Blue Shield (www.bcbsm.com), as an account representative and then transitioned into a new business representative position. I spent 15 years working on landing new accounts. Now I'm a labor relations liaison who handles all of our labor union accounts."

Luther's mother taught first grade and his father worked at the high school; all of his brothers and sisters are well-educated as well. "Just before I entered the 9th grade we moved from Florence, South Carolina, to Muncie, Indiana. My dad was also a high school football coach so I grew up loving football. I would go to practice with him and travel with him to watch his team play. I started playing football in junior high and was surprised at how good I was. I played basketball and ran track as well. I ran the 100 meter, 200 meter and 4x4 relay (mile). I was a sprinter who loved track, but I was really good at football."

Luther's aspirations did not always feature playing Division I football in the top spot. He first had his sights set on becoming the next big Olympic track and field star. "One day I told my dad that my goal was to compete on the Olympic Track and Field team. In all seriousness, my dad replied, 'Son, football speed and track speed are totally different. Stick to football.' That was a humbling discussion. But that's just what I did."

Anyone who talks to Luther realizes the great influence of family in life. With his father's wisdom and guidance he returned his goals to football and began looking at where he wanted to attend college. Notre Dame, however, was not on his original list. "Had we stayed in Greenwood, South Carolina, I'm sure I would have gone to school in South Carolina. Even after we moved to Indiana I really had no desire to attend or play football at Notre Dame. One of my high school football teammates actually introduced me to the school, both his father and his brother went to Notre Dame and he started talking with me about it. One Saturday, our junior year of high school, he invited me to go with them to South Bend to watch a game. Notre Dame was playing the University of Missouri and got completely crushed. Even though they got hammered by a bad team we had a terrific time at the game. The game was exciting, the place was gorgeous, and that trip really turned my head."

Luther's recruitment is not atypical from many of the men in this book, "I only took official visits to Indiana, Purdue, Cincinnati and Notre Dame." His father's encouragement to look at only four schools helped make the decision process less complicated, "My dad set limits for me. It could get overwhelming very quickly if you did not set limits on how many schools you were going to visit. He felt if I limited myself to four schools, I could get through the process sooner and get to decision-making. Even with looking at four schools you still had a coach calling you or stopping by almost every night."

In the early 1970s Notre Dame was the ultimate destination for the best of the best. And Luther was one of the best of the best that enrolled in the Notre Dame Value Stream in 1973. This was only the second year in NCAA history that freshman were permitted to don the uniforms of their chosen school to do battle on fall Saturdays across the nation. This was a unique year for Her Lady who recruited the largest contingent of African American football players to date. Luther and Ross Browner were at the heart of this elite contingent of 9, both quickly breaking into the starting lineup. But other freshman like Willie Fry, Tim Simon, Marv Russell and Elton Moore would also contribute in this new era that would change the landscape of this institution and other universities across the nation. College football was different in those days and Luther, as one of the top football recruits in the nation, along with these other young men, could have played college football at any school of their choosing, yet they found and were embraced by the Notre Dame Value Stream.

Luther commented on his official visit to Notre Dame how the veteran players had a way of making the recruits feel that they already were a part of the Notre Dame family. The Notre Dame Value Stream always seems to come shining through, even when you least expect it. "My official host during my visit to Notre Dame was Cliff Brown, but he was too busy that weekend with some lady problems that he was dealing with and so I ended up spending most of my time with Greg Hill. The Notre Dame players really knew how to make you feel welcome during your recruiting weekend, as though you were already a part of the Notre Dame family."

Recruiting in today's digital age is much different from what the recruiting process was like in the 1970s when Luther was being recruited. Some of today's influences make the process easier, and some more complicated.

"When I was being recruited to play college football there was no limit on how many schools you could take official visits to."

"Today with social media the recruiting process is much more complicated. We used to do everything face-to-face or over the phone. This gave you a chance to really get to know the coaches well, how they thought, and what their coaching strategies were. At the same time, they got to know what kind of person you were as well. The recruiting process helped me understand where I was going when I chose Notre Dame, what the people around me were going to be like, what the academic requirements on me were going to be – essentially, what the overall culture of the University was. Today it's not nearly as personalized as I think it should be. Through the recruiting process I really came to understand what each school was all about, not just from an athletic standpoint but from an academic standpoint as well. At Notre Dame you are a student first and your education at Notre Dame gives you the tools to achieve success in life."

The first play of the 1973 USC game when Luther leveled Lynn Swann for a loss and set the tone for the game and the rest of year, or his 99 yard interception return against Purdue in 1975 may be the first things you think of when someone says the name "Luther Bradley;" but when you ask "The Ole Man," that's not the first thing he thinks of. "When I think about my ND career the first thing that comes to my mind is being a starter as a freshman. I started every game that year. When I first realized that I was going to start the first game I was a bundle of nerves. I went to the pregame meal and after we ate my stomach was so messed up I had to go to the restroom and throw up. When I got to the stadium Coach Parseghian stopped by my locker as I was getting ready and asked me how I was feeling. I said, 'Coach, I'm nervous.' And Coach Parseghian replied, 'If I didn't think you could do this, I would not put you out there.' The first play of the game was a pass that was thrown to me and hit me in the hands and I dropped it. But after that I was able to calm down, focus, and play my game."

"Playing Southern California my freshman year is one of my favorite on-the-field memories. I was going up against Lynn Swann and I knocked his helmet off on the first play on a quick pass to the flat. I guess John McKay (USC Coach) figured he'd pick on the freshman. I had a couple of interceptions that game as well. That game pulled us into the conversation of being national championship contenders. People ask me all the time about that hit on Lynn Swann. When you're 18 years old, you see the blimp flying overhead before the game, you are so pumped up to be playing in a game on such a huge national stage. All I knew, I was ready to get out there and hit this cat, and I did! And then winning the national championship my freshman year against Alabama, that was the perfect culmination of a great season!"

While there were many great moments for Luther during his time at Notre Dame, the journey also had its uphill climbs. Fortunately for Luther, and every other student at Notre Dame, the Notre Dame Value Stream carried him through the rough waters and back to smooth sailing. "The biggest challenge for me was my first year and a half. To find a way to balance academics and playing football on a big-time basis was a definite struggle. Maybe if I hadn't started my freshman year it would not have been such a huge adjustment, but there is a great deal of pressure put on you when you start as a freshman. The expectations are just so much greater. And not only are the expectations on-the-field greater, you are still expected to be successful in the classroom. One day I decided that I should start going to the library every day right after practice. I had learned that if you went back to your dorm to study, people would stop by your room and then the next thing you knew you were goofing off and not studying. I started by going to the library for two to three hours every day after practice and I realized that it was exactly what I needed."

"I had a friend at Notre Dame, his first name was Bradley, and he ended up flunking out freshman year. I saw him walking across campus with his head down, and I asked him what was wrong, and he told me he had flunked out. There I was thinking to myself, I am the one who should be flunking out of Notre Dame, not you! He said not to worry, he would be back, and that's exactly what he did. He went to Bradley University, got his undergraduate degree (and straight A's), and came back and got his MBA from Notre Dame. Sometimes it just takes people a little bit longer to figure out how to get their priorities in order. Notre Dame certainly does help you learn how to do that."

As a student-athlete at Notre Dame, Luther was constantly reminded that he was a student first and an athlete second. He tells a perfect example of just that philosophy. "When I was a senior in college I was in this finance class that had a team project and your team had to present to the class at the end of the semester. At the beginning of the semester the professor had assigned each team their presentation date and you had to be there. The only way you could get out of this presentation was if there was a death in the family."

"My senior year I was invited to go to New York. They had the Heisman Trophy dinner at the New York City Athletic Club and I was one of three defensive backs who was going to get accepted as the best defensive back in college football. They had me scheduled to travel to New York City on Thursday and the dinner was on Friday. As it turned out, the day of the dinner in New York City was also the day that my team presentation was scheduled. I went to the professor to explain to him that I had been invited to participate in this event and he replied, 'I told you at the beginning of the semester that you had to be in class for your presentation. Unless your mother or father passes away, you cannot get out of this.' So I had to go talk to Moose Krause, who was the athletic director, and he ended up calling the dean who called my professor and told him that I had to go to New York for this dinner. We ended up getting it all worked out to present when I came back. My team ended up getting a B on the presentation and I was very excited about getting a B! But it just showed that education was really critical and it is very important to the culture here at Notre Dame. You made a commitment to your team and to the class and they wanted you to hold firm to your commitment. "

Luther had the good fortune of playing college football under two national championship winning head coaches, Coach Ara Parseghian and Coach Dan Devine. "Coach Parseghian recruited me and I signed with him. They called him 'The Man.' When I first got to Notre Dame one of my teammates had asked me, 'Did you get a chance to talk to The Man?' What? And then they explained, Ara is 'The Man.'"

"Whether you like it or not, ... you're a national figure after five games at Notre Dame." ~Ara Parseghian

"Coach Parseghian had this aura about him. He had a certain presence when he walked into the room. You always knew he had everything under control. He was extremely intelligent. He was a great motivator. He knew both offense and defense. He could coach the Xs and Os. He could motivate the second-stringers to play like the first team, the bench guys to play like starters, and keep the superstars in check; and he did it all without insulting or humiliating you."

"Dan Devine didn't possess the same skills as Ara Parseghian. He was a smart guy but very different. Don't get me wrong. He was just not an Xs and Os guy like Ara. However, he knew his limitations and his strengths. He knew that because of his lack of detail, he needed to surround himself with good assistant coaches, and he knew that he was a strong recruiter and that he needed to be the face that sold Notre Dame football. That was what made him a great coach. Dan Devine was a terrific person, but he was a leader who knew how to delegate and he knew how to stay out of the way. He knew he was not a play-calling guy and that he needed to have the best offensive and defensive coordinators to take care of that for him."

"Know Your Limitations." ~Luther Bradley

Like so many of his teammates, Luther could not say enough about Coach Parseghian. Coach Parseghian was the perfect role model for these men and did so much to mold and shape them and prepare them for the futures that were ahead of them. "Ara is such a phenomenal guy. He was not my dad, but he taught us a great deal about being prepared, committed, and how to perform at the highest level. You expected it out of him, and he expected it out of you. He was the difference maker. I always said, we knew if you gave Ara two or three weeks to prepare for a game, the other team was going to be in trouble and you were going to beat them. He is in a class above the rest. Coach Holtz is in that class as well."

As a Division I college football player, you work hard during your college career to hopefully get that precious opportunity to play football at the next level. Luther received just that opportunity. "My brother-in-law played football for the Steelers. I was slated to go in the first round and one of his coaches said that I would definitely go high in the draft. I had already taken a job at Merrill Lynch in New York City and the Steelers had called me a couple of days before the draft to express to me that they were very interested in picking me, and to get the best phone number in which to reach me. Merrill Lynch was so thrilled to have one of their employees in the NFL Draft that they had sent over a television crew to record the day. The draft started and as I'm anxiously awaiting the phone call from the Pittsburgh Steelers the phone rings and it's the Detroit Lions. The Lions had the 11th pick in the draft and the Steelers weren't up until pick No. 22 so they swooped in and stole me. I was a bit disappointed. The Steelers were really good at that time, but it all worked out for me. I ended up meeting my future wife in Detroit. God has a way of knowing exactly what you need and looking out for you."

While every professional player cherishes the opportunities they have been given when they reach that next level, it is still accompanied by plenty of trials and tribulations. There are often very few moments to let your guard down and actually enjoy the experience. You are constantly watching your back and making sure you are at the top of your game. It's only later that you can actually reflect on how tremendous the experience really was. "When you play football in the NFL you always feel like you have to prove yourself every week. It doesn't matter how well you performed the week before, you continually feel as though you could be cut at any moment. I always felt as though I needed a second career while I was playing in the NFL, so that I had something to fall back on in case I got cut one week. That was why I took the job at Merrill Lynch, you never felt like you were safe. They'd trade you away as if you were a piece of meat. There were no commitments to retain players on a long-term basis."

"Another low of playing in the NFL was the fact that they never really treated you as a person. You were more of a commodity to them. They didn't care if you were playing injured. It was all about the money to them. They'd give you a shot or some smelling salts and push you back out there. They are starting to be much more cautious these days about sending people out there injured. They have learned over the years the long term dangers of continuing to play people with injuries and/or concussions."

Luther and anyone else in the NFL would tell you there are also many great benefits playing at this level, coast to coast travel and playing in front of tens of thousands each week is just a start. But more importantly those that played in the NFL cherished being able to play against the best players in the world every week as the great test of courage and perseverance. Luther explained this point, "In college, you might have a couple of big games each season, but in the NFL you played the best of the best every week. At the professional level everyone was at the top of their game. I liked the fact that you got a lot more publicity at the professional level. I was used to the interviews and the phone calls from when I was at Notre Dame, but at the professional level it's even more intense. When I made the All-Rookie team my first year in the NFL, that was a huge accomplishment for me. When you are told that you are one of the top 24 rookies in the league that is pretty big."

Luther learned some very important lessons during his time playing in the NFL. Lessons that the Notre Dame Value Stream had already imparted on him but that he put to good use in the NFL. "Surrounding yourself with good people that you can trust is tremendously important. Always making sure that you are prepared for the next phase of your life is key. When it was time for me to move on from my football career, that's when I appreciated the education that I got from Notre Dame. When you are a product of Notre Dame, you are taught early on that there is more to life than football."

Heading into his fourth season in the USFL (Bradley played for the Chicago Blitz, Arizona Wranglers and Houston Gamblers and was the USFL's all-time interception leader) Luther came to the realization that it was time to move on from playing football. "I was doing some weight-lifting at camp and I wasn't able to lift as much as I was accustomed to lifting. I reduced the weight and tried again and I still couldn't do it. Very quickly I came to the realization that my body was just not going to let me do it anymore. I knew that if I couldn't lift and get my body into shape that it was time for me to move on. At that point I knew it was time to transition to my next career."

Luther has always made it a life priority to give back when he's able. His passion for working with kids made his connection with Youth for Christ (www.yfcdetroit.org), an easy one. "I've been on their Board of Directors for about ten years now and my work with Youth for Christ is an integral part of my life. It's my passion, I love working with kids. We have three hundred kids that we minister to on a weekly basis. We provide tutoring, take them to camps, conferences to equip them with life skills, we have moped (mini-bike) ministry (www.yfcdetroit.org/ministries/nypum); all of which give them a chance to experience things they would never experience otherwise. Of course, our ultimate goal is to introduce each kid to the gospel of Jesus Christ. I believe that if we can convert one child to the gospel, we will have fulfilled our mission. In reality, we convert hundreds per year. We meet them where they are."

"My executive director gave me this book written by Billy Graham, who founded Youth for Christ fifty years ago. The most amazing thing that I took from this book is as follows: Billy Graham's girlfriend at the time (now his wife) asked him the killer question when they were in college. She said 'Billy, What are you going to do with your life when you get out of college?' To which Billy responded, 'Be an evangelist.' She said, 'that is good Billy,' but then she gave him the killer response. She said 'Billy, if your life is not lived for something greater than yourself, your life is not worth living.' That is the legacy that I want to leave." And what a great legacy to leave.

Luther Bradley and his wife Sylvia

Lessons from Luther's Notre Dame Value Stream of Life:

- Make academics a priority in your life. When you prepare for your future you will be ready for whatever life puts in front of you. Make a commitment to your future and it will pay off tenfold.
- Surround yourself with good people. If you do this they will be there to catch you when you fall and support you during your successes.
- Know your limitations. Not everyone has the same strengths and weaknesses. Recognize both and use them to your advantage.
- Live your life for a greater cause!

Notre Dame vs. Michigan, 1994. Oscar McBride (# 80) and Derrick Mayes (#1) in between plays. (Photographer: Joe Raymond, photo courtesy of Notre Dame Archives.)

CHAPTER ELEVEN

The Mentor, Author, Speaker, Coach Oscar McBride

Kristene Burns-Saraiva, a writer and expert on role modeling and mentoring, wrote, " Mentoring is an understanding between two or more people. It is a way for people to learn from each other. Even though most think mentors are older, I think it's a bond and no matter age, race, or gender. It's a way for people to communicate!" It is Oscar McBride who is in constant pursuit of creating this mentoring relationship to help young people find their role in life. Through his non-profit organization Fit4Life Youth Foundation (www.oscarmcbride.com), and coaching high school football, Oscar is the role model every parent desires for their child. Oscar's message is not just behaviors but also the words in his book, "Relentless Wisdom: A Collection of Thoughts, Ideas and Opinions." His book examines the world of sports and athletics and encourages the reader to critically think about its evolution. Oscar's written words encourage coaches, parents and athletes alike to "step up" their level of responsibility with regards to sport and the powerful impact it has on society.

Oscar was born on July 23, 1972, in Gainesville, Florida. Growing up in Florida, he had always had his heart set on going to Florida State University. That is until he made his official visit to Notre Dame. It doesn't matter how well you thought you knew what Notre Dame was all about or stood for, you never completely understand all that is Our Lady's University until you make your first visit to the campus and meet the people who collectively are called the Fighting Irish. And each one of us whose path ended up under the Golden Dome has a specific moment that made us realize that ND was our destiny. Oscar's moment can be described quite simply. "Two words ... Irv Smith."

Setting out on a new journey can often be overwhelming and intimidating, but Oscar did not let either one of those things slow him down or get in his way. He set out to establish himself in the car industry in the toughest territory of all ... Michigan! "My first job (after football) was as a regional manager for a company that did sales training for people in the car industry. Basically it was an inside sales job, calling upon car dealers, and teaching them how to train their sales reps to be more efficient and effective in their jobs. My territories were Michigan (the car sales Mecca of the United States) and South Carolina. I grew a very thick skin from that job and definitely learned to not take things personally. My next job was in wholesale mortgage banking, and I did that for 11 years. I started out as a sales associate, progressed to national sales manager, and eventually made it to be a vice president."

After more than a decade in sales, Oscar decided it was time to try his hand at something a little different. He was ready to embark on a journey where he could give something back, and make a difference in young people's lives. He realized that coaching and teaching was something that he was passionate about and excelled at as well. The Notre Dame Value Stream taught us that we should do our part to give back any time we can, and that is exactly what Oscar did. "Then I decided to go back to school. I earned my Master's Degree and started teaching at the high school level as well as coaching football. I am currently working towards my Doctorate in Education, because I realize how much I enjoy working with young people. It is such a gift to be able to work with young people, to be able to help shape and mold young football players, both athletically and character wise. And because I have had similar experiences and have been exposed to many of the same situations that they are, I can impart upon them advice to help them make good choices."

On his journey to establish his career in education, his path took a turn towards a familiar place. One he had strayed away from, but that which was calling him home. "In 2008 I attended a National Catholic Educators Conference for teachers and coaches, and as I was looking over all of the seminars that were being offered, one in particular caught my eye. PLACT: Play Like A

Champion Today. I thought to myself, hey, I know that! So I went in to the seminar and Dr. Clark Power was giving a presentation on the importance of developing youth through sport. I am sitting in the front row, and am literally on the edge of my seat for the entire presentation. Following the seminar, I introduced myself to Dr. Power, 'Hi, I am Oscar Mc' … and before I can even get my name out he says, 'You're Oscar McBride and you played on the '93 Championship team! You need to be involved in this!' Within one year I was working with them as a consultant in the Los Angeles Archdiocese, and in October of 2010 they approached me about working for them full time, and by January of 2011 I was a permanent fixture on their staff."

"Adversity is another way to measure the greatness of individuals. I never had a crisis that didn't make me stronger." ~ Lou Holtz

"There was a point in my life when I was really bitter at Notre Dame for my limited success in the NFL, but then I realized that it was not Notre Dame's fault. I could have prepared myself better for the draft. I could have prepared myself better for the business aspect of the NFL. This was all a part of growing up and realizing that we all are in charge of our lives, and that you are given an opportunity to be the best version of yourself that you can possibly be."

For all intents and purposes, Oscar was headed to Florida State. His aunt had attended Florida State and it was at the top of his list. "When Bobby Bowden came to the house to visit my family, he helped my mom bring in the groceries and stayed for dinner. We were all sold on the idea of me going to Florida State. My official visit to Florida State was for the 1989 FSU - Miami game, a rivalry game that everyone looks forward to, and Florida State beat Miami that year in convincing fashion, 24-10. But when I made my official visit to Notre Dame, in the ever so appealing South Bend, Indiana (he says sarcastically), I met this dude with this big smile and dimples (Irv Smith) who just lit up the room. I met his best friend Nick Smith, and the rest of the guys on the team. I had an amazing weekend and left Notre Dame immediately feeling like I was already part of the Notre Dame family. Bye-bye Florida State." It's that family mentality that gave us that instant connection to Notre Dame and drew us into her clutches.

Oscar still remembers going to the Orange Bowl scrimmage with his mom. "I saw Chris Zorich tackle Ricky Watters, and saw a huge fleck of gold fly off his helmet, and thought … dude … there is no way that I can play here. Rocket Ismail came over to the sidelines and said to me, 'We can't wait to have you here! We are going to win a National Championship next year!' And that's all it took!"

Being a part of something such as Notre Dame is never easy. You have to do more than just show up to succeed. You have to put in the work day in and day out. There is no phoning it in on days you don't feel good. You still have to get up, go to class and go to practice every day. No excuses. But all the hard work is not without its rewards. Oscar shares the rewards that he reaped during his senior year at Notre Dame. "During the 1992 season, I played with a broken jaw and a fracture in my foot. There were all of these questions coming into the 1993 season. What kind of team will Notre Dame bring out this year? They don't have a quarterback. They don't have a tight end. They don't have a running back. Ron Powlus was new to the scene. There were just so many unknowns, and nobody expected us to be as good as we were that year. We just completely played for each other. We had an amazing bunch of guys ... Jeff Burris, Lake Dawson, Marc Edwards, Jim Flannigan, Derrick Mayes, Aaron Taylor, Kevin McDougal, Bryant Young, and Ray Zellars among others, and Coach Holtz did his best to downplay all of the questions and we just went about our business."

The biggest rewards for the blood, sweat and tears that you leave behind are the opportunities and open doors that you are greeted with in life. Not to say that life after college is easy, but people recognize the effort that it takes to survive at a place like Notre Dame and you are respected for your achievements. "Prior to draft day I had several conversations with teams who were interested in me. They would tell me things like, 'if you are still available by x round of the draft, we'd be thrilled to take you.'"

And then the NFL Draft finally arrives. "The first day, and the first two rounds, come and go, and I was not picked up by any teams. I was kind of bummed because the Chicago Bears had expressed a significant amount of interest, and instead took a punter in the second round. A punter? The third round came and went. Then the fourth ... fifth ... sixth ... Are you kidding me? The seventh round came and went, and still no one had chosen me. After the draft was complete, my phone started ringing off the hook with teams talking to me about their interest in picking me up as a free agent. At this point I say to myself, I am a Florida boy who has lived in freezing South Bend, Indiana, for four years, and I have my pick of several teams; I am going to pick somewhere warm! I signed to play tight end for the Arizona Cardinals, and by the fourth game of the season, I was the starting tight end."

Making it to the NFL is an accomplishment to be celebrated, but as many learn once they are there, it is still a job just like any other. It has its heart stopping moments of joy and its pitfalls as well. "The best part of playing in the NFL is that playing football, something that you love, is actually your job! The challenging part of playing in the NFL is the super long days. You get up early, come in, watch film, go to team meetings, go through each week's game plan, go out on the field for the walk through, change, practice, eat lunch, work out, shower, more meetings ... The day is long, easily a 12 hour day, but at the end of the day you are still playing football for a living."

"The worst part of playing in the NFL is the business side of the game. It's not a matter of being the best player out there ... it's about signing the biggest and best contract and making the most money. Regardless of anyone's talent level, if you are making the most money, then you are the man. I got signed at the league minimum of $119,000, and started 11 games as a rookie. I was told by coach Buddy Ryan that if I played, he would renegotiate my contract with me and compensate me with the equivalent of being a second round draft pick. We had a deal on the table, and then much to my surprise, after the 1995 season, Buddy Ryan was fired. They brought in Vince Tobin in 1996 and he drafted two additional tight ends, had no desire to renegotiate my contract, and that was the beginning of the end. Unless you are taken as a top draft pick, there is nothing guaranteed or set in stone. After the 1996 season, I signed with the Kansas City Chiefs. I was there from January until the first week of the season, at which point I was released."

Playing in the NFL is a lot like life. You must learn to work hard, do your best and treat every day is if it's your last, because you never know when someone will decide you are no longer needed. It's a tough business. Those who survive are the ones that realize that it is not a forever career, it is only a moment in your life. "After the first preseason game in 1997, I had gone in to talk to Marty Schottenheimer and his staff. I said to them, 'I know you picked up Tony Gonzalez in the draft. If you are going to cut me (which it seemed as though the writing was on the wall) please cut me now so that I have a chance to find a spot somewhere else.' But they kept reassuring me that everything was okay. They told me, 'You are great for us. There is nothing for you to be worried about.' We were getting ready to play the Rams, the opening game of the season. The trainer was headed over to tape me up when I get tapped on the shoulder, 'Coach needs to talk to you and bring your play book.'"

"I'm sitting there in Marty Schottenheimer's office, and he says to me, 'You were a big surprise to us in camp. You did a great job, but this is a monetary decision.' And just as I had feared, there was no team for me to go to. All rosters were set. Had they released me earlier, I could have found something else, but this was all about the money. And there I was, stuck without a job. When I left the NFL I was really bitter for a long time. I couldn't watch football. I went through a period of depression. Finally one day, it dawned on me. You graduated from Notre Dame, go get a job. You are only 26 years old, go get a job. And that's exactly what I did!"

Whether he realized it or not, preparation was a key aspect of his time both on and off the field at Notre Dame. Coach Lou Holtz was very instrumental in making sure that his players were prepared for not only what was happening on the field, but in the rest of their lives as well. A prepared individual is a successful individual.

"There are no secrets to success. It is the result of preparation, hard work, and learning from failure." ~ Colin Powell

"In December of 1991 we were down in New Orleans getting ready to play in the Sugar Bowl. No one expected us to win this bowl. No one even thought we belonged in this bowl. They kept telling us that we belonged in a cereal bowl. Our last team practice before the game was held in the convention center in full pads, on concrete, because it was raining outside. Coach Holtz calls us together after practice and gives us his rallying pep talk. Lou began, 'We have a big game coming up and I want to tell you about Steve Spurrier and our opponent. Now here is what is going to happen tomorrow. We are going to get the ball on offense, we are going to give the ball to Jerome Bettis, and he is going to score on the first drive. Then we are going to come out on defense, we are going to get the ball back on a turnover, Jerome is going to get the ball back on offense, and he is going to score again. Then I want you to look across the field and you will see Steve Spurrier throw his headset on the ground and start to pout.'"

"January 1, 1992 ... we take the field and Jerome gets the ball on offense. Jerome then scores on a 45 yard touchdown play. The Gators get the ball back on offense, and Demetrius DuBose gets the interception giving us the ball back. Then Jerome comes back out and scores again. We look across the field and right before our eyes Spurrier throws down his headset, crosses his arms and starts to pout."

"We all look at each other and say ... 'What just happened??'"

"After that moment, my level of respect for Coach Holtz went through the roof. I knew that not only had he studied the team and knew their tendencies, studied what they were going to do on offense, defense, and special teams; but he also had studied the manners of Coach Spurrier as well. He really went above and beyond in doing his job."

Oscar and Kevin Dugan (ND '01), helped found Play Like a Champion Today's Uganda initiative, which is promoting sports as a form of physical, moral and social development for the children in Uganda. His newest project is the release of his radio show on the TNNDN Radio Network to help teach others the importance of the development of character through sports. "The most important part of being a good coach is imparting upon your players (and often times their parents, too) that making good decisions on the field can be translated into making good decisions in life."

Oscar McBride

Lessons from Oscar's Notre Dame Value Stream of Life:

- Find something you love, and then find a way to make that your career. You may have to think outside the box a bit but when you love your job it is much easier to give it your all.
- Do your best to prepare yourself for your future. The best way to set yourself up for future success is hard work and preparation in advance.
- In life, as in football, you have to do more than just show up to succeed. You have to put in the work, day in and day out. There is no phoning it in on days you don't feel good. No excuses. But all the hard work is not without its rewards.

Mike McCoy, in a white uniform jersey, 1969. (Photo courtesy of Notre Dame Archives.)

CHAPTER TWELVE

The Motivational Speaker and Youth Empowerment Mike McCoy

Ralph Waldo Emerson must have been thinking of a person such as Mike McCoy when he wrote, "Passion is one of the most powerful engines of success. When you do a thing, do it with all your might. Put your whole soul into it. Stamp it with your own personality. Be active, be energetic and faithful, and you will accomplish your object. Nothing great was ever achieved without passion." Mike's life today and his work is one rooted in passion, his passion to empower young people to find their vision for the future through a faith-based message of hope and confidence to overcome the obstacles of life. The Notre Dame Value Stream gave Mike the tools he needed to be able to help arm young people with the tools they so desperately needed to make good decisions amidst the pressures of today's society. The biggest reason that young adults make poor decisions is that they have not been prepared for the challenges they will face. Mike helps equip today's youth with the skills needed to make good decisions. "Notre Dame and the NFL had given me this great platform to reach people and spread my message. I took a pay cut, and a huge leap of faith, and set out to make a difference. I started on Bill Glass' staff (Champions For Life: www.billglass.org), speaking in prisons, public and Catholic schools. I now have Mike McCoy Ministries reaching students in Catholic Schools with the message of Hope, Faith and Encouragement. I have partnered with Notre Dame's 'Play Like a Champion Today' Educational Series." Over the last 20 years, Mike has spoken around the world, from schools in Scotland to prisons in South Africa.

Being larger than most is usually an asset when it comes to football. But for former Notre Dame and Green Bay Packers standout lineman Mike McCoy, being larger meant being told at an early age that he wasn't able to play a sport in which he would eventually excel at the highest level. Mike was not allowed to play football in elementary school for fear he may hurt someone. Once he reached Cathedral Prep High in Erie, Pennsylvania, Mike finally found an ally in head coach Tony Zambrowski. Zambrowski and other coaches helped Mike learn to turn his size into an asset, a weapon that with learned aggression would push him toward a college scholarship and eventually a job in the NFL. Mike was a three-year letter-winner at Notre Dame who earned consensus All-American honors under former Irish coach Ara Parseghian.

Mike was selected second overall in the 1970 NFL draft by the Green Bay Packers and played 11 seasons with the Packers, Oakland Raiders and the New York Giants. His pro football honors include:

- Packers Rookie of the Year
- Packers Dodge NFL Man of the Year
- Notre Dame Pro Player of the Year
- Erie, Pennsylvania, Pro Hall of Fame
- Cathedral Prep Hall of Fame
- Pennsylvania Sports Hall of Fame.

He also received the Harvey Foster Humanitarian Award from the Notre Dame Alumni Association. Another prestigious honor was the Bronco Nagurski Legends award, which recognized the top defensive players in the last 40 years. Mike now is the driving force behind the inspirational Mike McCoy Ministries program, lives in Jefferson, Georgia and has four children: Molly, Maggie, Katie and Caleb, along with six grandchildren and another on the way.

Mike did not start playing football until his sophomore year in high school at Cathedral Prep, because he had always been told that he was too big to play football. His mom used to always tell him, "Don't sit on your friends' bicycles because you will break them." Coach Tony Zambrowski was a driving force in his high-school football career. "After a very successful junior year a lot of colleges began to look at me. Coach Zambrowski asked me where I was looking to go to college. I told him that I had no idea where I wanted to go. He asked me if I had ever considered going to Notre Dame (Zambrowski's Alma Mater) and at that point I did not even know that Notre Dame existed. He took me on a trip to visit the campus, and I knew very quickly that Notre Dame fit me perfectly. I was the first person from my high school class to sign a letter of intent to play college football. I also visited Syracuse, Penn State and Indiana."

"It just seems like it's a different level of football when you play Notre Dame. I'm not sure if it has to do with the rivalry or the tradition of Notre Dame. But it seems like it's a different type of game."
Brandon Kirsch (quarterback, Purdue University)

The best part of playing football at a school like Notre Dame is the heated passion with which each game is played. Everyone is a rival. Everyone feels as though you are the team to beat. Everyone gets up just a little bit bigger the day they play the Fighting Irish. It's what comes with the territory when you put on Our Lady's shining gold helmet. "The rivalries with USC and Michigan State were very fierce during my time at Notre Dame. We didn't do so well against Purdue when I was there, so we won't talk about that. (laughs) The game we played against USC my junior year, however, has to be the best game during my (college) career." It was the last game of the 1968 regular season against defending national champion USC, and prior to the game the Los Angeles media had proclaimed Mike as a sure bet for All-American honors in 1969. "The media said I was a 'dominating force on the line of scrimmage' against USC that day, and the Notre Dame defense held Heisman Trophy winner O.J. Simpson to a career-low 55 yards on 22 carries. At one point during the fourth quarter, Simpson looked up at me and said, 'Oh no, not you again.' I guess I left quite an impression on him."

"My senior year we were invited to play the Texas Longhorns in the Cotton Bowl, which was the first time that Notre Dame had been invited to a bowl game in 45 years. That was pretty special. When we were recruited to play football at Notre Dame, we were told that Notre Dame never went to bowl games, so to receive that invitation was quite an achievement for us as a team." (Texas beat Notre Dame 21-17 and won the national championship.)

In today's current era of football, time spent in the weight room is a normal part of the routine of a football player. Back when Mike played football, working out with weights was unheard of and definitely not promoted or supported. That's where Father Lange came into the picture. "South Bend was a very small town, and other than school and football, there wasn't much to be offered. Father Lange's gym was right behind Keenan Hall, and on my own I started going over there to lift weights. This was not an activity that was encouraged by the football coaches. It was a different era. Father Lange's gym was such a unique environment and Father Lange was such a force that it drew us back to his gym. Our time was precious. Between football and school work we did not have a lot of free time, but I really enjoyed going over to the gym and spending time with the other guys who were there. More important than lifting weights was the time that I spent getting to know Father Lange as a person. He was such a remarkable person. I remember one time I went over to the gym, Father Lange was in his 80s and he was partially blind from being a diabetic. He asked me to help him down onto his bench. Then he said, 'Can you hand me those dumbbells so that I can do some flys?' I looked at him and said, 'The 35 pound ones?' And he replied, 'No, the 85 pound ones.' And then I did some flys with him. Even in his 80s he was still in amazing shape."

Anyone who has attended Notre Dame, stepped on campus or has had any interaction with someone affiliated with the University understands the meaning of the Notre Dame family. It does not matter whether you are a student, alum or subway fan, if you love Our Lady's University, you are part of the family. Some people however, have a knack of expressing this value of the Notre Dame family better than others. Coach Ara Parseghian was one of these people who did it best. "My time playing under Coach Ara Parseghian was a great experience. It has become more significant to me as I've gotten older and have had a chance to look back on it. When you are in school you are so busy with classes and practice, and at that point in your life, you really don't have a lot of experience with different coaches and game strategies. After playing in the NFL and having a chance to experience other coaches, it is then that you truly realize what a remarkable experience you had. When I look at the schools that we played when I was at Notre Dame, and the things we accomplished as a team, what we had under Coach Parseghian was really unique. You definitely appreciate it more as time goes by."

"My senior year in high school, when I signed my letter of intent to play football at Notre Dame, Coach Parseghian sent me a picture with a message saying, 'Welcome to the Notre Dame family.' That meant so much to me. We still have it framed in our house. Notre Dame really is a family that stays with you throughout your life. Parseghian also did a great job of surrounding himself with a great staff. He was an amazing coach, but his surrounding staff was made up of quality people, and that just enhanced what he could do on his own. This was probably the best group of coaches in college football at the time: Paul Shoults (defensive backs), John Ray (linebackers), Joe Yonto (defensive line), Tom Pagna (offensive backfield), Jerry Wamphler (offensive line), John Murphy (prep team), George Sefcik and Wally Moore (freshmen)."

Mike was fortunate to have an opportunity to play in the NFL for the Green Bay Packers. He never expected a career in the NFL. In fact, he was so busy making plans to attend law school that he did not pay much attention to the NFL draft. That is until he got the phone call from the Green Bay Packers telling him that he was the second overall pick in the draft (behind Terry Bradshaw who was the No. 1 pick, selected by the Steelers). "The NFL back in the 70s was a totally different ball game than it is today. We all worked during the off-season because the NFL did not pay enough to be our sole form of income. I worked in several different fields - sales, banking, and real estate - all the while trying to figure out what I wanted to do when I grew up. It was quite the balancing act. During the off season you worked in your alternate career for five or six months, working from 8-to-5, and then trained in the evening so that you would be ready to jump right back into the NFL. You didn't even see your fellow teammates in the off-season until training camp started back up. The team owners assumed that you would stay in shape during the off-season and come to camp ready to play."

Blessed with a professional football career that lasted over a decade, Mike was ready to move on and get back to his family roots in Pennsylvania. "I knew the end of my football career was coming when I got traded to the New York Giants for my 10th and 11th seasons. When I was no longer wanted by the NFL, we decided to move back to Pennsylvania to be near the grandparents. Five years into retirement, my daughter (who was in seventh grade at the time) came home and began to tell me about all of the pressures and temptations she was being exposed to in school. At that moment I had a great epiphany about what I could do to help. I decided to join a friend of mine who was putting together an organization that was sending former NFL players around the country to speak at schools and serve as positive role models."

"It brings me great satisfaction going into the schools and getting feedback from the kids; to hear exactly what they are going through and figure out how we can help them. A lot of students open up to me through our comment cards, about a lot of serious subjects including depression, drug and alcohol abuse and other problems they are dealing with at home. This feedback allows me to help kids who are in tough situations get the guidance and trained help they need. I believe every student in America is currently at risk regardless of their race, creed, or financial situation. Whether they attend a public school, private school, Christian school, or a Catholic school, they are all at risk due to the influences of our culture. The shift started in the late 1950s and early 1960s from faith, family and friends to what we have today – friends, maybe family, and where faith is almost irrelevant. It's my job to stand up against the influences that are undermining the future of so many. We get some referrals through Notre Dame Alumni Clubs but the majority of our speaking engagements come through recommendations from schools we have previously visited and my Notre Dame contacts. The Ministry is basically me! I have a great board of directors who help guide the Ministry."

If you'd like to help out the Mike McCoy Ministries visit his web site at www.mccoy77.com. He would love to come to speak in your Catholic

Schools. He only asks for expenses. You can also visit the NFLPA site (www.sotl.com). Search Mike McCoy in the upper right search field and he will get a donation for every visit to his site. It costs you nothing!

Shortly after my interview with Mike, his wife Kia succumbed to a long battle with cancer. Our prayers and thoughts are with Mike and his family.

Mike McCoy and his beloved wife, Kia.

Lessons from Mike's Notre Dame Value Stream of Life:

- What we do in life and how we affect others comes from our heart and the passion we have to serve one another.
- Always give everything you do your best and you will never have any regrets.
- Face life with faith, passion and good preparation and you will find success.

NOTRE DAME 1957 FOOTBALL SQUAD

FIRST ROW: (left to right) Tom Gordecki (Associate Senior Manager), Richard Shulsen, Patrick Dolan, Richard Lynch, Robert Gaydos, Richard Prendergast, Edward Sullivan, Robert Ward, Aubrey Lewis, Charles Luna, Frank Kuchta, John McGinley, Matt Aiben (Head Manager of Football). SECOND ROW: John McFadden (Associate Senior Manager), Frank Reynolds, Richard Royer, Gary Myers, Allen Ecuyer, Ronald DeNardo, William Owens, Carl Hebert, Paul Djuisasak, Bronko Nagurski, Robert Wetoska, Robert Williams, Frank Geremia, Michael Muehlbauer. THIRD ROW: Peter Sabich, Michael Dugan, William Hickman, Kevin Burke, Neil Seaman, James Colosimo, Charles Puntillo, Donald Lawrence, Norman Odyniec, James Schaaf, Ronald Toth, Nick Pietrosante, Richard Selcer. FOURTH ROW: Michael Gorham, Oliver Flor, Michael Lodish, Robert Pietrzak, Patrick Doyle, Richard Beuchen, Donald Costa, Charles Frederick, Louis Manno, David Hurd, Kenneth Adamson, Patrick Healy, George Izo, Monty Stickles, Donald White. FIFTH ROW: Thomas Rini, Douglas McGinn, Robert Nicolazzi, Donald McAllister, Paul Weber, Lawrence Pring, James Cratty, Edward Nebel, Robert Carson, Henry Wilke, Paul Loop, Robert Scholtz, John Quinn, Allan Chonko, Gary Steckler, Albin Sabal, John Harerisk.

Notre Dame team photo, 1957. (Photographer: Bagby Photo Co., photo courtesy of Notre Dame Archives.)

CHAPTER THIRTEEN

The Football Coach Pat Dolan

Pat Dolan grew up in Throop, Pennsylvania, a predominately Irish Catholic community outside of Scranton, surrounded by Ireland-esque rolling green hills and overlooking the Lackawanna River. The youngest of eight children, Pat had many family and community influences urging him to attend Notre Dame from an early age.

Both of his parents were widowed early in life (his father left with three children and his mother left with two of her own) when their parish priest intervened to introduce them and suggested that they marry each other, which they did fairly soon after. They had three more children together to make eight, Pat the baby after his younger brother Paul died as an infant. His older sisters were all nurses and paid for a lot of his clothing when he was in high school and college. Even though he was probably one of the poorest kids on the team at ND, his buddies used to borrow his clothes because his sisters had such good taste, some of which were never returned. Bob Williams (Notre Dame quarterback) showed up at their house in New Jersey years later wearing one of Pat's shirts that he had tailored to fit his slimmer build!

Unforgettable wins are what Notre Dame is all about and Pat can lay claim to one of his own: the upset over Oklahoma in 1957 ending an OU 47-game winning streak. Following his Notre Dame career, Pat married his high school sweetheart Katie and pursued a career in coaching. They have one daughter, Erin Dolan, and Erin has three children: Connor ND 2012, Mary Fiona ND 2015 and Faelen who is in high school and hoping to be ND 2020.

"Throop, Pennsylvania, was a very strong Irish Catholic community and many friends of our family and parishioners influenced me to attend Notre Dame. Not necessarily to play football, but to receive an excellent Catholic education. I was also exposed to Notre Dame football early on when they came to my high school, Scranton Technical High School, when I was a freshman to recruit one of my teammates, Bill Hollenbeck. Bill went on to become a specialist kicker at ND. After that exposure to the Fighting Irish I became much more interested in playing football there. Even though there were many top football programs who were recruiting me, the only other school that I was seriously looking at besides Notre Dame was the University of North Carolina."

Pat's experiences at Notre Dame taught him early that Notre Dame was more than just a school, more than just a football program, but a family. The connections and friends he made at Notre Dame stayed with him throughout his life journeys and were a support in good times and bad. "Just playing for Notre Dame, and traveling with the team itself was an amazing experience. We played some very talented teams, and there were some great players that I played with (too many to list, Pat says). I would not trade my time at Notre Dame for anything."

"One of my best friends on the team was running back Dick Lynch. He went to Phillipsburg Catholic High School in Phillipsburg, New Jersey, and I was familiar with the area even before I got to ND because my high school played Phillipsburg High School in football. When we got to Notre Dame, Dick reached out to me being that we were from the same area and we became lifelong friends. Dick was the hero in our big upset over Oklahoma in 1957. He was a defensive standout (played defensive back), but he also scored the only touchdown in that 7-0 win over the Sooners which broke their 47-game win streak. Dick went on to have a successful career in the NFL playing for the Washington Redskins and the New York Giants."

Pat and his teammates learned much about hard work, success, and supporting each other during their time at Our Lady's University. The Notre

Dame Value Stream not only guided them during their football playing days, but throughout their lives and was the glue that held them together. "Our quarterback, Bob Williams, and I were also very close. He is the godfather to my daughter, Erin. There is nothing quite like the Notre Dame family. It stays with you forever."

Though the media has changed tremendously over the last 50 years, the hype that the media placed on that Notre Dame – Oklahoma match-up was quite intense. What made the story even bigger was the fact that in the previous 48 games Oklahoma only had one loss, and that one loss was at the hands of Notre Dame. And here come the Irish, headed into Norman to try and do the same thing that their 1953 counterparts had done when they upset the Sooners in their season debut by a score of 28-21.

"Oklahoma was ranked No. 1 in the nation. Notre Dame had been 2-8 the season before in 1956 and headed into the Oklahoma game, the Fighting Irish were 4-2, but were still not on anyone's short list as being world beaters by any stretch of the imagination. So here was this nobody team from South Bend coming into Norman and we turned their world completely upside down."

"The secret is to work less as individuals and more as a team. As a coach, I play not my eleven best, but my best eleven." - Knute Rockne

When push came to shove, even though they weren't the best team out there by any stretch, the Notre Dame Value Stream carried them through the test that was Oklahoma and brought them out victorious. "When you play for Notre Dame, you think you are capable of anything. That is what our coaches taught us. Go out there, do your best, and good things will happen. And that's exactly how we ended up doing it."

Everything about that day was unforgettable. "It was an incredible situation. Oklahoma was No. 1 and undefeated and no one truly expected us to come in there and pull off the upset. It was absolutely unbelievable. We were supposed to stay overnight in Norman after the game but because of the extraordinary situation they decided to fly us home for the various celebrations that were waiting for us (and to get out of Dodge before the place erupted)."

I can only imagine the Notre Dame days of the 1950s when the team arrived back from those great wins. Just like in *Knute Rockne All American*, the crowds lined up waiting for Rock and the team to arrive, Pat and the Irish flew back to South Bend with the crowds awaiting their arrival. In the Knute Rockne days the crowds lined the South Shore Line station in anticipation of the team's arrival. In 1957 the fans lined up at the South Bend airport to welcome the team back from Norman. "As we were flying back to South Bend, the pilots kept announcing to us what the plan was and what was waiting for us when we got home. The towns below us kept turning their lights on and off in celebration of our big win and they even sang the Fight Song for us on the plane."

"The airport was loaded with people when we arrived in South Bend, and there was a parade-like atmosphere driving down the streets on our way to campus. When we arrived on campus, the students were waiting to welcome us at the circle. It was unforgettable." Absolutely unforgettable.

Finishing his collegiate career on such a high note, Pat could have pursued a professional football career, but decided coaching was the road he preferred to take. "I could have had a shot at it, but I decided to pursue a coaching career instead. My first coaching stop was at a little high school in Mt. Clemens, Michigan, St. Mary's High School. I coached the football team there for three years. Then I moved to Franklin Township, New Jersey, and took a job coaching the football team at Franklin Township High School. I started out coaching the football team, was eventually promoted to be their Athletic Director and stayed there until I retired in 1992."

It's amazing, how at any point in your life your Notre Dame ties can come in to play. Pat Dolan was able to give a fellow Notre Dame graduate an opportunity that helped propel him towards future successes. "In 1989 we were looking for a new head coach for the high school football team, and my old friend Dick Lynch gave me a call. He knew we were looking for someone, knew a fellow Notre Dame alum that was looking for a job and suggested that I take a look at him. That alum was Charlie Weis, and we gave him his first football head coaching job. He coached our football team for one year and the team broke the state record for touchdowns that year as well as going to the New Jersey State Championship. Tremendous start to that young man's career!"

At the end of my delightful conversation with Pat he asked me if I had ever heard of the Irish Blessing. Well, as an Irish girl, I'm sure I had but I asked to hear it from him all the same. And so I received an Irish blessing from one of Notre Dame's greats. There truly is nothing like the Notre Dame family. God bless!

May the road rise up to meet you.
May the wind always be at your back.
May the sun shine warm upon your face,
And rains fall soft upon your fields.
And until we meet again,
May God hold you in the palm of His hand.

Pat Dolan

Lessons from Pat's Notre Dame Value Stream of Life:

- Whether it's sports or life, go out there, do your best, and good things will happen.
- The support of your family and friends is what gets you through life, in good times and bad.
- The keys to success are hard work and supporting one another.
- Whenever possible, help others. I was able to give Charlie Weis his first coaching job. Always do your best to help out your fellow man. You never know when you'll need their help in return.

Notre Dame vs. Tennessee, 1991. Pete Bercich (#47) making a tackle. (Photographer: Joe Raymond, photo courtesy of Notre Dame Archives.)

CHAPTER FOURTEEN

The Color Man of the Viking Network
Pete Bercich

Color Commentary has become the new art form of college and professional sports across America. These men and women use their whit, athletic experience and zany personalities to amuse us, describe the action and provide opinionated insights into why the coaches did what they did, what a player did and why they did it, why a team won and why a team lost and finally what they would have done differently if they were the coach or player. And, of course, they also help confirm why we all hate those guys in zebra stripes. Their job is to provide excitement and the first reaction to the action on the field. Whether on television and even more so on the radio, they provide "color," they blend hues seen and heard in the form of words, making what we watch interesting. Pete Bercich's playing days with the Minnesota Vikings are over. Today, he is no longer black and blue from the bruises you get playing in the "Black and Blue" Central Division of the NFL. Pete has added a whole new set of colors to his repertoire using his voice, whit and knowledge of the game to provide "The Color" of game and analysis for the Vikings. Pete is the voice that all those Vikings fans hear. What a treat for his wife Amy and their three children to listen to dad tell it like it is on Viking's radio Sunday afternoons.

Many opportunities present themselves when you least expect them. As Pete was deciding where the post-football path of his journey was going to take him, a friend helped guide him in the right direction. "After I was done playing in the NFL I spent a year working for a company called Bremen Castings (www.bremencastings.com). Bremen Castings, Inc. (BCI) is a precision CNC (Computer Numerical Control) machine shop with our own green sand foundry under one roof. BCI knows that *Status Quo Sucks*, and our partners/customers cannot achieve "World Class" status without companies like BCI. The owner and I became friends during my NFL off-seasons while I was working out in South Bend. We met through a mutual friend, and he told me when I was done playing ball that he'd have a job waiting for me. My wife and I bought a house in Granger, Indiana so we could be close to her parents in southwest Michigan, and I took the job at the foundry. At the same time I was trying to get a job as a coach. During my last year with the Vikings, Denny Green had pulled me aside and told me that I should think about coaching. My first go at it didn't work out so well, which is how I ended up at the foundry. In January of 2002, Mike Tice was hired as the head coach, and they asked me to come back and try my hand at coaching again. We sold our house in Indiana and moved to Minnesota so that I could coach full time. I was an assistant coach for the Vikings. I spent one year doing quality control and four years as a linebacker coach. Coaching taught me even more about the game."

"When Tice was fired they brought in Brad Childress, and I was let go with 10 days left on my contract. I tried to get on somewhere else, but it just didn't work out. I took a job at Merrill Lynch as a financial advisor in 2006, and then on Monday mornings I would go into the local radio station (for free) from 6 am – 7 am and do analysis of Sunday's game, so that I could get to work for an 8 am meeting. At the end of that season, the Vikings' radio analyst retired and in 2007 I was offered the job." Today Pete enjoys the best of both worlds. He is able to split his time and talents between working on the radio for the Minnesota Vikings and doing sales for Bremen Castings. This past season was his first year as part of the Viking radio network. "This past NFL season was my first as a part of the Viking radio network team (Analyst Minnesota Vikings Radio Network at KFAN AM 1130 Minneapolis). The Vikings are getting more involved in the entertainment aspect of the game. Currently I fill-in on the radio during the week. Mark Rosen (Co-host on Mark Rosen's Sports Sunday at WCCO-TV) and I do his show on Sunday nights, and in the meantime I am back at Bremen Castings as an Account

Manager in the upper Midwest. I kind of just fell into the radio broadcasting stuff, but I really enjoy it."

"The impossible we do every day, miracles take a bit longer."
4404th CSG/PERSCO Dhahran AB, Saudi Arabia (USAF)

Pete had one dream as a kid growing up in Joliet, Illinois – to fly fighter planes for the Air Force. Though his path may not have taken that route, he can still cross flying in a fighter plane off his bucket list. A baseball kid who quickly learned that football much better fit his explosive temperament, Pete had a successful football career at Providence Catholic High School which set him up for opportunities at such schools as Stanford, Notre Dame, and his family's favorite Michigan State. Pete's determination and Midwest work ethic set him up for success both in his collegiate career and beyond.

Believe it or not, football was not Pete's favorite sport. He started out as a baseball kid but soon came to realize that his temperament was much better suited for football than for baseball. "Baseball was what I loved to do, but then I realized in high school that mentally it was not what I wanted to do. It did not suit me. Baseball is all about dealing with failure. Effort means a lot, but it does not mean as much in baseball as it does in football. How I dealt with failure (in both baseball and football) was getting pissed off. I didn't deal with failure well at all. In football, if you work hard, you will probably have success. I also learned that it was much easier to take out my frustrations in football, than it was in baseball."

Football success came early to Pete in high school and his aspirations of playing football for a Division I school and beyond became a definite reality. "At the end of my sophomore year in high school I realized I could play with the seniors and hold my own. We won State that year, and I felt like I was definitely part of the turning point of that team. During my junior year letters started showing up from big schools ... Miami, Southern Cal, Michigan, Penn State. My father played in the NFL. He played on the original Dallas Cowboy team, and both my parents went to Michigan State. My dad never talked about football, though. He maybe had one football picture in the house. I think that took a lot of pressure off me."

When it came time to looking at colleges, Pete's parents did a great job of not pushing him in the direction of their alma mater, Michigan State. They wanted to make sure he chose a school that fit him, and that he wasn't selecting a school just based on comfort level or family tradition. "When my dad played football at Michigan State, he played with MSU coach, George Perles, so when I was looking at MSU I already had some familiarity. Not to mention the fact that we had been to campus for several games, we would go to MSU to watch camp, and my uncle had done some work with the hockey team. I didn't watch a ton of college football when I was a kid, but the main reason I liked Michigan State so much was a result of my huge dislike for Michigan football. MSU was a consideration for sure. I took an official visit there, but my parents were good about not putting any pressure on me to follow in their footsteps."

"The number one school on my list was Stanford. Denny Green was one of the coaches at Stanford, and came and made a visit to my parents' house. We had this gigantic Rottweiler, and the dog would go bananas any time someone would come to the house. We could not lock him up, because he would just claw his way out. So there we sat, trying to talk and have a meeting while this dog was going nuts. Yes, we were a little bit country, we had the dog out. You should have seen the look on Denny's face when this gigantic dog came out. Going out to California was quite a trip for me when I took my official visit. Half of their weight room was outside. It was a totally different atmosphere for me. But it was just too far away from my folks and they would not have been able to see me play. Being accepted to Stanford was a big accomplishment for me, though."

Notre Dame had tough competition with the caliber of schools that Pete was looking at. Not only was an academically rigorous Stanford tops on Pete's list, but he had childhood aspirations of attending the Air Force Academy and being a fighter pilot. "I was also really interested in Air Force because I wanted to fly fighter planes. Saying no to Air Force about broke my heart."

"Stanford was my No. 1. Notre Dame was my No. 2. Barry Alvarez was the offensive coordinator at Notre Dame; he said Notre Dame was a no-brainer for me. 'You're a Chicago kid, from a Catholic High School. You'll get a good education and get to play football,' he told me."

During the recruiting process, Notre Dame's defensive coach Barry Alvarez gave Pete an early lesson on the Notre Dame Value Stream. "Alvarez told me many things, but this is one of the things that still sticks with me today. I knew that Notre Dame was a top football place, and that lots of great local Chicago kids went there. But at the same time, the amount of playing time that I was going to get (or not get) at ND was a big concern for me. Why would you want to go there if you were not going to get the opportunity to play? That was the only real objection that I had to attending Notre Dame. And then Coach Alvarez said, 'If you are good enough to play Division I football, then you will play in high school. If you are good enough to play football in the NFL, then you will play in college. And by the way, while you are here you will get one hell of a good education.' That really hit home with me. I knew that Notre Dame was the right place with me. And my objection was definitely proven wrong as nine guys in my class were drafted, five of whom were selected in the first round, including Jerome Bettis and Tommy Carter."

As Pete can attest, you just never know where your life's journey is going to take you, "My dad also played in the NFL and never dreamed he would end up a parole officer. I always dreamed of flying fighter jets, just like Tom Cruise in Top Gun, flying Mach 2 with my hair on fire. When I got the opportunity to fly in a Navy Blue Angel plane, I was ready. That was probably the most awesome 50 minutes of my entire life. That was the number one thing on my bucket list. When I was a kid all I could think of was the Air Force Academy and then fighter pilot training. I have a friend who is a pilot and we fly up to Canada all the time. Flying with the Blue Angels was incredible. We burned 10,000 pounds of jet fuel, had 7Gs of positive force, came close to a negative three ... amazing."

Pete's time at Notre Dame had its share of successes as well as bumps in the road. His senior year he played on the team that many say should have won it all. But like so many stories, the 1993 team did not get the fairy tale ending. "After we beat Texas A&M in the Cotton Bowl, we thought we'd win the coaches poll and Florida State would win the AP poll, and that we'd be co-national champions. We didn't think we'd win it outright, but we did feel slighted that we got nothing at all. We had a good idea of what the media felt about us during the week going into the Notre Dame - FSU 'Game of the Century.' There was a certain color that everything was looked through. 'There is no way ND can beat FSU. Why do they think they can beat FSU?' That week was a bit of an awakening for a lot of us. The great football minds at large didn't give us any chance to beat FSU. Just like when we played Florida in the Sugar Bowl in '92. The big joke was, 'What's the difference between Notre Dame and Cheerios? Cheerios belong in the bowl.' And that team did not let the media stop them from getting the job done either."

Pete's first week at Notre Dame had a few bumps in it as well! "I'll never forget the first day of football training camp. John Witmer was on the training staff, and Jim Russ was the head athletic trainer. The first day you go from station to station and get fitted for your uniform, pads and helmet. John Witmer was putting shoulder pads on me and I asked for a neck roll. He looked me and said, 'What the (expletive) do you need a neck roll for?' At that moment I realized that college was totally different than high school. You go through the recruiting process and everyone is kissing your butt, and then Lou (Holtz) gets up and gives a speech after practice about how terrible you all look and you're sitting there thinking, who is this guy?"

"As a freshman at ND, I remember the first round of tackling drills that we did at that first training camp. I was looking across from me at whom I was going up against, and I see: Ricky Watters, Rodney Culver, Lee Becton, Tony Brooks, Reggie Brooks, Jerome Bettis, Anthony Johnson, and all I could think was, 'Oh crap.' You're counting down the line to see who you are going to face, hoping that you get the walk-on. At that point you realize that this is for real. This is no joke. This is serious business."

If you think a football program like Notre Dame creates humility in a young man, the NFL has a way of doing the exact same thing to its rookies. "My first NFL mini-camp (with the Minnesota Vikings), I show up, and I remember sitting in the meeting room after the first day of practice. I remember looking over at John Randle, who is sitting up against the wall, and he's just bouncing up and down. He can't even sit still. I start thinking to myself, I do not belong here. I remember thinking, if they cut me today, I will be okay. When I came out of college, I hated football. You really didn't get a chance to enjoy it at Notre Dame; you were just under so much pressure. You were worried about the carpet getting pulled out from under your feet." The NFL has a way of taking the tools that you gained during your time at Notre Dame and putting them to good use. It is during the struggles of everyday life that the Notre Dame Value Stream teaches us how to adapt and survive.

Along with its trying moments, playing at the professional level also had some uplifting moments for Pete. "Tackling Barry Sanders was probably the biggest moment of my NFL career. Most of the time you tackle somebody and don't even think twice about it. After I tackled Barry Sanders my first thought was, 'Oh my God, I just tackled Barry Sanders.' The 1998 NFC championship game was definitely the worst moment. We lost the NFC championship game to Atlanta after having gone 15-1 that year. That was a tough loss."

"I definitely became a better football player during my time in the NFL. From a mental aspect, I kept learning. I loved the strategy of the game. The Xs and Os. The whole thing just fascinates me. As a player I was able to learn multiple positions. I not only played special teams, but I could be a backup at five different spots. They would put me in there and trusted me that I was not going to make any mental mistakes, or blow a coverage. That was my niche in the NFL. New guys would come in who were bigger, stronger and faster. But from a mental standpoint, they couldn't beat me."

The Notre Dame Value Stream equipped Pete with the tools and the perseverance to give the NFL his all, be prepared for whatever faced him, and be the best possible version of himself. It pushes all of Her students to find their limits and reach their ultimate potential during their time under the Dome and in life. "In the NFL, you are basically holding on for dear life on a daily basis. Notre Dame prepared me for that. You threw yourself into it and did the best you could to hang on. I was ready to work when I got to the NFL because they worked us to death in college. In the NFL, you are treated like an adult. Like a man. You go home to your families after practice. It's professional. It's a job. It's a livelihood."

Pete attributes his humble mindset back to the lessons he learned from Coach Lou Holtz at Notre Dame. Coach Holtz was quick to make sure you didn't think too highly of yourself and took advantage of turning almost anything into a teaching moment. "We were in practice one day and I was on special teams running a punt return. We were doing middle returns, and my job was to make sure that the guy does not go down the middle of the field. I was blocking the left guard, and his job was to shift behind the center. When I blocked him, I pushed him off in the wrong direction. After the kick, Coach Holtz blows the whistle. He looks at me and says, 'Who are you blocking?' And I respond, 'that guy.' Lou says, 'And what way are you supposed to be blocking?' and I replied, 'To the left.' Then Lou asks, 'And which way did you go?' And I answer, 'Well I had to go this way because …' when Lou cuts me off, 'I'm going to have to take recruiting a little more seriously.' Public humiliation was his biggest tool. There was no way you would get a big head with Coach Holtz around. He would just tear you apart."

Lessons from Pete's Notre Dame Value Stream of Life:

- You never know where your life will take you. One day you may want to fly jets but the next thing you know here's the NFL. Things change and you never know where the excitement will come from. Learn from your experience and take advantage of every opportunity.
- The struggles of everyday life are what teach you how to adapt and survive.
- Life is not always going to be full of successes and accomplishments. Take the bad along with the good and know there is something good waiting just around the corner.

Notre Dame vs. Tennessee, 1991. Irv Smith (#84) set in position before the snap. (Photographer: Paul Webb. This photo was published in the 1991 Scholastic Football Review. Photo courtesy of Notre Dame Archives.)

CHAPTER FIFTEEN

The Smoothie King and Asset Manager Irv Smith

He lights up the room as soon as he walks in with that smile and signature dimples. He's a friend to everyone, would give you the shirt off his back, and always found a way to talk the dining hall ladies out of an extra steak on "steak night." (Even though none of us were sure they were really steaks.) Irv Smith worked his way from being a three-sport star at tiny Pemberton High in New Jersey to becoming the 20th overall pick in the first round of the 1993 NFL Draft. At Pemberton High, Smith earned all-division, all-county and all-state accolades as a tight end, linebacker and safety in football and also starred in baseball and basketball. Irv originally committed to play football at Clemson until the Notre Dame Value Stream got a hold of him and he changed his path. He played football and baseball at Notre Dame and was talented enough on the baseball diamond to be drafted by the Houston Astros after his junior year at Notre Dame, but he decided to stay for his senior year to focus on football. Irv was drafted by the New Orleans Saints with the 20th pick of the first round and went on to play seven seasons in the NFL with the Saints, San Francisco 49ers and Cleveland Browns. Smith finished his NFL career with 183 receptions for 1,788 yards, averaging 9.8 yards per carry, and had 15 touchdowns. Now a vice president with Primerica, Irv enjoys being able to help others grow their money and lives in Phoenix, Arizona, with his son "Little Irv."

While he was still playing football in the NFL Irv set out on his first business venture. He realized that playing professional football was not going to last forever so he began to prepare for his future. "From 1995-2007 Nick Smith and I owned some restaurants together called *Smoothie King*. We also owned some tanning salons. After that I became a real estate agent and then a real estate broker." Today Irv is a financial advisor for Primerica Financial Services (www.primerica.com). He works with NFL players, teaching them how to manage their money. "Being that I was there once myself, I feel that I can help them make good decisions and protect their assets. I have been a vice president with Primerica for seven years now and I enjoy being able to help others grow their money. I also hire and train other people, which is great because there are so many players who need the services that we provide. It is our job to give them good advice and help keep them on the right path." The number one advice Irv has for rookies is to save their money because they will live a long life after football is over. "You could have another 50 years left after you turn 40. You need to truly be smart with your investments. Make sure you are cautious about to whom you give your money."

Notre Dame very clearly told Irv that he would be riding the bench behind Derek Brown for his first three years, and yet the Notre Dame Value Stream still managed to steer Irv towards becoming part of the Fighting Irish family. "Notre Dame was actually my last choice. It was my last choice because Derek Brown was a freshman at ND when I was a senior in high school, Notre Dame had just won the national championship, and they flat out told me that I would be Brown's backup for my first three years. All of the other schools that I was looking at promised me a starting position. I was looking at Florida State, USC, UCLA, Clemson and Auburn. When I took my visit to FSU, it was for the FSU - Florida game and 'Neon' Deion Sanders was a senior at FSU. Auburn was supposed to be my fifth and final visit. I was getting ready to commit to Auburn during my official recruiting trip when they called me the Monday prior to my visit and told me they had just signed two tight ends that weekend (one of whom was Fred Baxter) and they no longer had a scholarship for me. I was getting ready to sign and they said 'no thank you' to me. Once Notre Dame got wind of this, they put some pressure on me to make my fifth visit there. I told them that I would take my fifth visit there, but firmly told them that it was my intention to commit to Clemson."

Irv took his official visit to Notre Dame even though he verbally committed to Clemson that very same day. Just when Irv thought he had everything figured out, he soon came to realize he didn't have anything figured out. "I verbally committed to Clemson the Friday that I left to make my official visit at ND. The entire weekend I was at Notre Dame I fought the fact that I really did love the place. Before I took my visit, I didn't even know what state Notre Dame was in, and here I was falling in love with the school. The players I met that weekend not only told me about how great it was to play football at Notre Dame, but that it was a place that would literally change your life. That Notre Dame was so much more than just a football school. I went home and told my parents that I had changed my mind. I was going to Notre Dame. I was a backup tight end for three years, but it truly did change my life."

Just as the football players at ND won Irv over during his official visit, he did the same thing for many other young men visiting Notre Dame for the first time. "When I was at Notre Dame, I became that guy who convinced the visiting recruits that Notre Dame was the place they wanted to be. Some of the guys that I helped bring to Notre Dame included Jeff Burris, John Covington, Oscar McBride, Tommy Carter, Jerome Bettis, Oliver Gibson, Ray Zellars and Bryant Young. The recruits would get dropped off to me Friday night and we had them until Sunday morning when they met Coach Holtz and Coach Vinny Cerrato. We made them see all that Notre Dame had to offer, and that you were also making lifelong friends along the way."

If you spent any time watching Notre Dame football during the early 1990s, the image of Irv dragging multiple Indiana defenders into the end zone is surely emblazoned in your mind. It's one of his best memories of his time at Notre Dame as well. "The Indiana game (Sept. 7, 1991) when I dragged two Indiana defenders 20 yards to score a touchdown, I'm not sure anything could top that. It was a home game, the opening game of my junior year and I had worked so hard to prove that I was good enough to be out there. I played baseball and football my first two years at ND. I liked baseball, but I loved football. I eventually gave up baseball to pursue football full-time, and that play made me realize that playing Notre Dame football was exactly where I wanted to be. It gave me the motivation to work hard to get my opportunity to shine."

"It wasn't even so much the actual play that sticks out in my mind so much, but the moment when Derek Brown and the guys picked me up in the end zone and tried to carry me off the field. As I was getting close to the side line I realized that Coach Holtz was screaming at me, 'You're on the field goal unit ... get out there!' Derek Brown was the man, the starter, the stud, and to see him happy for me was a real turning point for me."

Football wasn't always Irv's primary path at Notre Dame. A two-sport student-athlete, Irv split his non-academic hours at Notre Dame between playing baseball and football. A wake-up call from head coach Lou Holtz helped Irv clarify his focus and narrow his path. "During my sophomore year I was playing both football and baseball. Both Coach Murphy (baseball) and Coach Holtz had signed off on this. As soon as the football season was over, and the bowl game behind us, I started working out with the baseball team. When March came around I had spring practice with the football team as well as baseball games and practice. I walked into Coach Holtz's office and said, 'I am currently in the middle of the baseball season, I need to figure out a way to work in spring football practice.' I wanted to make sure he knew that I wasn't just skipping out on spring football practice. Coach Holtz says to me, 'I love you Irv, but I think what is best for you is for you to focus 100 percent on baseball and skip spring football practice. In fact, when football comes around, I want you to continue to focus on baseball. With Derek Brown going to be a senior in the fall, and now we've got Oscar McBride and Karmeeleyah McGill, and in addition to those three we've signed a few new guys. I'm not going to take your scholarship from you, but I think baseball is best for you.'"

> "Show me someone who has done something worthwhile,
> and I'll show you someone who has overcome adversity." - Lou Holtz

"I looked at him and thought, 'Are you serious?' He's sitting there telling me, Irv, we don't need you anymore. I walked out of his office completely broken. I went next door to Coach Joe Moore's office and told Coach Moore what happened and he said, 'WHAT??' The two of us walked into Coach Holtz's office and Coach Moore says, 'What do we have to do to keep Irv on the team?' Then Coach Moore says, 'Coach Holtz, Irv is going to be at practice today. Please give him one more chance.' After Coach Holtz agreed to this, Coach Moore walks out with me and tells me, 'Go out to practice today and show Coach Holtz that you deserve to be on this team.' Then I go tell Coach Murphy what is going on and he gives me the OK to go to every spring football practice that week to show Coach Holtz what I've got."

"I go to practice the first day and Coach Holtz has me running fourth-string. He had Oscar McBride running second, Karmeeleyah McGill third, and me at the bottom of the barrel. I came out that day and absolutely killed it. I finished out that baseball season, but after that experience, I made the decision that I was going to focus 100 percent on football. When I told Coach Murphy that I was no longer going to play baseball, he told me, 'Go do your thing!' And when I called Coach Moore with my decision, he said, 'Irv, we've got ya!' Coach Holtz wanted to motivate me. He wanted it to be my decision, to play football full-time. He really knew how to push everyone's buttons. He knew that year was a critical time for me. That it was time for me to either put up or shut up, but he had done it in a way that the decision was on me."

Reenergized and focused on his future, Irv put everything he had into playing football. While baseball was his love, football was what he was truly skilled at and his performance on the field showcased that very fact. When it was time to move on to the next level he was ready to show the world he had what it took to be successful and thrive. "That was an amazing day. I was in New York City at the draft with Jerome Bettis and Drew Bledsoe. I was the 20th pick of the first round, chosen by the New Orleans Saints. Each team got 30 minutes to make their picks. The draft started at 9 am, and I was selected right around 5 pm. I was the last guy of the guys who were in New York City to get picked. Bledsoe went first, Jerome went 10th … it was the longest day ever, but it was so unbelievable to walk up to the podium and get my jersey from (then-NFL Commissioner) Paul Tagliabue. I flew directly from New York City to New Orleans the next day to do my meet and greet with the team. It's crazy how one day someone chooses you, and it determines the direction of your career."

Irv took full advantage of the opportunities placed in front of him and had a successful NFL career with the Saints, 49ers and Browns. He made the most of his time and took nothing for granted, always knowing that the ride could stop at any moment. "Being able to play at the highest level of football was a definite high. The NFL was the crème de la crème of football. It was an honor to be there. The lows included having to deal with the politics and all of the egos. One of my coaches with the New Orleans Saints was Mike Ditka. He had been a tight end just like me and was very tough on me. He was one of the main reasons that I left the Saints. I was not a fan of his coaching style. I loved New Orleans, but we did not work well together."

"When I became a free agent in 1997, I ended up signing with the San Francisco 49ers. I played one year at San Francisco (1998), and that year was definitely the highlight of my NFL career. I got the opportunity to play with an amazing cast: Steve Young, Jerry Rice, Terrell Owens, J.J. Stokes, Garrison Hearst. Some of my Notre Dame teammates were also there: Bryant Young, Junior Bryant, Anthony Peterson. It was an amazing group of guys. It was such a blessed season. I created such strong friendships with those guys. They are my closest friends to this day. Being in San Francisco that year was definitely my destiny. I was looking to go somewhere that I could win and have fun. We went 13-4 that year."

The Notre Dame Value Stream helped prepare Irv Smith for what he faced on and off the field, just as he helps his clients prepare for their futures ahead of them. Good planning and preparation give you the tools you need for success in the long haul.

Irv Smith

Lessons from Irv's Notre Dame Value Stream of Life:

- Whether you are a professional athlete, school teacher, or you work on Wall Street, start your financial planning efforts early. It is never too early to start saving for your future.
- Be smart with your investments and be cautious about with whom you trust your money.
- Take full advantage of all opportunities placed in front of you so that you don't look back and wonder "what if?"
- Good planning and preparation will give you the tools you need for success in the long haul.

Notre Dame vs. Michigan, 1992. Reggie Brooks (#40) running with the ball. (Photographer: Joe Raymond, photo courtesy of Notre Dame Archives.)

CHAPTER SIXTEEN

The Athlete Engager and Player Liaison Reggie Brooks

There are so many traditions around the Notre Dame football program, many of which the average fan does not know. One such legacy way of life is how the program continuously draws former players back into its fold to support the program, and most importantly to serve as an example and model to current players. Today, Reggie Brooks plays the role of Player Liaison. Each day this former All-American running back is in constant contact with former players via the Internet and in person. Reggie can be found each day roaming the great corridors of the Joyce Athletic and Convocation Center with a personality and demeanor that welcomes all back to Our Lady. Everyone knows from Friday Night Lights that football is larger than life in Texas, but high school football is equally as prominent in Oklahoma. Reggie was born in Tulsa, never dreaming of leaving the state "Where the Sun Comes Sweeping Down the Plains." Why leave? After all, leaving Booker

T Washington High School and playing at Oklahoma or Oklahoma State was football at its best. But Reggie was tugged by the influence of his older brother Tony and the Notre Dame Value Stream that has always carried great athletes north, ever closer to that Golden Dome in South Bend. Fortunately for ND fans everywhere Reggie found his way to our pure green 100 yard pasture where he is renowned for being knocked unconscious on his feet, yet finding the instinct and will to churn his massive legs to touchdown pay dirt against the great beasts of Michigan. This play in 1992 is forever burned in our minds and chronicled as one of the best in Fighting Irish football lore.

Reggie went on to find more immediate success in the NFL in 1993 as a rookie running back for the Washington Redskins where he racked up 1,063 yards in his first pro season. He now lives in South Bend with his wife and five children whose ages span twenty years from 2 to 22.

Reggie is a pure family man with a wife and five kids, not to mention his Notre Dame family where he parents hundreds of former football gladiators. For an Oklahoma-raised kid, where high school football stadiums were often equally as impressive as some collegiate stadiums, being drawn away from his home state to play football elsewhere was no easy feat. But after watching his brother Tony win a national championship in his first year at Notre Dame, that little school which is often buried in snow six months of the year suddenly moved to the top of his list. "I was very interested in playing for either Oklahoma or Oklahoma State, but by the time I got to be a senior in high school both of their programs were on probation. There were three other schools on my short list, USC, Miami and Notre Dame, but several factors caused me to lean towards Notre Dame. The biggest was the fact that Notre Dame had just won the national title. Also, the fact that my brother was already at Notre Dame and I had been there several times to visit him and had gotten to know his teammates. That really pulled me in."

"My brother was supposed to be my host when I made my official recruiting visit to Notre Dame, but I actually only saw him once that weekend. Since I already knew my way around campus, and knew most of the guys, I ended up being my own host that weekend, and spent time showing Dorsey Levens and Adrian Jarrell around. There was one thing they really fooled me on during my recruiting weekend. They wined and dined us that weekend on all of this fabulous food, and then when I got to school they stuck us with this awful dining hall food. They tricked me for sure."

For some, playing collegiate football with your older brother could cause conflict and heightened competition; it did not present any of these issues for Reggie and Tony Brooks. "Being in my brother's shadow was not really much of a challenge for me. I already felt like all of the upperclassmen on the team were my big brothers, so me playing behind Tony did not put any additional pressure on me. Also, when I started at Notre Dame I played defensive back, not running back, so we were not in direct competition. When I made the switch from defensive back to running back, I had already learned so much from my brother and guys like Ricky Watters and Anthony Johnson that I already knew what was required of me to play at that level. They helped make the transition easier for me."

For so many of us, what we love most about our days at Notre Dame does not revolve around the flashy moments, but more so the regular, every day ones. The Notre Dame Value Stream kept our feet firmly planted on the ground. It allowed us to celebrate in our successes but also reminded us that the little miracles were the most important. "This is not really a football memory per se, but this moment definitely left a big impact on me. It happened during the Notre Dame-Penn State 'Snow Bowl' game, and it was not 'The Catch.' It was very cold during that game and I was freezing my butt off. Offensive lineman Aaron Taylor came over to me, out of the blue, and gave me the biggest bear hug to warm me up as I was standing there shivering. I didn't ask him to, he just did it. That reinforced to me that we were more than just teammates. We were family. We looked out for one another. That was a great moment. It left a lasting and special place in my heart."

And then, of course, there are the flashing moments that you cannot remember at all. (During the 1992 Notre Dame - Michigan game Reggie broke six Michigan tacklers and stumbled across the goal line, scoring the touchdown, only to fall to the ground unconscious.) "I am not really sure how much of the play I was actually conscious for, because I do not remember any of the play at all. The head trainer came out to me with smelling salts, and when I came to the entire left side of my body was numb. They took me over to the sideline, told me to shake it off and get back out there and play. The media was asking me about the play at the postgame press conference, and I had no idea what they were talking about. Not until I watched the film the next day did I get a chance to see the run. After watching the play I thought to myself, 'Man, that was a great play!'"

"The price of success is hard work, dedication to the job at hand, and the determination that whether we win or lose, we have applied the best of ourselves to the task at hand."
~ Vince Lombardi

In addition to the concussion touchdown, Reggie has one other play that is a Notre Dame fan favorite and well entrenched in Fighting Irish Lore: the two-point conversion in the "Snow Bowl" against Penn State in 1992. Coach Lou Holtz had done with them what he had done with so many teams before, made sure they were prepared. He made practices a nightmare so that when it came time to play the game they were confident in their skills and ability to take care of business. That is exactly what happened that snowy day in

November. "We always practiced the two-point conversion in practice. It was nothing new to us. Holtz had us on the sideline, told us what the formation was, and we never had any doubt in our mind that we could successfully run the play. The funny thing about that play was I was not even the intended receiver. Irv Smith was supposed to run a pivot route and I was supposed to distract the safety so that he could make the catch. We had never practiced this particular formation before, we just knew that we needed to go out and execute it. We had so much confidence in ourselves. Aaron Taylor likes to say that he was the reason I caught the pass because he missed the block that caused Rick Mirer to have to roll right and throw to me."

When it came time to transition from playing college football to playing at the professional level, Reggie had no doubts in his ability to perform and compete with NFL caliber players. He had watched his brother take the leap the year before him and looked forward to accepting the challenges before him. "I had gone to the combine workouts and had done quite well. I was talking quite extensively with the Dallas Cowboys and they were planning on taking me as the last pick of the first round. Jimmy Johnson was known for trading down, and they had made such a move and had told me that they were now going to take me as their first pick of the second round (No. 46 overall). The 45th pick was quickly approaching and my phone rings. I assume it is going to be the Cowboys. I get on the phone, and it's the running back coach for the Washington Redskins and he says, 'How would you like to be a Washington Redskin?' It was the most awkward experience for me, as one of the reps from Dallas is sitting right next to me during all of this. The Redskins go on to choose me as the 45th pick, right out from under Dallas. They also chose Tommy Carter in the first round, and so the next day Tommy and I got on a plane and made our visit to the Redskins facility for our press conference."

While Reggie enjoyed his time in the NFL, it was quite different from his time at Notre Dame. Having the opportunity to play at the professional level was a dream come true for Reggie, however it had a much different feel than his college days. "It was not nearly as fun as playing at the collegiate level. You also did not have a lot of strong relationships with the guys on the team in the NFL. There is a big difference between playing ball at Notre Dame and playing ball in the NFL. Coming out of Notre Dame, you are prepared for the media attention and all of the attention in general that you get as an NFL player. But you are not prepared for the team atmosphere, or lack thereof. The locker room did not have the same family feel as Notre Dame."

"The highlight of my NFL career had to have been my rookie season. During my rookie year myself, Jerome Bettis and Rick Mirer (all former Fighting Irish stars) were leading the league in completions, rushing and yards per carry. It was also awesome to get to see lots of your former Notre Dame teammates playing with you in the NFL as well. It was very comforting to see those familiar faces."

Coach Lou Holtz may have prepared him for football playing days, but his business school professors prepared him for the next steps in his life's journey. "I did not have a difficult transition from the NFL to the next stage of my life. My degree from Notre Dame was in Management Information Systems. After I played in the NFL, and then for a few years for NFL Europe, I got a job as an IT (information technology) specialist. I eventually ended up coming back to Tulsa and worked for the Siegfried family, also alumni of Notre Dame. Since I only had a short NFL career, I knew I was going to have to go out and embark on my next career in order to take care of my family. I was young and knew I had a lot of life ahead of me, so the transition was pretty easy."

"Some years later, I saw there was a job open at Notre Dame in the Office of Information Technology and I decided to go ahead and apply for it. I was working as an IT Business Analyst, and Notre Dame had a position open in Change Management. My wife and I had just been talking about where we wanted to raise our family when I got the call from Notre Dame wanting to speak with me further about coming to work for them. My wife and I had met at Notre Dame and we really felt like this call was fate. Once I was offered the position (as an administrator of production systems) we jumped on the opportunity to come back to South Bend. Then a short time after being in that position, I was asked to take a position in the athletic department as the liaison between former Notre Dame athletes and current Notre Dame student-athletes. It was the perfect fit for me."

"My current job is to re-engage former athletes with the University and to create a synergy between former athletes and current student-athletes. A lot of these kids don't understand the importance of networking, or the importance of the Notre Dame family or how to take advantage of those opportunities. They are not thinking about what tomorrow has in store for them. I have been able to work with Tyler Eifert, Kyle Rudolph, Harrison Smith, and Michael Floyd, to pair them up with mentors who can help guide them on the next step of their journey. They are not being told how to play, but are being mentored on how to be a professional, how to transition to the next level."

Both Coach Ara Parseghian and Coach Lou Holtz knew how to get every ounce out of their players. They knew if they gave their all to their players in practice, that their players would give their all to them during games. Both groups of guys have remarked that even today their former coaches can bring out the competitive spirit in them. Reggie feels the same way about Coach Holtz. "When I played at Notre Dame, I could not stand Coach Holtz. He was an absolute tyrant. However, he was exactly what we needed. His level of discipline kept us on track. He would say the same things over and over for four years and yet they never got old. He could still get you jacked up to play right now. That little fellow really got you ready to play the game of football. He almost got me pumped up to play in the Japan bowl a few years ago. Fortunately for me, I got hurt and was not able to play. He was very instrumental in my life. Not necessarily about football, but about life in general. I live by the principles that he taught us day after day."

"Coach Holtz really rode us hard during practice. Game day was our sanctuary because it actually meant that you got Coach Holtz off your back! My freshman year, we came to campus early to get ready for the Kickoff Classic. Here you are, this kid who was just highly recruited as a high school football player. You have Coach Holtz in your living room telling your parents how great you are. Now here we are at campus the week before the upperclassmen get there. We are under the impression that we are going to learn the plays and get our feet wet before they arrive. Oh no. He has us out there running one rep after another. You have to run 15 yards every play and then jog back to get in line again. I got tired, and ran the wrong way. I turn around and this little dude was in my face ripping me a new one. I'm thinking to myself, 'You were just in my living room telling me how great I am and now you are ripping me a new one?' I called home and said, 'I don't think I can handle this.' But what happened was, you learned to listen to what he said, and not how he said it."

Reggie Brooks

Lessons from Reggie's Notre Dame Value Stream of Life:

- While accomplishments and successes in life are important, pay attention to the little miracles. They are often more meaningful than the major goals you will reach in your life.
- The more you prepare ahead of time the more successful you will be; not just in sports, but in life as well.

PATRICK TERRELL   FREE SAFETY   UNIVERSITY OF NOTRE DAME

Pat Terrell (#15) on the field in between plays, c1986-1989. (Photographer: Br. Charles McBride, CSC., photo courtesy of Notre Dame Archives.)

CHAPTER SEVENTEEN

The Pilot and Commercial Construction Entrepreneur Pat Terrell

Patrick Terrell may be best remembered in Notre Dame football lore for his one shining play in the 1988 Notre Dame - Miami game. In a game described as "Catholics vs. Convicts", No. 1 Miami pulled to within one point of Notre Dame with a touchdown, with less than one minute to go in the fourth quarter. Miami coach Jimmy Johnson made the decision to go for the two-point conversion, and called for a pass play to the right corner of the end zone. Pat batted down quarterback Steve Walsh's pass at the last possible second, securing the win for the Irish, and helping them roll onward to an undefeated 12-0 season and the national title.

Today he flies jets, builds runways and builds buildings. There might have been a time when he could "leap tall buildings in a single bound." Sorry, that might have been Superman or was it really Pat Terrell? One thing we know for sure, like his ND teammate Pete Bercich, Pat never wanted his feet to touch ground. Pat's first post-NFL job was in aviation. He had an opportunity to do some NFL commentating, but passed on that to become an airline pilot. "My wife supported me 100 percent. She told me, 'When I met you this is what you wanted to do so why not do it?' This made my transition into the real world much smoother. I don't think I watched an NFL game for the first two years of my retirement. I was too busy with my new life! I was flying corporate jets when I got the job with ATA. I loved it because they only hired captains. I flew a 757 all over the world. I had the opportunity to fly soldiers during Iraqi Freedom. Some of my ATA routes included flying to such places as Australia, Germany and Spain; it was a tremendous experience. It was the perfect way for me to transition into the next phase of my life. It was something I was truly passionate about. I did that for six years."

So is that enough for one former ND legend? No, not for this gridiron son of Our Lady. After Notre Dame football, nine years in the NFL for the Los Angeles Rams, New York Jets, Carolina Panthers and Green Bay Packers and piloting commercial 757 jets for ATA, Pat now owns and operates a multi-million dollar construction firm headquartered in Chicago, Illinois. "While I was flying jets (for ATA) the construction company I started while in the NFL was also taking off, pun intended. I pooled all of my resources as an entrepreneur and it really started growing. Terrell Materials (www.terrellmaterials.com), builds freeways and runways, and right now our current project includes building one of the biggest runways at O'Hare Airport and the reconstruction of the CTA Red Line tracks in Chicago. We're not only manufacturing all of the concrete for this project, but we're doing all of the concrete recycling as well. We've been manufacturing concrete for years, and we've done a lot of work on freeways in the Midwest. We have approximately 87 employees and right now we have been presented with great opportunities even in the current challenging market." Pat currently resides in Chicago, Illinois with his wife Elizabeth, and their five children.

Selling South Bend, Indiana, to a kid who grew up in Florida is no easy feat, but it was something about which head coach Lou Holtz was no stranger. "Lou Holtz told me it was only cold a couple months out of the year and I believed him!" (laughs) But as Pat continued to look at Notre Dame during his recruiting process, he realized what a great tradition ND had, both academically and athletically. "Notre Dame is one of the most awesome football programs ever and the school academically is unparalleled. It has such a great reputation." Pat's father was a great influence to him in any big decisions that he had to make in his life. "I was fortunate enough to be recruited by most of the top football programs at the time. I decided that I would narrow the schools down to five and ask my dad for his opinions on each school. He looked at me and said, 'Son, you are 18 years old now, it's time to make your own decisions. You're being recruited by some great academic institutions, and I want you do to some research into how much each of these schools cost.'"

At that point Pat and his family had looked at graduations rates and all of the normal things you look at when you're looking at colleges and football programs, but he had no idea how much it cost to attend each one of these schools. One of his final five schools was the University of Florida. With in-state tuition, it was four thousand dollars per year to attend UF. Four thousand dollars times four years came out to $16,000 in tuition. "My dad extended his hand to me and said, 'Congratulations, you just earned yourself sixteen grand worth of education.'" Next he looked at Notre Dame. Notre Dame was $25,000 per year, times four years, came out to $100,000 in tuition. Pat's father then said, 'Son, you can get a $16,000 education or a $100,000 education. You do the math.'"

"I looked at choosing where I was going to attend college as a business decision. I thought Notre Dame would give me the greatest opportunity to not be locked into a certain region of the country. It's a nationally known school. It's not a Hollywood-type answer. It's four years of your life. If I go to Notre Dame, I know that I can keep up with guys who are going in the right direction. If I go to other schools, not to say that they are bad schools, but if the majority of the guys are not focused on graduating in four years, it would be more difficult for me to keep focused on my education. If the crowd is headed towards graduation, that's the crowd I want to be with."

There were five other schools that Pat looked at besides Notre Dame: Minnesota, Purdue, Georgia Tech, Florida and Miami. Why on earth would a kid from St. Petersburg, Florida, want to go to a school like Minnesota? "Mostly because I had never been that far north before and why not take the trip if you have the opportunity!" During his official visit to Notre Dame Pat's hosts were Reggie Ward (wide receiver) and Mark Green (running back). "How was my visit to Notre Dame? It was freezing cold during my trip. I got to the airport in South Bend and there was no limousine waiting for me. I'm not trying to be arrogant, but based on past trips I was used to staying in the Penthouse of the Ritz Carlton. When I visited most schools I was on the front cover of the newspaper, I was wined and dined, there were pretty girls. It was the closest I've ever felt to being an A-List movie star. The graduate student who picked me up didn't recognize me, and I was kind of irritated by that. The other schools had set such crazy standards you kind of expected to be treated like royalty. It smelled funny when I got to South Bend because of the Ethanol plant. When we got to campus I couldn't wait to see the stadium and the locker room and I didn't even get to see the football offices until the second day. My first appointment when we arrived on campus was with the dean of the business school. Then I get to the Morris Inn, and it's not that it's not nice, but it's old and small, it doesn't have a city view, and they placed me with a roommate (Braxton Banks). I was sure I was in the wrong room because I had never had a roommate on one of these trips."

Pat very quickly came off his pedestal and learned what Notre Dame deemed important. Those situations he encountered during his weekend at ND definitely had a positive effect on him. "You're not going to decide to go to Notre Dame unless your priorities are in order. I was expecting to go to a fraternity party that night, and then I learned there were no fraternities at Notre Dame. Instead, Tim Brown, Reggie Ward and Mark Green took me bowling. What I realize now is that bowling allowed me to spend quality time with and get to know the guys who were going to become my best friends. Looking back on it, it was much better than screaming over loud music at a frat party. I really enjoyed the guys that I met at Notre Dame and they made my decision that much easier. I thought it was so cool that Braxton and I went to Senior Bar (a bar just on the edge of campus) and then they wouldn't let us in because we were not seniors. I was thinking to myself 'this is not the place for me.'" But Pat ended up making a mature decision.

Being a Notre Dame student-athlete comes with its challenges both on and off the field, but the Notre Dame Values Stream seems to always give them just enough support to guide them through and propel them forward to success. Pat talks about a few of his struggles. "To name just one is kind of tough. Being homesick is the first thing that comes to mind. Being homesick combined with the awful weather were big adjustments for me but you quickly learn that the world does not come to an end just because it's cold outside. One of the other challenges for me was probably getting moved position-wise. I got moved from being on the starting rotation of the wide receivers to being a defensive back. Being from Florida, I walked with some swagger. I just knew as soon as Tim Brown graduated that I would come in and win MY Heisman Trophy. Being moved my junior year to defensive back was a huge challenge for me. To have to break into the starting lineup, to play and perform well enough to be able to play at the next level, was a pretty tall order. I didn't even start at defensive back until the third game of my junior year."

Often times when you play football at a school like Notre Dame, at some point in your career you have your fifteen seconds of fame. However, not often does your fifteen seconds of fame propel your team into playing for the national championship. That is exactly what happened to Pat, "I played all of those years in the NFL and in so many big games at Notre Dame and I remember that game (Notre Dame – Miami 1988) more than any other. I remember it like it was just yesterday. The matchup between Notre Dame and Miami in 1988 was very tight. Every play was crucial, critical. When it came down to that last play, it was just one of many equally intense plays in that game. Our defensive coach, Barry Alvarez, was amazing. He always had us extremely prepared for what we were going to be up against. That game was only my second start. He had quite a challenge getting me ready. All he knew was that I was fast, crazy and wanted to hit people. For him to line me up in the right place, I owe so much to him."

"We ran that play several times in practice. We knew that was a big part of their offense. When I lined up, Leonard Conley was who I was defending, and he was actually from my neck of the woods. So here we were, across from each other at the collegiate level, just as we had been in high school. I'm right back at home going up against the same guy. I was fortunate to be in the right position to be able to make a play that ended up being very memorable. If it wasn't for George Williams putting the pressure on quarterback Steve Walsh, maybe he would have gotten the throw off sooner and maybe I would not have been there. There was a lot more to that play than the moment I batted down the ball." Tony Rice suggested I ask Pat why he only batted down the ball. Why didn't he CATCH it? "Tell Tony because I wanted to make it dramatic. ANYONE can catch the ball."

Football is a game of respect. Pat and his teammates had a feeling going into that 1988 season that they were going to be good and that they'd be able to compete for a national title. "When I talk about respect, you still have to go out there and earn it. Deserve it. Certain teams, Miami for example, had no respect. In fairness to them, we didn't deserve their respect. They beat us the year before, and the year before that they embarrassed us. Here they were, in our house. We were lined up pregame practicing punt returns and Rocket was lined up in the back. They came out, trampled over Rocket, and then ran right through our drill. I knew this was not going to be pretty. It was actually our third-teamers out there fighting. All of the first string guys knew better. I was all fired up for the game and I didn't want to expend any unnecessary energy fighting. I just stepped back and enjoyed the fight. In regards to Coach Holtz and Jimmy Johnson, Lou's pregame speech was true."

> *"Men, I have no doubt that you are going to do well today.*
> *You'll be fine, you'll be fine. But I have one favor to ask of you.*
> *Save Jimmy Johnson's ass for me." - Lou Holtz*

"The funny thing is, it was a very moving speech (like most, if not all of them, were.) Not once did Lou *not* have us fired up for a game. But after this particular speech, never was I so fired up and tickled to go out there and play a game. Here is this little guy asking us to leave Jimmy Johnson's ass for him. That was some serious confidence because Jimmy Johnson would have tossed Lou's ninety-pound ass all over that field."

Although the game winning play at the end of the Notre Dame – Miami game is most likely what you and I remember Pat for, it's not his most memorable moment from his time spent playing football for the Fighting Irish. "Probably the night after we won the national championship. You knew that you had done something special. It was fun to see your parents celebrating with you and excited. They realized, more so than you did, how big of a deal it was. Sharing it with my family was tremendous. To know that you and your teammates, with whom you accomplished this amazing task, would always have that in common for the rest of your lives – it's indescribable. We were all just floating on air. Not tired and sore, floating on air."

Pat was invited to go to New York to attend the draft, but he opted not to go. Things were changing in the NFL with the arrival of underclassman eligibility. Pat had been predicted to go in the first round, but after this change he had no idea where he would end up. So he decided he'd rather not be stressed-out in New York City sitting in front of all those cameras, and opted to be comfortable and watch it at home. "I remember being at home on draft day and being so nervous. I have a sister who is four years younger than me, so she was a senior in high school when I was a senior in college. At that time, there were no such things as cell phones, so on draft day the house telephone was the most sought after piece of equipment in the world. I don't even think we had call waiting back then. I made her sit next to me at all times so that I could make sure she was not back in her room on the phone. I needed to have my sister in eye contact at all times. I got more and more nervous as the day went on. The draft takes much longer than people think, especially back then. I kept quickly picking up the phone and checking the dial tone to make sure it still worked. Then I told my sister Kim to go next door and call the house to make sure the phone worked. I was so nervous that I forgot that I had sent her over there. The phone rings, and here I am sitting in front of these reporters. I smile and answer the phone only to find Kim on the other line. I start yelling at her, 'Why are you on the phone?' and she says, 'Because you told me to call!'"

Finally, Pat received the call he was waiting for. "I got a call from John Robinson with the Los Angeles Rams, who then put me on the phone with Georgia Frontiere, who asked me if I would like to be a Los Angeles Ram. The next phone call was from Frank Stams, who had been drafted by the Rams the year before me. I was excited to go to a place where I already knew a few people (and then the next year they drafted Todd Lyght, and after Todd, Jerome Bettis, so we had quite the Notre Dame group). They flew me out to Los Angeles immediately so that I could see where my new job was going to be. It was a great experience. I knew I was going to get drafted. I had experienced a lot of new things at Notre Dame and it was fun my family was able to go through it with me. I married my college sweetheart which is great because I don't have to tell her any of the stories; she was there for all of them."

Getting the opportunity to play at the NFL level is something that every Division I college football player strives to achieve. Pat was blessed to receive such an opportunity and looking back feels that the positives of successfully being able to compete at that level outweighed the negatives. "You're getting to do something that you absolutely can't believe you're getting paid for. That is a definite high. I remember, during TV timeouts I would literally take a moment, to *take in* the moment. I would look around, look at the kids in the crowd, look at the guys in the crowd who looked like my dad. My wife laughs sarcastically at me when I tell my NFL stories. She said, 'Pat, you were not a happy camper.' But that's because it's your job. You complain about this and that. You may not like the call a coach makes. You're trying to perform at a peak level to keep your job. The fact that you are able to reach that level and compete with some of the greatest athletes in the world, that is why you've worked so hard. It's painful and it hurts the body but I'd do it all over again given the chance."

"As far as lows go, I played with championship teams in college, but while I played on successful teams in the NFL I was never able to win a Super Bowl, and that still gets me. However, not winning a Super Bowl has made my national title all that more special to me. Some of the other lows? I'm dealing with them right now — the pain. I am in excellent physical shape still, but my body does not feel like it should feel at this point. I was in 850 car accidents (850 tackles) and I am paying the price. Football is a physical game, and what I am enduring now makes me look at the game differently with regards to my kids. I support them, but I am not going to push them into the game. The physical aspect of football takes a toll on your body, especially when you play it as long as I did. Football opened a lot of opportunities for me, but it took me a while to separate myself from being type-caste as a football player to transition into my next career. It was tough to not be identified as 'Pat the football player.' The positives of successfully being able to compete at that level, however, outweigh the negatives in my eyes."

Not many guys make enough money playing in the NFL that they can retire when they are done playing. Pat looked at his NFL "retirement" as a great start into his new life. "I worked hard while I was still playing in the NFL to set myself up so that when I was done with football I'd still have something else to do. It was tough to focus on life after football and football at the same time. At Notre Dame I started out studying aerospace engineering, but I soon learned that I didn't care why the plane flew — I just wanted to fly it. I switched majors and got a business degree and I am very glad that I did. It made my future opportunities more diverse. During the NFL offseason I got my pilot's license and started my construction company. So many people suffer from depression when making the transition from the NFL to the rest of their lives. I wanted to make sure that I had something else that I was passionate about to carry me into my future."

As Pat looks back on his time at Notre Dame he appreciates all the doors that Notre Dame opened up for him. He shares his words of wisdom for today's student-athletes. "First, really cherish the time you have during your college years. You have a great opportunity, especially the men and women who are on athletic scholarships. The University is getting a great deal out of your talents. Know the value of what they are getting and the value of the education that you are getting in return. It's like teaching your child value when you make them buy something with their own money. As a student-athlete, you go straight to college from high school and you've never seen a tuition bill. You're going through all of these emotions and adjustments, just like any other student, but make sure you take advantage of what the University is giving you in exchange for your ability and talents. This goes especially for football players at Notre Dame. You can sit down and really do the math. As a defensive player you may make 35 plays in a game, multiply that by 12 games in a season, and then times four years — that's 1680 plays. That is *if* you play every game all four years, which most likely you will not. Maybe you only play two years, which only gives you 840 plays. You've got a limited opportunity to show the world what you can do. Don't take any plays off. You should treat every play like it's the last play of your career. They go by so fast. Cherish every one because it is not going to last forever. I am glad I was able to leave it all out there on the field. I would have regretted it if I had not."

    Pat, like all team sport athletes, always has a story about his teammates. "I was an airline pilot during the terrorist attacks of 9/11. Shortly after 9/11 it seemed as if the TSA was changing our hijack procedures almost on a weekly basis. One week I was trained to do one thing, the next week I was trained to do something else. Roll the plane, no wait, do this instead. It was insane. At that point I was still in pretty good 'football shape' and decided I would have my own anti-hijacking procedure. My policy was that prior to every flight I would walk up and down the aisle of my plane so that my passengers could see me. Know this: if you intend to hijack my plane there is going to be one big angry dude in the cockpit."

    "One day, I'm preparing for a flight and I'm doing my little stroll and I see this guy leaning into the aisle and his eyes are as big as golf balls, it was Tony Rice! Tony knew I was a practical joker, and the last time he saw me I was still playing in the NFL for the Green Bay Packers. He could not for the life of him figure out why I was in a pilot uniform. Here I am, so happy to see him and so I invite him to come up and see the cockpit, and his eyes are still as big as golf balls. So I say, 'come up and meet the crew.' I have never seen Tony Rice drop an ounce of sweat. He is Mister Cool under pressure, and here was Tony sweating buckets. Tony looks at me and says, 'Man, you know how to drive this thing?' and I reply, 'I know how to fly it!' He looks back and says, 'Pat, uh, I'm gonna go back to my seat and I'll talk to you when we land.'" *(howling with laughter)*

    A pivotal moment in Pat's career at Notre Dame was the day that head coach Lou Holtz decided to move him from wide receiver to defensive back.

It was something that Pat never saw coming, but changed the course of his career and lead to the moment against Miami that is embedded in Notre Dame football lore. "I started my football career at Notre Dame as a wide receiver and in the starting rotation I was pretty good. But when you are wide receiver in a wishbone offense you do more blocking that you do receiving. This all happened during my sophomore year, which was the year Tim Brown won the Heisman Trophy and so my statistics were not looking all that good. I only had three or four catches on the whole season going into the Cotton Bowl. We were at one of our Cotton Bowl practices, and our practices were intense, to say the least. There were thousands of people piled into the stadium just to watch us practice and my parents had driven to Texas all the way from Florida just to see me play."

"Holtz calls my number and it's my turn to make a play. It was a middle crossing route from Tony Rice to me and it hits me right in the chest ... and I drop it. This was the end of a very long season, and there I go and drop the ball. Coach Holtz is standing behind the secondary and his face turns red and he starts yelling. He runs right at me, and then keeps running, right past me, and over to Tony Rice. He grabs Tony by the face mask and is screaming at him, meanwhile Tony is looking at me like, 'catch the dog-gone ball.' Lou screams at Tony, 'Tony, that is your fault! I don't care if Pat is so wide open that you can walk the ball up and hand him the football! Take the sack! I don't care

Pat Terrell

how open he is, take the sack. Do not throw Pat Terrell the ball!' After practice I walk off the field and feel just awful. Coach Holtz comes over to me and I am expecting him to apologize. He says to me, 'Pat, you're the best receiver I've ever coached. I have never coached a receiver with so much talent. You're great …until we throw you the football. I'm moving you to defensive back in the spring.' And that is how I found out I was being moved to defensive back. Coach Holtz made practice so much more intense than actual games, so much so that we looked forward to the games!" That was life for Lou's Lads and it was a great life.

Lessons from Pat's Notre Dame Value Stream of Life:

- Enjoy every moment in life because time moves by much too quickly. Learn to appreciate the here and now.
- Cherish the time you have during your college years. You have a great opportunity, especially the men and women who are on athletic scholarships. The University is getting a great deal out of your talents. Know the value of what they are getting and the value of the education that you are getting in return.
- Pursue what you are passionate about and you will always be challenged and happy in life.

Ryan Leahy (#72) on the field in between plays, c1994. (Notre Dame University photograph, photo courtesy of Notre Dame Archives.)

CHAPTER EIGHTEEN

The Bond Manager and Finance Marketeer Ryan Leahy

Ryan Leahy thrived on competition. It was a driving force for him while playing football at Notre Dame, in the NFL, and then he found that competition once again in a most unlikely place, a municipal bond trading desk. He discovered that working the municipal bonds trading desk was as close to a locker room as he could get not playing sports. There was a constant competition, communication and interaction. Now the Vice President at Incapital LLC (www.incapital.com), in Chicago, Ryan has found his niche working the bond market. With a grandfather and father who both played on national championship teams at Notre Dame, Ryan probably didn't need much of a nudge when it came to beginning his own career as an offensive lineman at Notre Dame. His grandfather is Irish playing and coaching legend Frank Leahy, who played for Knute Rockne, and his father, James Leahy, played on the 1966 national championship team. Frank Leahy won four

134

national championships at Notre Dame and had six unbeaten seasons. Ryan arrived in South Bend from Washington's Yakima River Valley eager to carve his own niche on the family tree. Brother Pat Leahy was already playing baseball at Notre Dame, so the brothers were in South Bend together. Ryan was twice elected co-captain of the Notre Dame football team (1994 and 1995) and he also received the Edward "Moose" Krause Lineman of the Year Award, which is named after the Notre Dame legend and one of his grandfather's close friends. After a brief career in the NFL with the Arizona Cardinals and Green Bay Packers, Ryan now lives in the Chicago area with his wife Becky and their two daughters.

When it was time for Ryan to change directions, he knew he already had the skills from his time at Notre Dame to make the transition an easy one. He may not have had a clear vision of where he was headed, but he knew he had the tools needed to find his way. "Immediately after retiring from the NFL, it was very challenging for me to figure out what the next chapter of my life was going to be. I studied to take the GMAT to possibly get a graduate degree in business. I had also taken some graduate classes when I was still at Notre Dame, but it was definitely a struggle for me to figure out exactly what I wanted to do. I knew that things were no longer happening for me in the NFL. I moved to Iowa to get into the finance field, and my first stop was working for ABN Amro (www.abnamro.com). I spent eight years working the municipal bonds trading desk, which I found out is as close to a locker room as I can get not playing sports. It's great; I get to hang out with a bunch of guys. We compete against one another. There is constant competition, communication and interaction. It's a life filled with competition which I very much enjoy."

"Then I went back to Northwestern Kellogg School of Management and received my MBA in Finance and Marketing. Most people don't combine marketing with finance, but somehow I felt that marketing would be helpful because eventually all financial products need to be marketed. Currently I am the Vice President at Incapital LLC (www.incapital.com), in Chicago. I work in the fixed income department focusing on municipal bonds. The president of our company is Tom Ricketts, whose family owns the Chicago Cubs. All of the White Sox fans in our office are 'encouraged' to root for the Cubs. Being in Chicago is great. I have family in the Chicago area, and I have been going to Cubs games since I was 13, so this is a great place for me."

If you are a Leahy, you would think it was a given that you were going to attend Notre Dame. This was not the case with Ryan. Growing up on the west coast he did not identify with Notre Dame and initially thought he'd attend school out west. That was until he made his official trip to South Bend. "I did take three other visits (Washington, Oregon, UCLA). Notre Dame was my first visit and to me, I really felt at home there. Even though I am a grandson of Frank Leahy, growing up in Washington State I felt pretty removed from Notre Dame. My older brother Pat was there when I was in high school. He played for the baseball team, and while he was there my parents flew me up for a two week visit, which gave me a good impression of what Notre Dame had to offer. Frank Jacobs and Irv Smith played baseball with my brother but were also members of the football team, and they helped recruit me. On my official visit to ND, I took my host (Bernard Manly) to a baseball get-together and introduced him to the guys that I knew on the baseball team. I never felt any pressure from my family."

"When the going gets tough, let the tough get going." -Frank Leahy

Washington was Ryan's second choice, but Notre Dame was so far in the lead it was not even close. "USC did call me a few times and sent some recruiting letters. After I received the first couple recruiting letters, I got a call from one of the USC coaches. His first question was to inquire if I was related to Coach Leahy, and after I said yes, that was the last call I got from USC. Notre Dame was not only just like family to me, it was the best place for me. The two coaches who came out to Washington to recruit me were Jay Hayes and Joe Moore. Coach Moore was selling me real hard on Notre Dame. 'The University of Notre Dame is the University of America. You go to any state and they know Notre Dame. Just like here in Wisconsin.' And then Coach Hayes says, 'Coach Moore, we're in Washington.' And Coach Moore says, 'See!' When I decided to go to Notre Dame, my dad told the coach, 'No special treatment. Treat him like the other players, or even worse.' Coach Moore made me crab 500 yards just for being related to Coach Leahy."

Being a Leahy may have been worse for Ryan and not better. Not only did he not get any special privileges, the coaches were often much harder on him than the rest. "I had such a deep respect for him (Coach Moore). He was hard as hell on us. Over the years, no matter what team he coached for, he made offensive linemen who were aggressive and physical. He always got his players to achieve their absolute best. I was lucky enough to run into him while he was coaching at Iowa (after Notre Dame) somewhere around 1999. He and Chris Doyle (strength coach) were leading a football clinic at Iowa with about 500 in attendance. I am watching from the sidelines in a suit and a tie. Coach Moore sees me and yells, 'Damn it, Leahy. Go show those offensive linemen how to double-team (how to snap the ball step and do a double team between the guard and the center).' When Coach Moore was on the field, for him it was not about anything but football. The most important thing to him was line play. It was all about blocking people. This was how he taught us to win and be physical. Coach Moore understood that the other players on the field cannot perform if your offensive line is not blocking to the best of their ability. He was so hard on us in practice. I got called for holding in a scrimmage and Coach Moore made me stand on the side of the practice field with my arms straight out for an hour and a half."

The coaches at Notre Dame understood there were going to be big games but they always made sure their players knew they were students first and foremost and football players second. Amidst the media hype that often accompanied big rivalry games, the coaches kept their players focused on the day-to-day academic requirements before football could be addressed. The Notre Dame Value Stream, which held the concept of the student-athlete in high regard, always kept these young men on the right track. "The play that stands out the most in my mind was the reverse in the '93 Florida State game. Everything surrounding that game was quite memorable, though. The campus turned into a zoo the week before the game with all of the media frenzy, but of course you still have to go to class because you have academic requirements. Coach (Lou) Holtz told us, 'yes it's a big game, but we still have to do things the way we always do things. Missing class to go to an interview is not an excuse.' The RVs were already showing up on campus on Monday. I had just come back from a knee injury, and the FSU game was my first game back. When Adrian Jarrell ran that reverse play, Todd Norman, Aaron Taylor, and myself were all up on the line, with Jarrell behind us. The entire FSU defense bit on the reverse play except for their defensive back, Clifton Abraham. All I can remember is seeing Abraham's eyes get really big as he saw the three of us coming at him. Then you hear the crowd light up and you knew that it was going to be a big play. You just pray there are no flags."

Having an older brother to share these special moments with meant a lot for Ryan. His brother had already left school when they played FSU in '93, but his Notre Dame family made sure that his brother could be there to share the moment with him. "The year we played FSU, my brother Pat had left Notre Dame early to go into the baseball draft (he later came back to finish his degree). He couldn't sign up for football tickets because his minor league baseball season ran into the first week of school. Our family had run out of tickets for that game, and we didn't have a ticket for Pat. There was a stadium usher by the name of Bob Schultheis, who used to mow my grandfather's lawn when he lived in South Bend. He and I had gotten to know each other, and so I asked him if by any chance he would be able to get Pat into the FSU game. Not only did he get my brother a ticket, the ticket was one of the seats down on the field. (Back then they had benches down on the field in between the boxes.) I'm coming off the field after a play and I look up to see my brother sitting on the sidelines. It was such an exciting win. After the game I snuck Pat into the locker room with the rest of the team and we sang the Notre Dame fight song together. 'Notre Dame, Our Lady, Queen of Victory ... pray for us!' Being able to sing the fight song with my brother was a huge moment for me.

When we were kids, my Grandmother Leahy would give us ice cream money if we would sing the fight song for her."

Sometimes life brings us along paths we did not expect. As a Leahy, with football in his genes, Ryan took his skills and Notre Dame preparation and tried his hand at the NFL. His body, however, was not on the same page as his mind and heart. With the injuries he had sustained at Notre Dame, his body was not able to compete at the next level as he had hoped it might be able to. "I was a free agent and so I didn't get chosen in all of the draft day craziness. I had good coaches at Notre Dame. I felt that Coach Moore had us very prepared to play in the NFL. I played for a year with the Arizona Cardinals and was mentored under Coach Carl Mauck, and further developed my skills under his instruction, but my knee surgery slowed me down. Unfortunately, I didn't have the talent level to be able to slow down."

Even though his time at the professional level was brief, Ryan is still thankful for the opportunities given to him and feels blessed for the experiences he was given. "Then I played over in NFL Europe with guys like Jake Delhomme, Jay Fielder and Kurt Warner in Amsterdam. I remember that my teammates were just like me. They wanted so badly to make it back to the NFL. I remember Warner saying to us, 'I just can't go back to bagging groceries.' I didn't earn a huge sum of money playing football professionally, but it was a great experience, and I'm so glad I got the chance to play at that level. I feel very fortunate that I got the chance to play and had a lot of fun doing it. There was a three-week period where I got the opportunity to play against three all-pros. Because of injuries to other players on our team, I got the start and that was definitely my NFL highlight. I was able to hold my own, have some fun and actually really compete."

Sometimes your journey is redirected by the actions of someone else and not those of your own. It is during these moments, when we lack clarity, that the Notre Dame Value Stream takes hold of us and points us in the right direction. "The NFL is weird. It does not have the atmosphere that a college game does. No marching band. No student body. It is definitely more of a 'job.' And then there is that moment when someone tells you, 'Coach needs to see you, and bring your playbook.' Having disappointments like that helped me become the person that I am today. I was always among the last to be cut, and at that point in the selection process all of the NFL teams already have their rosters pretty much set, which makes it almost impossible to find a spot somewhere else. It just forced me to figure out where life was going to take me next."

During his time at Notre Dame, head coach Lou Holtz left quite an impression on young Ryan. Coach Holtz knew just how to reach these young men, motivate them, and bring them to an even higher level than they ever thought they could reach. "What were my best moments with Coach Holtz?

Definitely all of the motivational stories. 'When your wife leaves you, or your kid is sick, you have to have the confidence to carry on when life throws you that curve ball. You always have to believe that momentum will carry you forward. You've got to be able to pick yourself up and fight to figure it out.' Coach Holtz was such a great motivator. He made sure that we did things the right way. That we went to class, went to practice. He was a huge disciplinarian. That's what he did."

"Some of the funniest parts of Coach Holtz were the sayings and stories that he told about my grandfather. He would get so mad at me at practice. Would look straight at me and say, 'There is no way you can be related to Frank Leahy.' Then he would look up to heaven and say, 'I'm so sorry, Frank. I can't teach your boy the offense.' There was this fundraiser in New York for an organization that I belong to called 'Lou's Lads.' They had me up at the podium and were asking me about being a Leahy and playing for Coach Holtz. After I gave my response, I finished with my Coach Holtz impression, singing the Mickey Mouse Club song with a lisp. The crowd goes wild. Then Coach Holtz says, 'Every time I hear you talk like me, I realize how bad my lisp is.'"

There was more to Coach Holtz, though, than his motivational speeches and laughter inducing lisp. The following touching moment between Coach Holtz and his grandson left quite an impact on Ryan. "This, however, is my best Coach Holtz memory of all. One day, we were at practice and we were a sweaty, muddy mess. It was late summer or early fall, and the season had just begun. Coach Holtz had his grandson, Trey, at practice. He had Trey with him on his golf cart and they were sitting off to the side watching practice. He was pointing out players to Trey and explaining to him what they were doing. That moment was pretty remarkable to me. There was no jealousy or contempt on my part. I just thought it was really great for him to be able to share that with his grandson, and for his grandson to see him coach. That is something that I did not get to do with my grandfather, as he passed when I was only 13 months old. But seeing Coach Holtz with Trey like that is an image I won't ever forget."

Lessons from Ryan's Notre Dame Value Stream of Life:

- Make sure you keep your priorities straight ... school should always come before athletics.
- Work hard and put forth the effort and you will reap the rewards in the long run.
- Use your disappointments to motivate you and find the positives in life.

Ryan Leahy

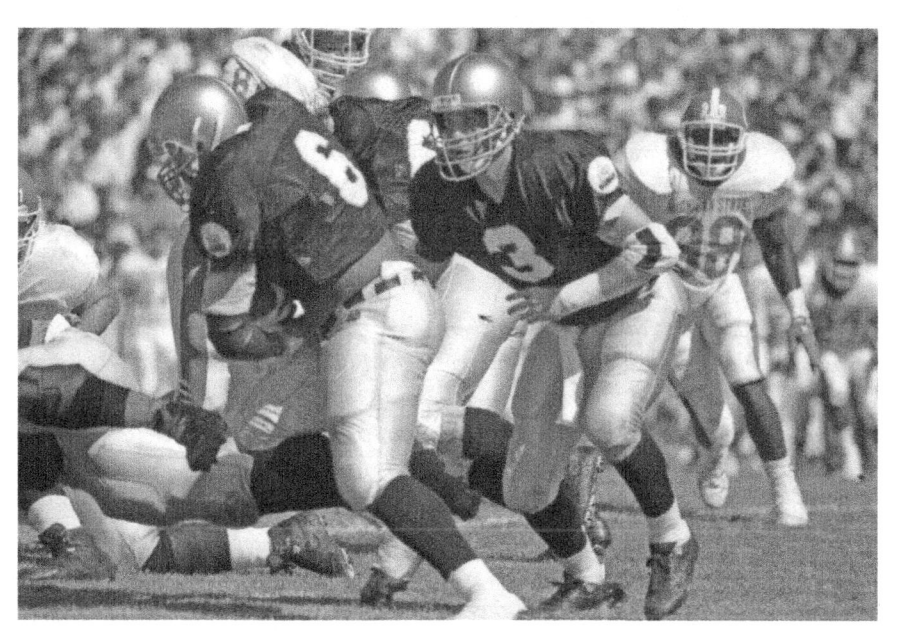

Notre Dame vs. Michigan State (MSU), 1991. Quarterback Rick Mirer (#3) handing ball off to Jerome Bettis (#6). (Photographer: Jim Hunt, photo courtesy of Notre Dame Archives.)

CHAPTER NINETEEN

The Vintner and Philanthropist
Rick Mirer

When I think about Rick Mirer I am reminded of my years growing up in California and the many trips we took to Napa Valley. I remember looking at the endless rows of grapes and thinking about the intricate process that is required to make wine. From vine, to press, to barrel, to someone's glass. How the sun shines lovingly on the grapes to nurture them and how those pure, simple grapes are transformed into this wonderful, sparkling wine that we sit down with today at our kitchen table. The steps that the grapes must go through from the fruit hanging on the vine until the finale when the bottle is opened and the rich ruby red beverage is poured into the glass. A process very similar to the development that Rick received during his time at Notre Dame. Today Rick creates and nurtures his own wine (www.mirrorwine.com), created from the grapes of his Mirror Wine Vineyards in the California Napa Valley.

Goshen, Indiana, is barely an hour from Notre Dame Stadium. This is a small town known across the nation for the horse and buggies of bearded, traditionally dressed Amish farmers and family that mosey into town on Saturday morning. Rick was probably invisible to these religious people who shun the benefits of our hi-tech world. But he was not invisible to the fans who watched his precision throwing arm take him west a few miles to ND and a 29-7-1 record as a starter and then on to a successful NFL career, achieving AFC Rookie of the Year honors.

Rick was the second overall pick in the 1993 draft, selected by the Seattle Seahawks. He was traded to the Chicago Bears in 1997 and played for a total of twelve NFL seasons with seven teams: the Seahawks, Bears, Packers, Jets, 49ers, Raiders and Lions. He threw for 11,969 yards, 50 touchdowns, and 76 interceptions. When he is not making wine, Rick coaches his own boys in the Torrey Pines Pop Warner Youth Football League. He and his wife Stephanie have three children ages 14, 12 and 9.

Once Rick decided what he was going to pursue in his post-football career, the next priority for him was to give back to the University that gave him so much. Notre Dame not only taught us to be prepared for what is ahead of us in life, but to help those around us if we are able. Rick did just that. "From way back when, even before attending Notre Dame, I've always felt that if you were in a position to help, you should. The NFL gives us a lot of connections to charities such as the United Way, and the Boys and Girls Clubs; they set a great example for us to give back when we are at a point to give back."

"In 1998 we quietly gifted some money to Notre Dame and started our own scholarship foundation (Mirer Family Foundation www.mirerfamilyfoundation.org), to help kids be able to attend the university. The wine-making business is a great vehicle for growing the foundation. We don't want to punish the business by giving everything away, but at the same time we need to use it to make a difference with the foundation. Our new concept to integrate the winery and the foundation together is to offer some of our customers several of the 6-liter bottles of wine in return for them making a donation to the foundation. This gets our wine out there and helps the foundation all at once. We also want to take advantage of the charity grant that the NFL has in place. We'd like to get to a point where the NFL grant is matching donations to our foundation, so that we can help the most children reach their education goals."

"A soft spot for the foundation is being able to help out military families. In the San Diego area we see a lot of families where a parent is deployed and does not come back. We think it is important to help out these military families and their children."

"We've had 18 kids now receive scholarships to Notre Dame from the donation that we made to the University in 1998. We may not be able to pay their entire way through school, but we are still able to make a difference. We get letters from the kids during their time at Notre Dame. One of our students, Katie Washington, sent a letter every semester and she ended up being the valedictorian in 2010."

With Rick having grown up in the shadows of the Dome, it was a natural fit for him to play football for the University of Notre Dame. The fact that they had just won the national title in 1988 made ND a very appealing choice as well. "Timing was key in my decision to play football at Notre Dame. Being recruited as a senior in high school while the '88 Notre Dame football team was winning game after game was unbelievable. I felt really comfortable when I went to campus and met the guys. I knew I was joining a very competitive team that was going to win. Plus I would be getting a great education from Notre Dame. It was a fun group to join. To have the opportunity to become a part of that group of guys was incredible. Being that it was so close to home, I didn't realize the magnitude of what Notre Dame was. Plus at the same time the NBC (television) contract was coming together and Lou Holtz was such a great leader."

Surrounding himself with good people was something that drew him to Our Lady's University by way of the Notre Dame Value Stream and has been a guiding force throughout his life. In his career path today as a vintner in Napa Valley, his successes have come from the support network which he has built around him. "I have surrounded myself with good people, and that adds to our success as well. Our expectations are not out of whack; we are just building our business, one customer, one person at a time."

Rick's time at Notre Dame was filled with many successes as well. While there are always a few on-the-field memories that stick out in his mind, the behind-the-scenes memories are what he most cherishes about his days as a Notre Dame quarterback. "I have so many great memories. Some of the simple things are what make up some of my best memories: the camaraderie, the travel, spending Thanksgiving together. My all-time best football memory, however, has to be the 1992 Penn State game."

"There was so much drama at the end of that game ... going for two points to win the game, playing our last game in Notre Dame Stadium. We ended our time at Notre Dame on a huge highlight. The one we got to sleep on was the Penn State game, and we could not have asked for a better ending. (Final score: Notre Dame 17 – Penn State 16.) After the Michigan game ending in a tie, and being left with such a weird feeling after that game, I just felt that we had to go for it. We're either going to win this thing, or not."

Being a Notre Dame quarterback comes with a certain amount of fame and glitz, but a trip to New York City to attend the NFL draft seemed like a little too much spotlight for the product of small town Goshen, Indiana. "I decided to not go to New York City to attend the draft in person. The NFL draft process today is much more of a spectacle, a televised circus, than it was when we were being drafted. I decided to stay home and watch it with my close friends and family. Drew (Bledsoe) and I knew we were going to go one and two, what we did not know was the order."

"The moment his choice was made I knew where I stood." ~Rick Mirer

"The whole experience was kind of a blur. Unlike some of the other guys, I didn't have to wait very long, but it was still a surreal thing. We knew all along that it was going to happen. It was the goal, the end game, but it was a huge relief when it actually happened."

Getting the chance to play in the NFL is the dream of most college football players. Most know that only a select few actually get the opportunity to play and a long NFL career is a rarity. To play at the professional level is a blessing and a curse. You are blessed to just be there, but the ride is often bumpy and filled with potholes. Only those with thick skin survive. This is where the Notre Dame Value Stream gives us the strength to sail the choppy seas. "Getting selected high usually means you go to a team that has not been winning. That was the tough part. I was happy to get the opportunity to play right away, but it didn't really help me learn. I was busy trying to survive. My time in the NFL was pretty interesting. I would have enjoyed staying with one team for a longer period of time. The frequent team changes meant that I had to deal with lots of ups and downs, and I believe that makes you stronger in the end."

"Playing in the NFL for me was an emotional roller coaster. It was very difficult to go from a winning team, to a team that won only two out of 16 games. We were still having the same discussions in the locker room, that we were going to win a championship, but for whatever reason that was not becoming a reality on the field. When you are in a situation like that, you figure out what you are made of. I have no regrets at all. I was lucky to get out of there without injuries or any other health issues. I am one of the lucky ones."

"The best thing (about playing in the NFL) is having the opportunity to keep playing your game, to make a living while doing it, and all of the interesting people that you meet along the way. Today more and more the injuries are a big negative about playing in the NFL. All of the head injuries and tragedies happening to the guys is a huge obstacle for players right now."

Even through the rough seas and murky waters, Rick did have some shining moments in his NFL career. Today he uses the lessons that he learned from playing in the NFL to teach kids how to play the game of football. "Having a productive rookie year was something I was proud of. Unfortunately a coaching change affected me and I started to bounce around a bit. Getting to see what a Super Bowl is like (with the Raiders) was a rush. I wish I had more of those years. I coach younger kids these days and really enjoy it. I could have coached in college and maybe even the NFL but chose to spend as much time with my family as possible. The guys coaching have to devote so many hours to the job that it scared me away. Now I am able to get my fix, but with Pop Warner hours."

All NFL careers come to an end at some point, and Rick's was no different. Making that transition to life after football is not always easy. Trying to find something that brings the same challenge and spark that football gave can often be difficult. Rick was able to take some time off and evaluate where he wanted to go in the next stage of his life. "After I decided to retire from the NFL, my wife Stephanie and I were fortunate enough to enjoy a lot of time off. Our children, now 14, 12, and 9; were little and we didn't have any school schedules, so we took the opportunity and traveled a lot. I never struggled with missing the game all that much. I was relieved to have some free time and to be able to spend it with my wife and children."

"After a while, though, I decided I wanted to create something else; something of my own. While playing football in the bay area, I developed a passion for wine. After my retirement, I decided to reach out to some of the people that I had met along the way, one of which was Rob Lawson, who worked in the wine business and could help me get started up and help with the process. They were able to open some doors for me that might not have been there had I still been in Seattle or Chicago."

"Wine making was not only something that I was interested in, but it was something that I thought I could use the marketing skills that I had been taught at Notre Dame and apply them to my brand, Mirror Wines (www.mirrorwine.com). I don't have the Hall of Fame name, but our winery is not structured that way either. We want our wine to be accepted by wine people, and to not be accepted just because some former NFL (or) Notre Dame player is behind it. My name is not the lead-in. It is not how we want to introduce ourselves."

"I have surrounded myself with good people, and that adds to our success as well. Our expectations are not out of whack; we are just building our business, one customer, one person at a time." -Rick Mirer

"I am not the technical guy in this wine making process. I rely on my wine-maker's experience and I am learning on the run. Rob Lawson is my technical guy, but at some point I definitely want to dive more into that. It's been such a race to get the product out there, to reach out to friends and family in order to market the business. The daily grind does not leave much time to learn the techy stuff about wine making."

As it has done for Rick and so many of us, the Notre Dame Value Stream teaches us how to go out and chase our dreams and to not be afraid of a challenge. It teaches us that a little hard work is good for the soul, and success often comes with failures along the way. "I didn't want my career path to be easy, but at the same time I did not anticipate starting a business in the worst recession of our lives. But even through it all, we've built this winery up in the worst possible situation, and we are looking forward to getting our chance to catch some momentum."

Since creating Mirror Wines, Rick has realized that the hard work that he put in to achieving his goals at Notre Dame also apply to the hard work and successes you attain in your post football careers. He knows that his wine may not be the number one wine brand, but he also knows that what he has is something special. "We don't pretend to be one of the big guys. We don't have the advertising budget. It is our friends, family, and word of mouth networking that is growing our brand. We have created something we like and enjoy, but not much happens with our brand when I am not there. I don't want someone else to represent their version of what we are at Mirror Wines. I am the outward brand of the winery. The sales force is basically me."

A great deal of Rick's work ethic came out of the leadership and discipline imparted on him and his fellow teammates by head coach Lou Holtz. "Coach Holtz was always a fair guy. He was hard on us, but we needed it. We did fine, but he was the one who kept us grounded. We didn't celebrate and he didn't turn us loose, but he made us work hard and I appreciate it. The conversations that Coach Holtz and I have had in the last year or two are probably some of my best Coach Holtz experiences." What makes Rick happy about and comfortable with his position today is when a man like Coach Holtz tells him that he's proud of what he's doing. It makes him humble.

You sense the pride he has in the hard work. "When he (Coach Holtz) sends me a check to support my foundation, now that is cool. He told my parents when I was 18 that he'd make sure I graduated, and that's exactly what he did. Now we are both adults and we can talk man-to-man, I greatly appreciate the consistency in which he did things to help us, to make us grow up, be responsible, and hold us accountable. This last year has probably been as rewarding as any, being able to reconnect with him."

"I was never really all that stressed out in all of the close games that I was a part of, but when I'd come over to the sideline and get the one-on-one conversation with Coach Holtz he was a great strength to me. I'm not sure if he knew whether I was OK or not, but we'd always seem to have a little laugh in the middle of a tense moment. We were so close, and in those crucial game moments he never made me feel like they were bigger than life moments."

"In a perfect world, if we caught lightning in a bottle with the winery, we'd want to help out more kids. The winery could really become something powerful, to fund the foundation, and maybe someday one of the kids will run the foundation. We are just doing our best to set a good example for our kids, to teach them to appreciate what you have, but at the same time to give back if and when you are able."

Rick Mirer

Lessons from Rick's Notre Dame Value Stream of Life:

- Always remember the challenges in life and bumps in the road make you stronger in the end.
- Surround yourself with good people. This will add to the level of success that you can achieve.
- Don't be afraid of taking on a challenge, in pursuing your dreams. A little hard work goes a long way in getting you to your goal.
- Set a good example, appreciate what you have and give back when you can.

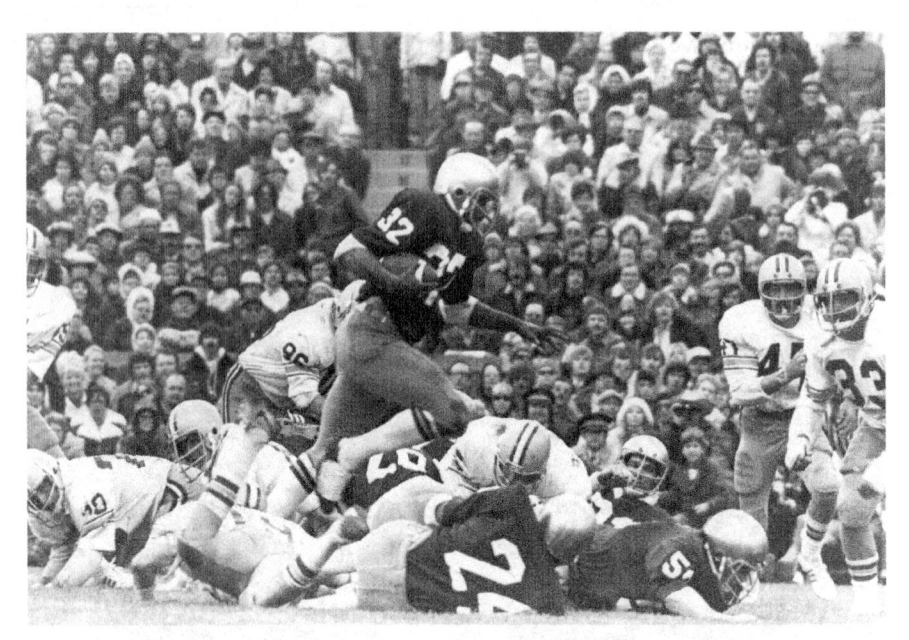

Notre Dame vs. Oregon, 1976. Player Vagas Ferguson (#32) running with the ball. (Photographer: Paul Joyce, photo courtesy of Notre Dame Archives.)

CHAPTER TWENTY

The Athletic Director and Youth Engager Vagas Ferguson

In 1991 Vagas Ferguson was ready to return home to Richmond, Indiana, when a phone call changed the direction of his life. Twenty years later he is still the Athletic Director at Richmond High School. This is rural America with all of its finest traditions. It's one of those towns that makes you feel like you've just stepped back in time. Main Street, farmland, truly the heartland of America, a place where people have their priorities straight. Vagas epitomizes this Midwestern town mindset. A hard worker who has always put great importance on family as well as education. "It's not easy transitioning from the NFL to the real world. You have to find yourself and find your place in life and prioritize what matters." What has always mattered to Vasquero Diaz "Vagas" Ferguson is his family.

When Vagas was ready to move on from the football world, he was living in Chicago, Illinois. He was looking for something that would allow him to stay in the big city, but still allow him to keep connected to his small town roots, and he found just that. "Believe it or not, there was a Fortune 500 company in Richmond, Indiana, called Belden Wiring Cable Company (www.belden.com). They did wiring for computers internationally and all over the U.S. I was looking for a job once I finished playing football and I had sent out a lot of resumes in the Chicago area without much luck. It's all about who you know, and I didn't know many people in Chicago. A friend of mine recommended that I call the president at Belden and I landed an interview. I went to Richmond for the interview and they really liked me. They needed a salesman in Chicago and I was already there, so it was a good match. They trained me and I worked there for six and a half years, until 1991."

After getting his career established and feet off the ground in the sales industry, Vagas realized the need to take care of his family back in Richmond. Family, love, respect and appreciation are powerful forces for a man like this with strong family values. Those values and ties kicked in and his roots began to call him home. "Going into 1991, I decided that I needed to get back home. My grandparents were getting older and I had gone through a divorce and wanted to move back home so that my kids could be around family. I also wanted to go back to school and get my Master's, but without a support network I could not continue to work, raise kids and go back to school. So in December I went home for Christmas and a family friend who worked at the local Richmond school system called me. She was in HR/Administration and she asked me if I'd be interested in coming in for an interview. They were creating a new position, to have someone oversee the non-sport extracurricular activities at the high school and thought that I would be perfect for the job. The timing could not have been better. Here I am trying to move back home and a job practically falls into my lap. The Lord blessed me indeed. I went in and spoke with them and told them that the job sounded great but I'd need a little time to think about it. They told me to take my time as they were in no rush. They were not even going to implement the program until the following school year."

"When I got back to Chicago after Christmas, the HR woman from the high school called me yet again, and this time she asked me if I'd be interested in taking over as the interim athletic director at the high school. I asked her if I could think about it and she said, 'Don't think about it too long!' I hung up the phone and was literally jumping up and down. I called her right back and said, 'Yes!' I explained that I would have to give my company notice and couldn't start until February, and she replied, 'We'll hold the job for you until February 1.' I moved my kids back to Richmond, moved in with my grandparents, got the kids enrolled in school and started as the interim athletic director ... and I've been here 20 years now. Taking that job allowed me the opportunity to go back to school and earned my Master's in Education and

Certificate of Principal through the University of Miami of Ohio, which I never would have been able to do if I had stayed in Chicago. It allowed me to take care of my grandparents, and my kids were in a much less hectic environment and surrounded by family. Blessings all around."

Notre Dame was nowhere on Vagas' radar when he began looking for a college. Yet this dashing, slashing, darting, powerful running back finished his career with the Fighting Irish as the nation's fifth-leading rusher, fifth in Heisman Trophy voting and with All-American honors. (He ranks third all-time for total yards (3,472) among Notre Dame running backs, averaging 5.2 yards per carry. He was a first-round pick in the 1980 NFL Draft and played for five seasons with the New England Patriots, Cleveland Browns, and Houston Oilers; and is a member of the Indiana Football Hall of Fame.) Notre Dame discovered him, in this small town near the Ohio border, and won him over with some Fighting Irish magic. You would assume, if you were a great player and you grew up in Indiana, you were familiar with Notre Dame, but this is not always the case. "To be truthful, I didn't hear about Notre Dame until my sophomore year of high school. The schools that most of us talked about were Purdue, Indiana, Michigan and Ohio State. Those schools got a lot of local coverage."

"I had the chance to visit Notre Dame during my sophomore year in high school because my cousin Lamar Lundy, Jr., a tight end, was being recruited by Notre Dame through a Notre Dame alum who lived in Richmond. He was a senior when I was a sophomore and I got to tag along on his visit to Notre Dame. My cousin ended up going to California – Berkeley, but that trip to Notre Dame left quite an impression on me. I took official visits to Big Ten schools primarily. I went to Indiana, Purdue, Ohio State, Michigan and Iowa; Notre Dame was the last school I visited." The concept that student-athletes at Notre Dame are students first, and athletes second, was very appealing to Vagas and his family. This was a huge selling point used by ND recruiter Brian Bulac, who was the driving force behind Vagas' decision to attend Notre Dame. "He came to my home to speak to my grandparents (Vagas' mother died when he was eight, and his father lived nearby). Education was top on my grandparents' list. They wanted to make sure we got a good education, and that was the first thing he talked about when he walked in the door. 'You will be a football player at Notre Dame, but you are a student first.' That impressed my grandparents, and impressed me as well. Most schools only talked about what I could do for them on the field."

The cultural make-up of Notre Dame in the late 70s was very complicated. While the University, much like the rest of the country, was doing its best to move forward it still had growing pains during the process. "When I was at Notre Dame in the late 1970s, we were in a time of awareness. Racial issues were very much being addressed and it wasn't any different at Notre

Dame than it had been at my high school back home. You tended to hang out with people who looked like you. You congregated as a group, black females and males. Women had not been at Notre Dame very long at that time either, so they had an especially tight bond as well. The black students that I met the first few weeks I was at Notre Dame, guys and girls, we became really close. We were new and didn't know any of the upperclassmen so we just kind of took each other in. We still stay in touch today. You gravitate to people who are more like you. It's not a negative thing. You renew yourself through people who have similar experiences as you do. Today, that is changing. I can see it in my kids and grandkids today. I have bi-racial grandkids. They don't even see that kind of stuff at all."

The Notre Dame Value Stream became ingrained in Her students' lives without us even noticing. We all had highlights during our collegiate careers, students and student-athletes alike; whether it was a big play on the football field or a successful presentation in class. But the moments that we hold most dear of our time at Our Lady's University are really much more basic than any of those big moments. "The most important thing that I took from Notre Dame was the development of relationships, and crossing the barriers of race. Football did that for us. We had to play as a team and support one another and that broke down a lot of racial barriers that we were facing during that time as players."

Not only did Vagas learn the value of hard work as a Fighting Irish football player, he also learned that *quit* was not a word in his vocabulary. His favorite on the field moment is a shining example of the *never say quit* attitude that he and his teammates shared. "My favorite memory on the field had to have been the 1979 Cotton Bowl against Houston. It was below zero; so cold, in fact, that they had to put salt down on the field to thaw it out. In the fourth quarter, we were behind 34-12 with seven minutes left. Late in the game the defense made a big play (a Tony Belden blocked punt) and got points on the board which really changed the momentum for us. (Quarterback Joe) Montana, who had been sick with the flu and missed most of the third quarter fighting below-normal body temperature, returned to execute an unforgettable fourth quarter comeback."

"Down 34-28 with six seconds remaining, we had just enough time to run two plays. The first play was a pass pattern where myself and receiver Kris Haines went to the flat and we had to get across the goal line from the 20-yard line. With the limited amount of time remaining in the game, if we caught the ball, we had to score. The first play we ran was not successful. At this point there was only two seconds on the clock. On the next play, Montana looks over to the sidelines and the coaches, including Coach Devine, put up their hands as if to say, 'Do whatever you want to do. Joe, you call it.' He got down on one knee and drew the play (the same play we had just run), just like you would in the school yard, and told me and Kris Haines how to run it. Haines said he could beat the guy that he was covering. Joe told him, 'I'll hit ya in the corner of the end zone.' We ran the play, scored and won on the last play of the game. Incredible."

Vagas reminisced about what made Coach Devine such a great Notre Dame football coach. "What made Dan Devine good as a head coach is that he surrounded himself with good position coaches. These guys had great instincts and tremendous knowledge of the game. You dealt with your position coach way more often than you actually dealt with Coach Devine. He was not very outgoing, didn't talk to people a lot and was kind of withdrawn. He would talk to us, but he didn't talk to the public very much. He and his family had previously had some bad experiences with the media and I think that was part of why he was so withdrawn. We didn't know that, we just accepted him the way he was. You have to be able to delegate to people and trust them. Coach (Gerry) Faust, unlike Coach Devine, was not able to do that."

"I had two backfield coaches when I was at Notre Dame, but my primary coach was Jim Gruden. Indiana had recruited me starting in my sophomore year of high school all the way through, and Coach Gruden was there before he got the job at Notre Dame. During the recruiting process he told me, 'I'm gonna coach you someday.' During my junior year of college he left Indiana and came to Notre Dame. He taught me more about the running back position than any other coach and took me to another level of play. I absolutely contribute the success I had my junior and senior years at Notre Dame to Coach Gruden. I try to stay in touch with him to this day."

"Always bear in mind that your own resolution to success is more important than any one thing." -Abraham Lincoln

After playing football and receiving an education at Notre Dame, most students leave South Bend with a great internal compass as to what is ahead of them. They are well grounded, and realize that success in life is attained through hard work, and that success is not something one is entitled to, but something one achieves. Vagas realized that playing in the NFL was not a guarantee, but regardless of what his future held, he was grateful for his experiences at Notre Dame. "I was dating my then-fiancée at the time and she was a student at Purdue. Most of the guys were in their rooms watching the draft, but I really didn't even think about it. I never got into that stuff. If I got drafted and got the chance to play in the NFL it was just an added benefit. All I knew was that it wasn't going to make or break me. It wasn't that important and I wasn't worried about it at all. I had always told the guys, 'I don't care where I go, but I really want to go some place warm.' And where did I end up? New England. My buddies ended up in San Francisco and New Orleans. How the heck did they end up there and I'm stuck in New England and I played there for three years (1980-82). Going into my fourth year we had a new coaching staff come in and I didn't get along with them, so I got cut. After New England I played a little bit for the Houston Oilers and a little bit for the Cleveland Browns. After that I moved to the USFL in 1984 and played for a year in Chicago. Then the USFL went under and I was pretty much done."

There are many things that one can take away from playing at the NFL level, but some of the most important takeaways are not learned skills, but the relationships that are cultivated. "The friendships you make and the people you meet are definitely one of the best things that I took away from the NFL. If I think of anything it is those relationships that I developed. I still keep in touch with many of the guys I played with in New England. Looking back you don't remember the records or the individual touchdowns, but you do remember people. It's a blessing to know I can go anywhere in the country and run into people that I know. It's no longer about football, it's about relationships."

The importance that Vagas' family put on education served him very well and he believes that all young people should make their education and academic successes a priority. "Get your education and get that degree! When it's all said and done and you have to put sports away, you will have to make a living for the rest of your life. The effort you put into your school work will determine the quality of life that you're going to live. My grandparents always told me, 'Don't always hang your hat on football, you have to get your degree.' I had to remind myself constantly that I had to get the education piece so that I at least had that going for me. I knew that as a Notre Dame graduate I could get a job anywhere. That degree meant a lot to me. It's with me each day and will be apart of me forever."

Lessons from Vagas' Notre Dame Value Stream of Life:

- Get your education and get that degree! The effort you put into your school work will determine the quality of life that you're going to live.
- Success in life is attained through hard work. Success is not something one is entitled to, but something one achieves.
- Never give up and never quit.

Vagas Ferguson

Notre Dame vs. Michigan, 1986. Tim Brown (#81) running with the ball. (Photographer: Lucian Niemeyer. This photo was published in the 1986 Scholastic Football Review Issue. Photo courtesy of Notre Dame Archives.)

CHAPTER TWENTY ONE

The Enzyme Booster and Fund Raising Driver Tim Brown

When you think of 1987 Heisman Trophy winner Tim Brown, you might describe him in the following manner: great leader, successful, confident, demands respect, role model. But if you had met Tim as a freshman at Notre Dame, you might not have used any of those words. Today, Tim uses his confidence and talents to run two successful companies: Smart Giving Gift Cards (www.sgcfundraisers.com), a program in which gift card users are able to contribute to their favorite charity just by using their gift card; and Tim is currently launching sales of a nutraceutical, enzyme product which promotes good health without medication.

Tim came to Notre Dame from Texas primarily to get an education, and secondarily to play football. When Fighting Irish Coach Lou Holtz took over the program, many felt Tim was not even the best player on the team, let alone someone who would go on to become the best player in the country. Thankfully for Tim, Coach Holtz was able to see his true potential and help him develop into a superstar. He played at Notre Dame from 1984 to 1987, earning All-American honors his senior year and capping off his college career by winning the Heisman Trophy. He had 137 catches for 2,493 yards with the Fighting Irish, also scoring 15 touchdowns. Tim was chosen by the NFL's Los Angeles Raiders with the sixth overall pick in the 1988 draft and finished his 17-year NFL career (all but one with the Raiders) with 1,094 catches for 14,934 yards and 100 touchdowns. He was a nine-time Pro Bowl selection from 1988 to 2004 and in 1997 he led the league with 104 pass receptions. Tim now lives in his home state of Texas with his wife Sherice, and his four children: Taylor, Timon, Tamar, and Timothy.

Tim made the transition from his NFL playing days by moving from one sport to another. "I dabbled with a NASCAR team (as a team owner) for awhile, and came really close to turning the corner with that. We had two teams and two major sponsors (Red Bull and Burger King) ready to sign the deal but Toyota came in and swooped them up giving them free racing and that killed the deal. Then the downturn in the economy adversely affected many businesses, including racing and it was a blessing that we did not pursue that any further." Following his venture with NASCAR Tim started with FOX Sports and worked on a NFL recap show with Jason Sehorn and Eddie George for three years. "They cancelled the show even though we had great ratings. Our show was actually doing better than the 'Best Damn Sports Show,' but they had more sponsors than we did, so they cancelled our show to send people over there, and then the next year they cancelled the 'Best Damn Sports Show.'"

Tim's latest business venture is a company he has started called Smart Giving Cards (www.sgcfundraisers.com). He struck a deal with Visa to offer a reloadable Visa Gift Card that would be connected to the charity of the consumer's choice. Every time the consumer uses their gift card, a percentage of their purchase is donated to the charity of their choice. He also is involved with a company that sells enzymes. "Enzymes are the second most important thing in our bodies behind oxygen. The older we get, the fewer enzymes our bodies create. When you get old, get wrinkles, it's because you don't have enough enzymes. This company sent me some products my last year in the league - nutraceuticals - but I decided to wait until after the NFL to try them. Since I have retired from the NFL and have been taking these enzymes, I have not taken one Advil or Aleve. I manage everything with these enzymes and I'm trying to spread the word about this fantastic product and help them get to the next level."

The time that Tim spent at ND under the influence of the Notre Dame Value Stream reinforced the already grounded views he received from his mother on the importance of getting a good education. "Make sure you get your education. It is the most important thing that you will always have in your back pocket. I talk to kids all the time and they say to me that I don't use my education, but that is not true. I tore my knee up after my first game in my second year in the NFL and I really thought my career was over. Life is short and you just don't know what is going to happen. I would have been sad if I could not have played in the NFL any more. When they told me I was about to have major reconstructive surgery, I reached down and kissed my class ring because I was so thankful that I had my education, and that I had something to fall back on. It's a beautiful thing to have a college education. You'll always be respected for it, and no one can take that away from you. Your education is what helps you communicate with others. If you can't communicate, what's the use of being in the room?"

When Tim was in high school, he knew nothing about Notre Dame. His brother was the person who introduced him to Our Lady's University. "He was eight years older than me and did not live at home when I was in high school. Unknown to me, he absolutely loved Notre Dame and watched the game replays on Sunday mornings. When I was in high school, he did a little research and found out that Notre Dame was all about education, and at that point he knew I had to go to there. He came over to the house one day and I had all of the letters from the schools that were interested in me spread out on the kitchen table. When he saw the ND letter, he said, 'That's where you want to go.'" Tim did not want to be 1,500 miles away from home, but once he figured out what Notre Dame was all about, the Notre Dame Value Stream had him sold. "My mom was the one who needed to be won over. In my house it was about convincing mom, not dad."

Tim took unofficial visits to SMU and Oklahoma, and official visits to Iowa, Notre Dame and Nebraska. Going into the other four visits, Tim was already pretty much focused on Notre Dame, but his visits really sealed that for him. "I could very quickly tell that my recruiting weekend hosts at the other four schools were not people that I would want to be friends with, and I did not share interests with them. All they wanted to do was drink, smoke, and use foul language and that was not me. (At) Notre Dame, my host was Alvin Miller. Even though my decision to attend Notre Dame was pretty much already made at that point, he solidified my decision for me. Alvin was a really great guy who was interested in the same things that I was ... he was funny, loved his teammates, talked about church and God. Right away I knew this was where I belonged."

When Tim moved to South Bend to begin his freshman year he was not so sure that this move to a small college town in Indiana had been a good one. "Initially, being that I was a momma's boy, being away from my family was a big challenge for me. Having to wait three, four, five weeks at a time before I could see them was a very difficult adjustment for me freshman year. The other big adjustment was the pressure of being a football player. When we first got to school and we were the only ones there, there was no pressure at all. You went to practice, hung out with the guys and everything was great. Once everyone got to school the pressure increased. When you were around your teammates, there was very little pressure. But when the students got there and everyone started asking you questions, things changed. All I wanted to do was play football and get a good education. I never wanted to be under the spotlight. I just wanted to go to school, learn and play football, not be under the spotlight. The academics were not as tough for me as they were for some of the guys. I was very motivated and focused on my education. I got a dual degree from the Arts & Letters and Business Administration departments, sociology and management."

Before the very first game of Tim's freshman year, the coaching staff had told him that he would not start right away, but rather that they would work him into the game. Then all of the sudden, they decided to put Brown out there for the opening kickoff. "I was nervous as all get out and feeling the pressure. So there I am standing out there, completely in shock, and I dropped the ball. I dropped the ball and I didn't even realize I had dropped the ball until I saw people running after me. I took about three or four steps at which point I realized that the ball was behind me. After that rocky start, the coaches were doing their best to keep me out of the game. They rotated players in and out of the game, and every time my 'group' went in they would hold me back. Eventually I got in on a third-down play, mostly because they didn't get a chance to hold me back, and I ended up making this great catch down the middle. That catch was probably the most memorable moment of my entire career because without that catch, nothing else would have happened. Football is all about confidence, and that play showed me that I could do it; that I could rebound from a terrible play and actually do well … that I had it in me to make a good play, keep my momentum and keep going."

Tim loved head coach Gerry Faust. Coach Faust recruited him to come play football at Notre Dame, and without him he never would have gone there. "He was a great inspiration for me, for my life. If I felt sad, he would always say, 'Come on in here and call your momma.' Gerry Faust was a passionate coach, and he loved the game with all of the passion in the world. He loved the players and he loved Notre Dame. I'm not sure there will ever be a coach who will love Notre Dame as much as Gerry Faust. He may have been in over his head. Notre Dame seemed to get a little bit too big for Coach Faust, and as more and more people became negative, they lost confidence in him and then he lost confidence in himself, and it just snowballed from there. Once the coaches and players lost confidence in him it was pretty much over." There was quite a change when Notre Dame transitioned from Coach Faust to Coach Holtz. "Coach Holtz was so full of energy. He had a different kind of passion. He was a very smart football coach who knew how to put you in the right position for your individual talent, and he was a fantastic motivator. He could make you believe you could run through that brick wall. We were so impressed with his vast football knowledge. He was definitely capable of doing everything that we thought a head football coach should be doing."

A defining and often misunderstood moment of Tim's career occurred during the 1987 Cotton Bowl matchup between Notre Dame and Texas A&M. Halfway through the fourth quarter, after the Aggies had taken a 28-10 lead over the Irish, Tim returned an A&M kickoff 14 yards before being stopped. At that point, Warren Barhorst of Texas A&M took Tim's towel from his belt. Tim then chased Warren across the field toward the Aggies' bench and grabbed Warren from behind, tackling him to the ground. *"I wanted my towel back," Tim said. "It had my initials on it. It had my number on it. I didn't know I'd be called just for trying to get my towel back." The Aggies' special teams had a thing for towels. They waved them all the time when they would go onto the field, and the crowd would go wild. "The towel was there, my mind thought of it, and I went for it," Warren said. Tim was called for 15 yards for a personal foul.*[3]

"All I knew was that they were not going to take my towel away that day. Cedric Figaro's girlfriend made us that towel. (Cedric was one of Tim's teammates.) Not everyone got one of the towels, but many of us did. Two weeks before the game she was in a serious car accident and so that towel had taken on a completely new meaning for us. They could have taken my helmet that day and it would not have been a big deal. But don't mess with my towel. I was not frustrated at all. They just were not going to take my towel. (Television sportscaster) Brent Musburger was making fun of me, but he didn't know the entire story behind the towel and what it meant to us."

In the late 80s, the NFL draft was not the media circus that it is today. Often top players would not travel to New York City to watch the draft. They would stay at home and follow the draft on television surrounded by family and friends. "I remember sitting in my little apartment in South Bend with a couple of friends around me. I had no idea where I was going to go. I knew I was not going as the first pick to the Atlanta Falcons, as they were taking Aundray Bruce. There was a chance I could go second, third, fourth or fifth before the Raiders, who were the sixth pick, but I really did not want to go to any of those teams. (Kansas City, Detroit, Tampa Bay, Cincinnati). I looked at the Raiders' roster and saw Bo Jackson and Marcus Allen and I knew that was where I wanted to be. To be able to play with Jackson and Allen, and learn the game from that caliber of players, was exactly what I was hoping for. I told my hopes to my agent, but my agent did not have a good feel for how this was all

---

[3] Quotes taken from New York Times article: www.nytimes.com/1988/01/02/sports/cotton-bowl-aggies-top-irish-by-35-10.html.

going to play out. Right before the fourth pick (Tampa Bay) the Raiders called me to say, 'If you are there at the No. 6 pick, we are going to take you … do you want to be a Raider?' Yes! After the Bengals made their choice at No. 5 and it was not me, the Raiders called back and said, 'We're bringing you to Cali!'"

For Tim, his rookie year was the high of his NFL career. "I was the new kid in town and that was a lot of fun. Being able to walk around town and do whatever you want because you are Los Angeles Raider Tim Brown. And whenever Marcus Allen said something good about me that just made life even easier for me. I was at a point in my life where I was able to take care of my family and do things for my mom that she never would have dreamed of and that made me extremely happy. Football is a very difficult game. You have to have fun at what you are doing, but at that level it's a job. It's what you are doing to make a living. It's not as enjoyable as you'd think. Monday through Saturday you are not only getting prepared for Sunday, but you also have to take care of family issues. It's a lot of pressure and stress. From that standpoint, it became a business more than a game. The weekly grind can become a very monotonous thing, especially when you are not winning. Fortunately a balance of up and down years made it easier for me to stay engaged."

"I always turn to the sports section first. The sports page records people's accomplishments; the front page has nothing but man's failures." -Earl Warren

"Another great highlight of my career would definitely be going over 1,000 catches. At the time that I reached that milestone, only two other players had done it before me, so it was quite the accomplishment for sure. I played in the NFL for 17 years. I would have liked to have gotten one more year in. I still felt like I was able to play at that level, but my twins were one year old at the time and the thought of dragging them to another city was just unfathomable. They were talking about trading me to Philadelphia or New England so I decided it was time to walk away."

Tim attributes a big part of his successes at Notre Dame and beyond to Coach Holtz's keen eye. When head coach Lou Holtz arrived on the scene at Notre Dame, Tim was not a Heisman Trophy caliber player. Well, at least not in his mind. He wasn't even a starter on the Fighting Irish squad. Coach Holtz helped Tim see himself in a completely different light. "Two days after we started spring ball, during Coach Holtz's first season, Holtz came up to me and asked me why was I not starting and playing every down. And I told him that I was not one of the regulars. He really challenged me on that, 'was it grades, did you get in trouble?' 'No, they just didn't play me.' At that very moment he told me not only was he going to play me all the time, on every down, he also told me that he thought I could be the greatest player in the country. He would show me films almost every day. 'Tim, normal guys can't do that. They can't make people miss like that. They can't run around and get out of the break like that.' I was totally blown away, and day by day I started to believe him. I started to walk that way, play that way, demand respect that way, like I was the best player in the country. When you have that kind of confidence, you carry yourself differently. From there it started to manifest itself on the field, and then it was over. I was like a little puppy dog that was so excited."

One of Coach Holtz's strengths was to be able to see the potential in his players and to help them reach that potential. "He saw something in me that I did not see in myself and his encouragement and guidance was what really took me to the next level. My high school coaches were great, but Lou showed me how to truly reach my potential. Before Lou I was not the best player on the team, let alone the best player in the nation. From there on out, the only way I was not going to get the ball was if they intercepted the snap from center. My life truly changed in April of 1986, because of Coach Holtz. People started looking at me differently, and started asking much more of me. Lou was the kind of coach who thought he was everybody's Dad. He was just what

Notre Dame vs. Army, 1985. Tim Brown (#81) running with the ball. (Photographer: Joe Raymond, photo courtesy OF Notre Dame Archives.)

we needed as young men."

Lessons from Tim's Notre Dame Value Stream of Life:

- Make sure you get your education. It is the most important thing that you will always have in your back pocket. You'll always be respected for it, and no one can take that away from you.
- The most important thing to learn is how to communicate with others. If you can't communicate, what's the use of being in the room?
- Have confidence in yourself and your abilities. When you start to carry yourself in a confident manner and demand respect from others, people will start to see you in a different light. Having confidence in yourself is your first step towards achieving success.

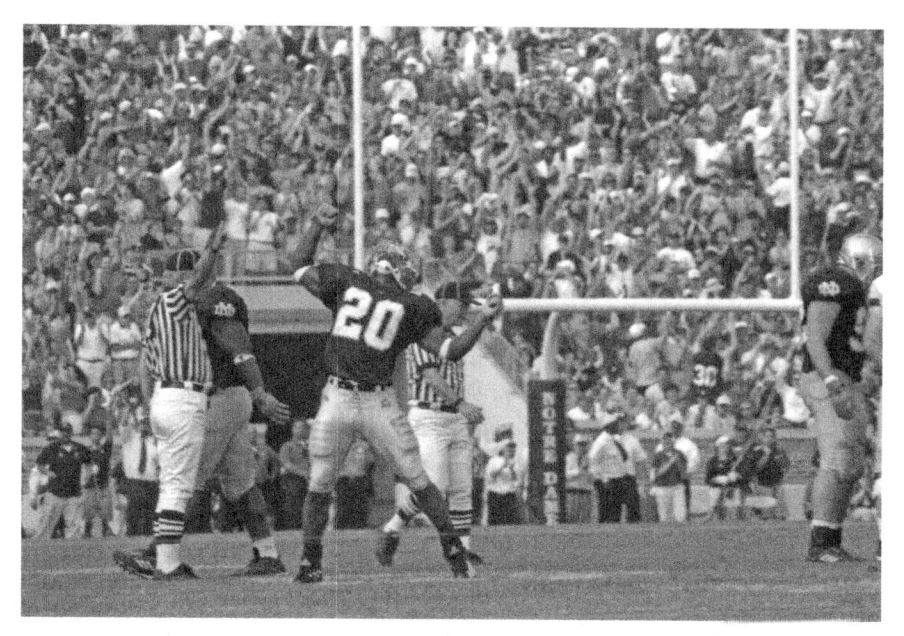

Notre Dame vs. Michigan, 2002. Gerome Sapp (#20) celebrating after a play. (Photographer: Brother Charles McBride, photo courtesy of Notre Dame Archives.)

CHAPTER TWENTY TWO

The Influencer
Gerome Sapp

Gerome Sapp grew up in a tough area of Houston, raised by his mother with little in the way of extras to be found. She helped steer him toward a successful path that later included an important role model in his high school football coach, Lee Malowitz. Gerome played football at Lamar High School in Houston where he became a Parade All-American defensive back as a junior and the top-ranked recruit in Texas as a senior. Acting on his mother's request to see the world, Gerome left Texas and became a part of a Notre Dame defensive squad that scored more points than the offense. He then went on to play safety for five years in the NFL for the Baltimore Ravens and Indianapolis Colts.

Gerome has the gift of gab. Quick to tell a story (or ten) and once he starts, a crowd is soon to form, with every single one of them all ears on Gerome. This gift also makes Gerome a born salesman and now an entrepreneur. His new company

Fluencr (www.Fluencr.com), says it all for this social media expert. He recently launched his latest business venture, which provides advice and consultation to consumers who need an active voice to interact with the brands and products that they already love. "My current business venture is designed to help people harness the power of social media. Social media allows the average person to have a huge voice that can be heard around the world. It gives people the opportunity to be ambassadors of their own brands. Even if you only know one person, and you tell them about your favorite brand or company, you can be an 'influencer.' For example, I am valuable if I tell one person to go to Legends (a bar on Notre Dame's campus), but by proclaiming it on social media I can amplify my influence. What I am doing with Fluencr is taking it to the next step ... helping people get rewarded for their influence specific to their favorite brand. This is good for the brand as well, because it allows the brand to cash into the consumer's social credibility with their friends. In a sense people end up getting endorsement deals just for simply supporting the brands they love."

Gerome's first memory of Notre Dame was when he was eight years old. He didn't initially understand the mystic that is ND, but soon enough he caught on to the Notre Dame Value Stream and was hooked. "I didn't really know much about Notre Dame as a kid. I thought they were a professional team, though, because they were always on TV. At about 13 I realized they were actually a powerhouse college football team. Growing up I did not really like Notre Dame. Florida State was my favorite team and I loved Charlie Ward. When the movie 'Rudy' came out, my whole perspective of Notre Dame changed. When you grow up in Texas, the only schools you are exposed to are Texas, Texas A&M, and maybe Oklahoma. Once I figured out what the essence of Notre Dame was, they moved to the top of the list."

For visitors from the south, South Bend can be quite harsh and uninviting. "My official visit to Notre Dame was the worst experience of all the visits that I made. There was absolutely nothing to do in South Bend. It was freezing cold outside. This compared to my visit to Texas, which was awesome. The weather was perfect. The Texas Angels escort you around. But there was something that was internally drawing me to Notre Dame. I knew I needed to be there."

Notre Dame quickly stood out from the rest. It became Gerome's opportunity to see, explore, live and discover what potential lie inside him. "At that point Texas was my second choice, and the rest of the list was USC, Miami and Michigan. As my mom and I were discussing my choices, she expressed that she really wanted me to get out of Texas and experience life. 'Experience the world.' After she said that, I knew I was going to Notre Dame. It was the perfect mix of tradition, athletics and academics."

The defensive core that Gerome had the opportunity to play with (Vontez Duff, Glenn Earl and Shane Walton) bonded quickly in the backfield and found success despite many other factors working against them. "Those were some of the best times. All four of us had such extremely different personalities, and yet despite that, we were a cohesive unit on the field. Glenn Earl was very intelligent but also quite crazy. He was the guy who would run through a brick wall because he wanted to get to the other side. Going around it be damned. He was very sarcastic and negative at times. He was my roommate on the road. Almost every Friday night before a game he would tell me, 'Gerome, you know something bad is gonna happen tomorrow? I'm just waiting for that bad thing to happen so that I can get over it.' However, Glenn was an amazing athlete and always seemed to make the plays that helped us win games. Shane Walton was another very intelligent guy, but also very personable and charismatic. He kind of went overboard, though. He would be the one to reprimand you on the field if you screwed up. He was our mascot. He represented us. He was our leader and displayed the swagger for the group."

"Vontez Duff was a southern boy. Very intelligent, very athletic, but was definitely the little brother of the group. Shane made sure to take him under his wing. I was the analytic professor type. I was the one who kept order in the room. I was the father of the group. Got everyone lined up. But once we hit the field, we really meshed. We 100 percent enjoyed making other teams look bad. We had a board where we put up names of guys from the other team, the ones that we were going to get in the next game, and after each game we checked their names off. It was definitely fun."

When you play for a team like Notre Dame, you are expected to win. You are expected to not only win, but to win a national championship every year. These pressures are felt from the top of the ND family food chain all the way through the team. What happens, though, when one unit is performing much better than another? Gerome and his defensive unit struggled mentally when their unit was outscoring the offense. "At first you don't think about it. We were so close. As a defense we just knew we needed to play as hard as we could. It wasn't like we knew we had to do it in order to win, it was how we played. If you're not scoring, you're not completing the play. It didn't really bother us until we got about midway through the season. At that point we realized that we were outscoring the offense. Here is the problem with that. When you are out on the field more, you become more physically tired. But beyond that, mentally you are not getting the time to get the intellectual knowledge during your time on the sideline to make the necessary adjustments and/or corrections that you need. When the offense continually goes three and out, you have no time on the sideline to figure out what is going on. It did not just affect us physically, but mentally and psychologically. It really put a lot of pressure on us to be perfect."

There is something about that first time you step out onto the college stage. The first time as a member of the Fighting Irish that you don the Blue and Gold and run out of the tunnel onto the lush green turf. "My favorite

(Notre Dame football memory) is the one I'll always remember. My first memory. The first time I ran out of the tunnel for the Kansas game, which was the first game of my freshman year. Amazing. Probably the next best memory was the USC game that same year. They came out of the blocks running and were handing it to us during the first half, despite the fact that it was storming. After we were given our adjustments at half time, we came out to start the second half and things changed. The rain stopped. The wind shifted in our favor. And we started playing our game. We all looked up and said, 'Wow, did that really just happen?' Divine intervention. We won that game, 26-24."

Football is a physical game, and quite often football becomes a practical application of Murphy's Law: *Anything that can go wrong will go wrong.* "I broke my wrist during the USC game, which was the last game of my senior season. I didn't know it was broken and I played the rest of the game. I also played with a broken wrist for the bowl game and the East/West game. They didn't discover the break until after that, and then at that point I had surgery. I attended the combine with a cast on, so many teams assumed that I would not play my rookie year."

"It was a very exciting time for me. The good part about getting injured the way I did was that when it came time for the draft there really was no pressure on me. I knew I was going to get drafted, I just didn't know where. I had received calls from the Colts, Steelers and Raven. The whole draft process is a huge chess match. They keep telling you, 'If this guy gets drafted we'll take you in this round' or 'If this guy is still on the board, we'll wait a bit longer before we take you.' I didn't even sit and watch the draft on TV. I was actually playing football outside with my brother when my phone rang. It was the Ravens telling me that they were about to draft me. We went inside and I turned the TV on and my name came across the screen."

The culmination of four years of hard work is getting to play at the next level. It's a dream come true, but it's not the fairy tale that many expect. It, however, is a good litmus test for what the real world is like. If you are able to survive and thrive in the NFL, you will do so in the next phases of your life as well. As Gerome quickly learned, his greatest asset was himself. "The best part was the competition. Being given the opportunity to play with the best people in the world, at such a high level and on that platform. That was the dream. Being able to compete in that arena and see how well you adjusted to the competition. There is a huge learning curve when you first start out, especially mentally. When you tackle that guy, yes, that is your job. But it's also his job not to get tackled. So at first it's a big accomplishment when you just tackle him."

"The worst part is the business aspect of the game. Most people don't understand the business side at all. It's more than just signing a contract and getting paid. It is such a completely one-sided business. You are contractually obligated to play for a team, but they are not contractually obligated to you. At any moment they can release you and be done with you. But you have to be committed 100 percent, at all times, and if they think you are not, they will attempt to expose you as some horrible, greedy athlete. The older you get, the more time you get to interact with the business side, the smarter you get. Being cut was a blessing. I felt like, you've done the worst to me, and I'm still here."

"My time playing in the NFL really helped me with my life. It taught me that we are all disposable assets. The more that you can increase your value, the harder it is for you to get disposed. My asset is me." –Gerome Sapp

Sometimes the moment when you are on top of the world can also be your lowest moment all at once. "My NFL highlight is a bittersweet one. The sweet part of my NFL highlight was my first game playing as a starter for the Ravens. The first time I actually got to not only start a game, but start a game after getting to practice with the first team all week as opposed to a starter getting hurt and getting thrown into a game. We were playing against the Saints, and we beat the mess out of them down in New Orleans. I caused Reggie Bush's first career fumble with a big hit on him in the back field along with several interceptions and pass deflections. It was definitely an 'I told you so!' moment. It was a vindication type thing for me, but not in a negative way. In a 'see what I can do if you give me the opportunity' kind of way. The bitter part was in that very same game I made a mistake, and got benched for it. Talk about a high and a low. My first start and I got benched. My family all drove down from Houston to see me play. Starters make a ton of mistakes all game long, but I only made one mistake and got benched. That was the nature of the NFL. For the first time, there was a hole in my armor. I realized that hard work does not always pay off in this league, and that the good guy does not always finish first."

The life skills that Gerome learned both at Notre Dame and in the NFL carried him toward the successful business that he runs today. "During my last year in the NFL I tore my hamstring, which pretty much ended my career. As that was becoming clear to me, two of my fellow Notre Dame teammates (Glenn Earl, and Chris Yura) and I decided to start a business called Morph & Thro (www.morphandthro.com). Morph & Thro produced high-performance sports apparel. The apparel was produced domestically using high-end materials which were made out of recycled plastic. We knew nothing about the rags business but we studied and learned on the fly. Our product line was so highly regarded the Navy Seals trained in them."

"I think I'm a born entrepreneur and with my gift to gab and my drive to succeed. I was very excited about my new company and this new chapter in my life. In preparation to launch Fluencr I have done a tremendous amount of research, watched webinars, done everything that I can to get my hands on information and individuals that allow me to learn everything I can about the social media marketing industry. I believe it's a win-win for the brand and the consumer. Not only does the company or brand win by getting the support of their customers, we will also provide them with a dashboard of analytics so that they can numerically see the return on their investment. The consumer gets rewarded for something they already do: talk about their favorite brand."

Gerome looked back on how Notre Dame and head coach Tyrone Willingham prepared him for his current journey in life. He talked about how he learned that you not only had to put in the hard work, but you also had to enjoy the successes as well. And he talked about the importance of having something *important* to say. "Following the beat-down that we put on Florida State down in Tallahassee, we were on the bus back to the airport. Everyone was happy and having a great time. We look up to see that Coach Willingham is actually dancing with joy. That was the first time I saw that our success actually affected him as well. He was actually letting loose and enjoying being in the moment! That left a big impression on me. Coach Willingham was a pretty quiet guy. He never really raised his voice, but that was because he didn't have to. He didn't feel as if he needed to either. He didn't talk just to talk; he talked when he had something to say. A lot of coaches just like hearing their own voice and what they say does not hold much weight. Everything Coach Willingham said was very much respected."

Notre Dame prides itself on doing its part to make sure each and every one of its students are ready for life. The time and preparation Her students put in during their four years will carry them through a lifetime of career as well as life changes. The Notre Dame Value Stream stays with them when they graduate and guides them through the hills and valleys of life. "I put in all the work and I did the best I could. You never want to look back and have regrets. I graduated from ND with a degree in Finance, I was the captain of ND football and at that point I had a sort of an inner peace about things. I was excited about the future. Someone is going to choose you, to pick you from a list of others to make a lot of money doing something you love. They are going to give you the opportunity to live in a new city and meet new people. The world was in front of me. It was time to take advantage of all that I learned."

Lessons from Gerome's Notre Dame Value Stream of Life:

- Don't talk just to talk… make sure when you say something that it's important.
- If you put forth the hard work and the effort you will reap the rewards.
- Learn early that your biggest asset is yourself. The more that you can increase your value, the harder it is for you to be disposed.

Gerome Sapp

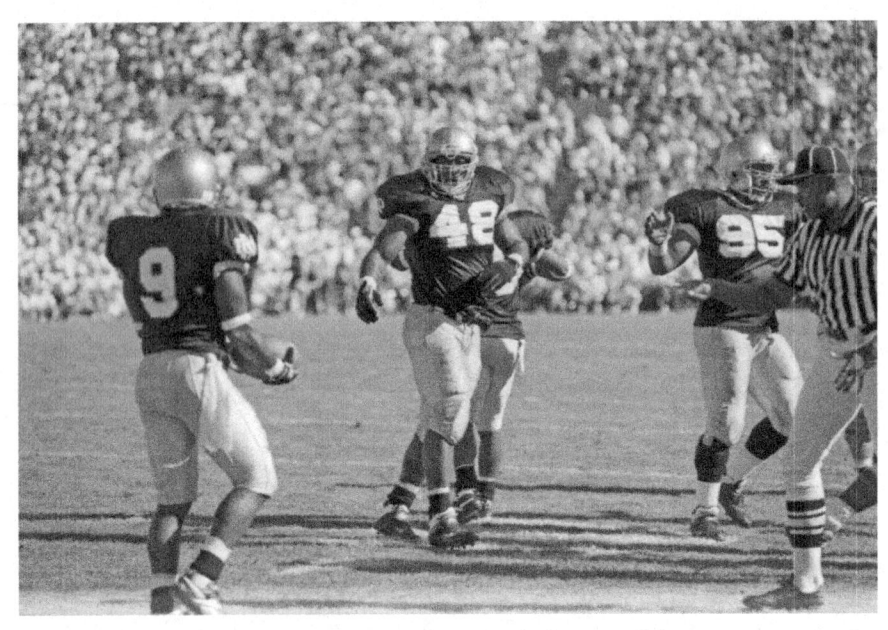

Notre Dame vs. Northwestern, 1995. Players including Renaldo Wynn (#48) on the field in between plays. (Photographer: Joe Raymond, photo courtesy of Notre Dame Archives.)

CHAPTER TWENTY THREE

The NASCAR Business Developer and Life Changer Renaldo Wynn

Renaldo Wynn's workplace does not consist of a desk, computer and office chair, but being trackside with the Joe Gibb's NASCAR racing team as the cars go whirring past him. Where the team's goals are to go fast, turn left and don't crash. He's come a long way from his days of playing high school football and trying to find a way out of his gang plagued neighborhood. Growing up on the South Side of Chicago and watching Notre Dame's rise to national title prominence, becoming a member of the Fighting Irish football squad was always at the top of Renaldo's wish list. A three sport guy in high school (track, basketball and football), Renaldo, an All-Catholic League and All City honors football player from De La Salle Institute in Chicago, was tops on Notre Dame's list as well. Renaldo was redshirted as a freshman and went on to have a successful football career at Notre Dame. He

170

started five games during the 1993 season and recorded 19 tackles. In 1994 he started ten games, including the Fiesta Bowl against the University of Colorado, recording 47 tackles and one sack. In 1995 he received All-American honorable mention honors with 57 tackles and 6.5 sacks and in 1996, his senior season, he made 61 tackles with nine sacks and was named the team's Most Valuable Player and Lineman of the Year. He played in the NFL for 13 seasons with four teams: the Jacksonville Jaguars, Washington Redskins, New Orleans Saints, and New York Giants. However, he finished his football career in the United Football League with the Omaha Nighthawks in 2010. Renaldo now lives in Charlotte, North Carolina, with his wife LaTanya and their daughter Kennedy, working with the Joe Gibbs Racing Team.

"Any transition is a tough one without a foundation in Jesus Christ."
- Renaldo Wynn

Like 99.9 percent of all NFL players, retirement didn't come on Renaldo's terms, it was decided for him. Very few guys are actually ready to leave, but eventually the ride comes to an end. Renaldo had a few goals in mind that he wanted to do moving forward. "I felt career-wise that I had several goals that I wanted to strive for. One was being a TV sports analyst. I had done some television in Washington, DC and wanted to try and make a go out of that. I interviewed with Comcast Sports Net in DC, but that was not the place where I wanted to live. I also interviewed with ESPN and that didn't work out. Then I thought about coaching, but I loved being with my family and didn't want to compromise that."

His transition from the NFL to life after football actually happened during the middle of his NFL career, when he was far from retirement. "In 2004, when I was still playing with the Washington Redskins, I got my first taste of NASCAR racing. Steve Spurrier had just stepped down as the head coach of the Washington Redskins and Joe Gibbs had come in as the new head coach. The first thing that Coach Gibbs did was announce a mandatory minicamp. It was very unusual for a head coach to come in like that and have his first interaction with the team be a mandatory camp. This was quite a statement by Coach Gibbs. Many of the guys were still on vacation and out of shape and knew that Coach Gibbs was going to come in and cut any guys who were not prepared for the season. At the time I was the player representative for the NFL Players Association and I was getting frantic phone calls from the guys telling me that what Coach Gibbs was doing was illegal, which it wasn't. He was just setting the tone."

"A winning effort begins with preparation." - *Joe Gibbs*

Renaldo himself was not able to make the mandatory minicamp. The NFL Players Association meetings were in Hawaii at the same time and so he called

Coach Gibbs to let him know that he would not be there. "He gave me quite the tongue lashing for not making the minicamp a priority and let me know that he'd be making decisions based on who was at camp. I told him that I had a responsibility to be at these meetings and that I was going to follow through with my commitment. On my way home from Hawaii I stopped at my house in Las Vegas. There happened to be a NASCAR race in Las Vegas that weekend, and I knew that Coach Gibbs had a racing team (www.JoeGibbsRacing.com). I called him and told him that I was in Las Vegas and would like to go to the NASCAR race and asked him if he could connect me with some passes. At that point I got another tongue lashing from Coach Gibbs for being in Las Vegas and goofing off, even though I had explained to him that Las Vegas was where my wife and I had a home. He got me in contact with his assistant and she set me up with passes for myself and my family to attend the race."

Little did he know, Coach Gibbs had already planned on making Renaldo's first exposure to NASCAR a learning experience. "When we arrived at the track I was supposed to ask for Marlin (who was with the Joe Gibbs racing team). I told him that I was to speak with him in regards to picking up my passes for the race that day, and Marlin told me, 'Yes, I have your passes, but there's only one thing. They aren't free.' I was not a race car fan, but I figured they couldn't be that expensive and so I asked him how much they were, to which he responded, '$1,800.' WHAT? I tried to explain to him that I was a VIP, an NFL player and to which he said, 'Coach left them for you, but told me that you'd pay for them.' And so I did. I saw Coach Gibbs down at the track and he didn't say anything to me, he just smiled. They won the race that day so I must have been their lucky charm. That was the last time I paid to attend a race."

Not only did that moment establish a good relationship between Coach Gibbs and Renaldo, it was a very good first impression for them both. From that day forward, Renaldo was hooked on NASCAR and in the offseason he would go to as many races as he could. "I loved going to the races and getting to experience race day. Coach Gibbs saw there was a sincerity in my interest in NASCAR and he approached me to come down in the offseason for 10 days to shadow him at the Joe Gibbs Racing facility in Charlotte, North Carolina. I spent 10 days with him and learned all about what goes into NASCAR racing. For the next six years that I played in the NFL I spent every offseason helping out with Joe Gibbs racing and learning more about NASCAR."

When it came time for Renaldo to retire from the NFL, the transition to working full-time with Joe Gibbs Racing was an easy one, considering the relationship that he already had with Coach Gibbs both on and off the field. "When he called me and offered me a position to come down to Charlotte and work with his ministry (www.gameplanforlife.com), and racing team, I jumped at the opportunity. I came down to Charlotte for an interview, and my wife and I prayed on it, and decided that it was the right move for us. Within six months we were moved and settled into our new life. We have three primary racing teams at Joe Gibbs Racing: the No. 11 Fed Ex/Toyota car driven by Denny Hamlin, No. 20 Husky/Home Depot/Dollar General car driven by Matt Kenseth and the No. 18 M&M car driven by Kyle Busch. We have four teams in the Saturday nationwide races, and MX Supercross; we've got a lot going with our racing teams."

"A life is not important except in the impact it has on other lives." - Jackie Robinson

Not only did accepting the job with Joe Gibbs Racing give Renaldo an opportunity to have a career doing something that he loved, it also gave him an opportunity to make a difference in the lives of troubled men. "On the ministry side we operate 'Game Plan for Life' (www.gameplanforlife.com). Game Plan for Life started out with the book that coach Gibbs wrote by the same name. The book was such a huge success that he took the ministry on the road. The ministry's mission is to get men off the sideline and into the game. We work with men who are already Christians and equip them to reach unsaved friends, and we work with men who have no relationship with Jesus Christ to introduce them to a new way of life. It's mainly an outreach for men. 40 percent of American families don't have fathers, and in minority communities it's 60 percent or higher. We need fathers to be responsible and accountable in their families, homes and communities. We do one or two events a month in different cities. We just did one in Greenville, South Carolina and we had 1,700 men show up."

"Coach Gibbs speaks to the men, testifying about his life, football, and the racing teams. He shares his successes and failures, and how God made him the man he is today. He shares what type of influence we have on those around us. Basically, we are disciples. Our mission is based around Matthew 28: 19 *Therefore, go and make disciples of all nations,* to make sure the gospel is heard by anyone we have an influence on. We also do a prison ministry. We go into prisons and talk to men there as well. We were just at Maury Correctional Institution and talked to many prisoners there. Most of the prisoners we talk to are guys who are in for life: murder, drugs, and violent crimes. These are men who have committed heinous crimes but deep down they are good people. They had no direction, they did what they thought they had to do to survive and now they live to regret the decisions they've made. Many of them had no fathers to direct them. They are so appreciative that Coach gets right in there with them, lets them shake his hand and look at his Super Bowl ring. I get to speak as well. I talk about my life and what God has done for me, how he has changed my life. I also speak in churches."

Renaldo did not look too far from home when he started looking at colleges. Growing up on the South Side of Chicago and watching Notre Dame's rise to national title prominence, becoming a member of the Fighting Irish football squad was always at the top of Renaldo's wish list. "Notre Dame was always a dream of mine, from day one. Even when people were telling me you're not big enough, you're never going to play, you should probably go to a smaller school; I still knew that Notre Dame was where I wanted to be. When head coach Lou Holtz came to Notre Dame and put them back on the map, winning a national championship in 1988, it piqued my interest in Notre Dame even further. Growing up on the South Side of Chicago, Notre Dame was such a big influence on us, especially playing football at De La Salle high school in the Chicago Catholic league. Everyone just wanted to go there. Several guys who had graduated prior to me went to Notre Dame: Lee Walker and Dan Hughes. And of course Moose Krause, a great pillar in the Notre Dame athletic department for so many years, was a graduate of De La Salle high school. Moose Krause also played a key role in my being recruited by Notre Dame. He basically told the recruiters that they were not going to pass up on a kid who hailed from his high school in Chicago."

The Notre Dame Value Stream started working on Renaldo early on, even when he was a high school student. A local priest at his high school was singing Notre Dame's praises long before Renaldo had even decided to apply. "We had a priest who was very active at De La Salle. He wasn't on staff but he was around a great deal and he was a huge influence on us as far as encouraging us to look at Notre Dame. There was even a local channel in Chicago that was dedicated to Notre Dame, so it was very visible to us growing up. I took two official visits. One visit to Notre Dame and one to the University of Illinois. Head coach Lou Tepper (Illinois) told me that I owed it to the area to at least come for a visit, and so I did. I knew I wasn't going to go there, but felt out of respect for my community that I needed to go. I had other visits set up, but after I took my visit to Notre Dame I cancelled them. At the end of my ND visit they put an offer on the table and told me that if I didn't take it they could not promise that it would still be there at a later time, and so I took it. I didn't want to risk letting my first choice slip through my fingers."

Renaldo may not have been a big enough high school star to warrant a recruiting visit from head coach Lou Holtz, but the recruiter who did visit him sold the importance of the Notre Dame Value Stream and how important it was to get a top notch education as well as the opportunity to play Division I football. "Former Notre Dame linebacker coach, George Kelly, who at the time was consulting for Coach Holtz and assisting with recruiting, came out to my house to recruit me. He was extremely crucial in getting me to sign. Plain and simple, I wasn't ranked high enough in high school to warrant a visit from Lou Holtz himself. Our Notre Dame recruiting class was number one that year with the likes of Cliff Stroud, Thomas Knight, Alton Maiden, Bobby Taylor and Derrick Mayes. I was just thrilled that they were interested in me."

Renaldo's student hosts during his recruiting weekend sold the Notre Dame Value Stream as well. They made sure to impress upon him that academics and football should be his priorities, and not his social life. "My hosts during my official visit to ND were Bryant Young and Anthony Peterson. Hanging out with two players like that for the weekend really sealed the deal for me. They were not only great players, but they were great people as well. They were straight up with me that weekend. Bryant told me, 'If you're coming here for the social life, this may not be the school for you. But if you're coming here to get an education, graduate and have a chance to play football at the next level, you're at the right place. A big selling point for the kids who weren't from the area was that ND was on TV every week. It was nice for them to know that their parents could see them play every week and not have to travel to South Bend in order to do so."

The Notre Dame Value Stream had been impressed upon Renaldo pretty much from every angle before getting to Notre Dame, but he soon found out, it's implementation is not always easy. Fortunately for Renaldo, he had a great support network which helped him navigate the rough waters. "Discipline was a big challenge for me as a student-athlete. I had two great parents who stayed on me in high school to keep me on my studies and get my work done. They didn't let me stray too far. Before I could go anywhere my work had to be done. When you get to college, you are completely responsible for balancing your studies, social life, and playing football. If you are not doing things right, bad things can happen in a short amount of time. I didn't have anyone telling me what to do or when to do it. I started out at Notre Dame as an Engineering major and balancing the tough academics was very difficult for me. I started blowing off labs, spending too much time working on my social life, and because of this my academics began to suffer. People can tell you that when you get to college you'll have to be accountable and responsible for your studies, but you don't really understand what that means until you actually get there. The quicker you figure that out, the better. I was lucky that I did figure it out in time and got my studies back on track. I ended up switching from Engineering and got my degree in Sociology. I really enjoyed the classes being from the South Side of Chicago. The different classes on ethnicity and overcoming racial barriers were very engaging for me."

"A big part of my academic turnaround is thanks to my wife. When I was at my lowest point in my academic career I turned to God. I prayed that He would give me the opportunity to stay in school and I asked Him to send me my wife (LaTanya, also a student at Notre Dame), and that's exactly what He did. We married three months later and moved into married student housing off campus. She was a determining force in my academic turnaround. She told me, 'If you don't get up and start going to class I'm going to leave and go back home to Las Vegas.' She told me, 'If you don't change, I'm going to make a change: my location.' And with that I started going to class on a regular basis. And once I was there, I decided I should actually do something with my education. It's amazing how much more you get out of class when you are actually there, compared to having someone else there and taking notes for you."

Sometimes memories are made by watching and not by doing. This was just the case for Renaldo. One of his best football memories of his time at Notre Dame does not consist of a big play that he made, but of a game that he watched. "It probably would have to be the 'Snow Bowl' when we beat Penn State in 1992. I didn't even play a single game that year. I redshirted and had a front row seat for every game. That game was amazing. The poster that they made from that game, with OJ McDuffie meeting Demetrius DuBose at the goal line, with the snow coming down, awesome. It was a head-to-head battle. Upsetting Florida State and Heisman trophy winner Charlie Ward in 1993 was a pretty memorable game as well. But probably the most memorable game for me would have to be the Boston College game the following week. I will never forget it. We were so close to going undefeated and playing for a national title. To lose to a team that we should not have lost to was heartbreaking. I would have rather been beat down or blown out than to lose by a last second field goal like that."

After a Notre Dame career full of twists and turns, ups and downs, failures and successes, Renaldo reached the culmination of his football goals by being drafted into the NFL. "It was all jubilation. A celebration of all the hard work I had put in. It was nice to be able to say that it (football) wasn't over at that point, and that the hard work finally paid off. To be able to see a childhood dream coming to fruition, it was unbelievable. I graduated from Notre Dame in December and right after graduation my wife and I went down to New Orleans so that I could train with this guy who had the reputation of being the best trainer to prepare you for the combine. The weekend of the draft my wife and I flew to Chicago to watch the draft at my parents' house with all of our family and friends. It was an awesome experience. I vividly remember the events of my draft weekend. I thought I was going to get drafted by the Dallas Cowboys. The Cowboys had sent a representative to Chicago who took me to dinner the night before so that they could talk with me about their strategy of how they planned to move up in the draft so that they could select me. They gave my dad a cell phone (he was a mail man and could not watch the entire draft with us) so that he could stay connected with us. They gave us Cowboy hats and welcomed us to the organization. I thought it was pretty much a done deal."

As often happens in life, Murphy's Law appears and what you had planned for is no longer your reality. "The day of the draft, the Jacksonville

Jaguars (pick 21) had the pick before the Cowboys (pick 22). The Cowboys were trying to work out some sort of trade to move ahead of Jacksonville. When there were only four picks remaining until Jacksonville was up, the Jaguars called me and kept me on the phone through all four picks, which was an eternity back then. Not only could the Cowboys not get through, but my dad could not get through on his phone either. They locked the Cowboys out so that they could make sure they were able to pick me. Jerry Jones was so pissed. I had a party planned later that night for my family and friends, but the Jaguars put my wife and me on a flight almost immediately to Jacksonville. I kept saying, 'I don't think there is a flight that leaves that late' but they already had the arrangements made. My wife and I flew to Jacksonville that night and they had me at press conferences the very next day welcoming me. It was quite the adventure."

As a young man who married his wife as a college student, being able to reach his goal of playing football at a professional level was not only a childhood dream, but a gift to be able to provide for his family in such a way. Renaldo appreciated the opportunities that the NFL had given him and his family and enjoyed every moment of his time in the NFL. "Among the highs are achieving a childhood dream which I never took for granted and for which I was always appreciative. Knowing that financially you are secure, that you can provide for your family and do things that you never thought possible is a huge blessing as well. You are able to travel, see different cities and you get a lot of perks and freebies. You get so many opportunities, and so many doors are opened for you that would never have been there previously." Along with the blessings comes it fair share of obstacles and forks in the road. "The lows include dealing with injuries. It's a physical game, and it's all about performance, so injuries are a big challenge. There is constant pressure to perform and succeed. I look back at it now and back then you didn't realize how much pressure was on you until you are outside the situation. Notre Dame prepared me for that, though. I felt a great deal of pressure at ND to perform and win. There is a lot of politics playing in the NFL as well. You see guys that should have made the team and didn't. Getting cut is a major low, and most of all losing. When you are losing it's not fun for anyone. No one likes to lose. You put in so much time in the off-season. It's difficult to deal with a losing season."

Like any journey in life, there are always lessons to be learned. Renaldo's biggest take away from his time in the NFL was to always remember what brought you to that particular moment in the first place. "One thing that I took with me (from the NFL) is the following. I had a cousin who played professional ball as well, and he told me 'always remember why you play the game. If you love it, politics and the rest of the lows will not matter. Don't ever let it become a job or a chore. Always play the game because you love it. Keep it simple and don't let the other stuff bother you.' And so as long as I continued to love the game, I continued to play it." And with all sincerity, Renaldo expressed that he never expected to play in the NFL for as many years as he did. "Overall, just being blessed to have had the longevity to be able to play longer than I ever expected to play, that would be my greatest highlight. NFL really stands for 'Not For Long.' I was expecting to play for three to five years in the NFL (three years is the average), and to play for 13 seasons is something I am very proud of; it's a tremendous personal achievement for me. Making an impact on younger players as I got older is something I pride myself on as well. To be able to make an impact in the locker room and talk about things other than football was important to me. I am also thankful that my daughter (Kennedy, 12 years old) got to experience some of my years in the NFL with me. She'll always remember getting to see her dad on the field."

Looking back on his time at Notre Dame, Renaldo remembered thinking that Coach Holtz was larger than life. He also remarked on how impactful Coach Holtz's words were on them as impressionable young men. He was a father figure to a group of young men who needed such influence in their daily lives. "Back then you didn't know any better. You were young and scared, and you were horrified if he said anything to you. During my freshman year, he could not remember my name. He would always call me Marcus Thorne. I thought he didn't even know who I was. Before my fifth year of eligibility, my wife and I sat down and discussed whether or not I should declare that I was going into the NFL draft, or if I would stay for my fifth year. I had talked to some so called 'experts' and people were predicting that I would go somewhere between the third and fifth rounds. Being married and living off campus it was difficult for us. We were only receiving a small stipend. So my wife and I decided that I would declare for the draft."

"She hyped me up and I headed over to the football offices to talk to Coach Holtz. I walked up to Lou's secretary, Jan, and told her that I needed to meet with Coach, and that I had something important I needed to discuss with him. I waited in the lobby for a few minutes before Coach came out and said, 'Come on in and have a seat,' (Renaldo tells the story in his best Lou Holtz accent.) He must have known something was going on. He looked at me and said, 'What can I do you for? What's going on?'"

"I said, 'Coach, I've had a good year. My wife and I have talked about it and we've decided that I'm going to declare for the draft.' Coach replied, 'I respect that. Are you sure?' And I responded, 'Yeah, I'm sure. I'm ready to go. They are predicting that I'll go somewhere between the third and fifth rounds. I appreciate all that you've done for me.' Coach Holtz said, 'I want to share a story with you. I had a guy just like you in your situation and he wanted to declare for the draft as well. He played on offense and he came to my office much like you did today. I told him I respected his decision, but I told him that if he leaves early a lot of coaches are going to call me and ask for my opinion, and when they call me I'm going to tell them the truth. At the end of the day, this player never got drafted, never played a snap in the NFL. I wish he would have played his final year as he would have been much better prepared for the NFL. Scouts are going to call me asking about you, Renaldo, and I'm going to have to give them my honest opinion. I wish you the best.'"

"I looked straight at Coach Holtz and said, 'Uh, I think I'm going to return for my fifth year.' Coach said, 'Okay, Renaldo, we'll see you in winter conditioning.' When I got back to the apartment my wife said, 'Did you tell him you're leaving?' and I answered, 'Uh, no, I said I'm coming back.' To which she replied, 'What??'"

"I slept on the couch for the first couple of days after that. (laughs)"

Renaldo Wynn

Lessons from Renaldo's Notre Dame Value Stream of Life:

- Whatever you pursue in life, don't ever let it become a job or a chore. Always do whatever you pursue because you love it. Keep it simple and don't let the other stuff bother you.
- Everyone has successes and failures in their lives. Always strive to achieve a better you in everything you do and every life you touch.
- When you are faced with obstacles in your life, always remember what brought you to that particular moment in the first place. Obstacles are usually opportunities that you just can't see yet.

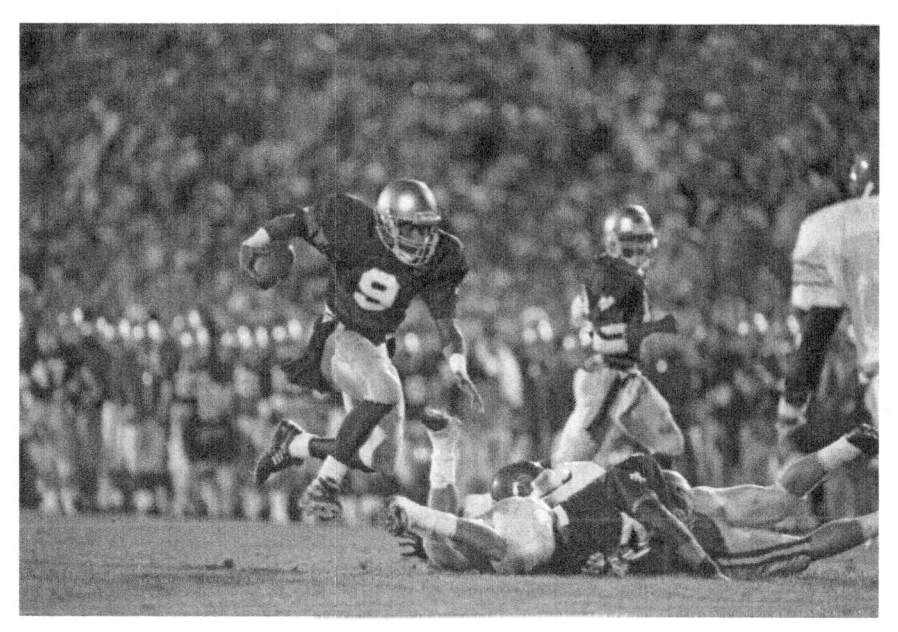

Notre Dame vs. Southern California (USC), 1989. Quarterback Tony Rice (#9) running with the ball. (Photographer: Joe Raymond, photo courtesy of Notre Dame Archives.)

CHAPTER TWENTY FOUR

The Insurance Broker and Notre Dame Personality Tony Rice

Tony Rice's main niche in life has become providing service and value to his Notre Dame family. This former National Championship quarterback is a legacy and has become a key face to everyone associated with ND. He is the man with a million dollar smile and personality, "When I am networking with people, once you find out that you both went to Notre Dame, you have an instant connection." Yes, Tony exemplifies the mantra "Play Like a Champion". You have to presume a guy that played the game like Tony, also plays the business game the same way – with intensity. "I tell people, 'Notre Dame allowed me to be one of its quarterbacks, why can't you allow me to be one of your business partners in the real world?' The first thing that a Notre Dame person asks you is, 'What dorm did you live in?' Notre Dame is such a unique community in which people stay on campus and there is a great deal of pride connected to the dorm you lived in."

Tony now lives in the second home of Notre Dame grads, Chicago, the Windy City; never far from where national champion quarterback Tony Rice tore through defenses with reckless feet and flailing legs. Today he fills the insurance needs of his Notre Dame family. Tony, an insurance broker for HUB International (www.hubinternational.com), in Chicago, currently has the resources he needs at his fingertips to service his niche market, his Notre Dame family. "Living in Chicago is great! I live about eight blocks from my office in the heart of downtown Chicago. I have to remind myself every couple of weeks that I need to take my car out, because I use it so seldom!" *Tony hails from South Carolina but decided to make the move north to attend the University of Notre Dame at the bidding of his grandmother. He attended Notre Dame from 1986-1990, graduating with a degree in psychology. While he did not play in the NFL, he did play professionally in the Canadian Football League and World League Football. He was previously married and has five kids — Alex, Madeline, Anthony, Michael, and Jasmine. Anthony is currently a wide receiver at Central Michigan.*

Tony's decision to attend Notre Dame wasn't his at all. "My grandmother decided that I would attend Notre Dame. Lou Holtz came in to our house and performed some kind of magic trick on my grandmother after which she told me, 'You're going to follow that little man!' He started out by selling her on academics, but more than anything what she was looking for was someone who could mentor her little baby and point him in the right direction. It had nothing to do with sports. She wanted me to be the first one in our family to graduate from a major university. That was her priority. During my freshman year I was not sure I was going to make it. There were several times that I was ready to pack it up and go home, but I found a way to stick it out. I was so far from home and everyone talked funny (when in reality it was probably me who talked funny being from the south)."

"When I called my grandmother to tell her that I wanted to come home all she told me, 'You've started something; you've got to finish it. Plus, we don't have the money to get you home.' She was definitely one of the people who inspired me to be the best person that I can be in life. She taught us to treat others the way that we wanted to be treated. When people ask me how I am, I always tell them, 'I can't complain.' My body hurts, and I have a pain here, and pain there, but you know what, I am just happy to be alive. I live day-by-day, try to keep my head above water and simply enjoy life. She made my future happen by pointing me in the right direction. When you are 18 years old you think you know everything, but until you start paying taxes and having kids, you don't know a thing! If you grow up in a right-going family, you should stay on that line. And at a fine University like Notre Dame, with great traditions both on the football field and in academics, you are trained for success."

"I expect to pass through this life but once. If therefore, there be any kindness I can show, or any good thing I can do to any fellow being, let me do it now, and not defer or neglect it, as I shall not pass this way again." ~ William Penn

Tony's biggest strength was that he was not afraid to ask for help. "The class sizes at Notre Dame were pretty small and you actually were a name and not a number. I used to ask people, 'What color is my nose?' They would respond 'Brown?' and I'd reply, 'Yep, I'm the biggest brown-noser around!'" Tony was a late bloomer. He was going to visit the University of Minnesota because of their coach, Lou Holtz, but when Notre Dame lost to Miami and they hired Holtz, Tony decided to follow Lou and look at Notre Dame. "When I found out he had been hired at Notre Dame my first question was, 'Where is Notre Dame even at?' When I made my official visit to Notre Dame my hosts were Ray Dumas, D'Juan Francisco and Mark Green. I also took official visits to the University of North Carolina and Pittsburgh; and unofficial visits to Clemson and South Carolina. My grandmother made me stop after three official visits because by that point she had already decided I was going to Notre Dame."

Tony made his official visit to Notre Dame in January. He showed up in South Bend with no coat because he didn't need a coat in South Carolina. He had no idea how freezing cold it was in South Bend, Indiana, and it was cold as can be during his visit. "Because I knew I was going to have to sit out of football my first year, I started mingling with people in the dorm during my official visit. I figured they would be the people I would be spending most of my time with freshman year, so those were the people I should meet."

Making the jump from South Carolina to South Bend, Indiana, was a big one for Tony. He grew up only an hour away from the state border of North Carolina, but never left the state of South Carolina until he was 18 years old. His hometown had a population of 5,000 people and they were a very close-knit group. "My high school football team was definitely a family affair. I had a first cousin who was the center, a first cousin who was a guard, I had a second cousin who was a tackle, one who was a receiver and my brother was in the backfield with me. We won two state championships and I went 40-2 as a starter. I also played basketball and track in high school, though I was not really a runner. I had a shot put record, and I also threw the disc, did the triple jump and ran the 4x100 relay. I ran a 4.8 when I got to Notre Dame, but by the end of my career at Notre Dame I was running a 4.48. They really worked with me on my speed. I was going to play basketball at Notre Dame as well, but I was told that I needed to stick with football. I didn't realize until my sophomore year how much of my time was needed to play football. It really was a full-time job. Even in the off-season you had to run and work out."

In 1986, Tony and fellow teammate John Foley were members of the first Notre Dame class which took Proposition 48 students. Tony fell 10 points below the minimum entrance-exam requirement to be eligible to play his freshman year so he had to sit out the season. He was not even allowed to practice. Tony often heard people say that he was not smart enough to be at Notre Dame, but that only drove him to succeed and prove them wrong. "I knew what I was getting myself into before getting there in having to give up that one year, but it didn't really hit me until I got there and saw all of my new friends being able to participate as freshmen. It really hurt because I was not able to communicate my skills as far as football went. I was extremely thankful that I had good people in my classes and dorm because they really were what got me through that year. My dorm mates, who would play catch with me during that year, they were my practice. I'm not sure what I would have done without them."

"You never forget the people that helped you cross that bridge. I am very thankful for my support network that helped me through that year and talked me out of going home. When you have to give up something that you've been doing all your life, you don't know what to do with yourself. I chose this path, and my grandmother kept telling me, 'You are going to do this. Football is not everything.' However, what you learn on the football field does translate into the real world. It was a very difficult year for me, but I surrounded myself with good people along the way who took the edge off." For Tony, the support network of the Notre Dame Value Stream really helped keep him afloat on his journey and gave him the skills that he needed to be successful both in college and in life. "You really don't appreciate the Notre Dame experience until you leave. To this day I stand back and think about my time at Notre Dame and think: It's a tremendous institution with a great football program. The longer you're away from it, the more you realize how tight-knit of a family it really is."

Today Tony can look back fondly on his time at Notre Dame, but while he was there it was not a walk in the park for him. "First and foremost Notre Dame is known for academics. Just graduating from Notre Dame was a big challenge for me. Football was easy. There is nothing compared to working hard and getting a degree after four years. You are made to become a big fish in a little pond because of the intense standards you are held to at ND. You are a Notre Dame man or Notre Dame woman and you are expected to succeed as a part of the Notre Dame family. When I was there I thought it was a prison, but now I recognize all that I took with me and the person it made me."

Winning a national championship was, of course, a great Notre Dame moment for Tony but playing the Service Academies was his most memorable experience. "Those guys (Air Force and Navy) never gave up. They went full speed ahead at you. Meeting those teams, who were extremely well-disciplined, those were great memories for me. It was a great honor to be able to say that you beat those teams because they never gave up. Everyone talks about the Miami game, but beating the Academies was quite an accomplishment. On any given day they could beat you. Often times you were up for the Miami's and USC's but maybe you took the Academies for granted because you outweighed them and were faster than them, and that was when you'd get beat. Air Force had this triple option quarterback, Michael 'Dee' Dowis, and I was the only quarterback who ran the option at ND, so I was a big part of getting our defense prepared for that game. I had two duties: being a quarterback and making sure our defense was ready to stop Dowis. He threw for 300 yards on us in 1989, but we knew what we had to do to win. (Notre Dame beat Air Force by a score of 42-17 and Dowis completed 15 of 24 passes for a career-high 306 yards and two touchdowns.) I had a chance to meet Dowis as we were both up for the Heisman Trophy in 1989."

Playing football at a professional level was both fun and challenging for Tony. The Canadian Football League, however, was an adjustment for him. "You play with 12 guys instead of 11. You get two timeouts instead of three. The field is wider. It's a completely different game. The team I played with, the Saskatchewan Rough Riders, had just come off a tremendous season when I arrived and they had a very talented quarterback. No matter how hard I worked I just never got the chance to play. I don't regret my time in the CFL one bit. That's just the way life goes. Then I got the opportunity to play with the Barcelona Dragons in the World League of Football. I played for them for two years and then the league folded. It was a great experience for me. I got to see a lot of places that a lot of other people never get the chance to see. I don't regret that I was not drafted into the NFL. You make the best out of the opportunities that you are given. Then you move on to the real world."

Tony's first post-football job was for a Notre Dame Alum, John "Jay" Jordan (class of 1969) and Jordan Industries. "I was a purchasing manager for two of his companies. Jay is one of the largest benefactors at Notre Dame (in 2005 he made a $40 million dollar gift to the University). I spoke with Jay and he encouraged me to get into sales. I really was not game for it but he pointed me in the right direction. I ended up being quite successful in sales and after two years I discovered I really was a good salesman. My next opportunity was with Louis Borders (of Borders Bookstore). Borders had a company which dealt with information systems and I was in charge of recruiting Information Technology applicants to fill positions within the company."

Tony then moved to South Bend and took an opportunity with DePuy Orthopaedics, a global leader in orthopaedic supplies. "I started out selling orthopaedic devices and supplies for ACL procedures and then added total knee, total hip and shoulders and eventually anything dealing with trauma, including gunshot wounds. It was a high pressure job and eventually it burned me out (http://www.depuy.com/about-depuy/depuy-divisions/depuy-orthopaedics). After that I worked for the University (Notre Dame) for a year in the Development Department. I worked in the Wrigley Building in Chicago, but it seemed too much like being back at school. Blue and Gold Illustrated, a newspaper which primarily covered Notre Dame football, then offered me a position in their public relations department, and I was a PR manager there for nine years back in South Bend."

In 2008 Tony decided to get his insurance license and took a job with a small company called Acrisure (an insurance brokerage firm that specialized in insurance solutions for small businesses to large corporations). "I enjoyed my time there but felt I needed more resources that could not be offered at a small company. Currently I work for HUB International (www.hubinternational.com), in Chicago and now I have all of the resources that I need to be successful." (HUB International Limited is a leading North American insurance brokerage that provides a broad array of property and casualty, life and health, employee benefits, investment and risk management products and service.) A combination of the influence of Tony's grandmother and the Notre Dame Value Stream taught Tony the importance of commitment and hard work. "Once you start something don't stop until you finish it. Always look at yourself as being a student first and an athlete second. You never know when your number is going to be called, or when it's time to give up athletics. You need to make sure you are prepared when it is time to move on from sports into the real world. With all of the technology today, you need to be aware of your surroundings. I tell my kids all the time, everyone wants to tell a story, so be aware of what you are doing."

Tony has always been active in giving back to the community. "There are multiple charities that I am involved with including Big Brothers Big Sisters and the Make-A-Wish Foundation. I am also on the board of an autism foundation in Pennsylvania for a friend whose son has autism. I've been a member of that board for six years. I do a ton of golf outings. They keep me very busy. I have never had a real vacation where I didn't have some sort of event to do when I was there. Someday I'd like to actually go somewhere for a few days where I can put my cell phone away and actually enjoy myself! I've been saying that for a few years, but really, if I wasn't as busy as I am I'd be bored as hell. I'm having fun in life and that's what is important."

When you played football for Coach Lou Holtz football practices were by no means a walk in the park. In fact, his practices were so rough that the players actually looked forward to game day because that was the easiest day of the entire week. "Coach Holtz got mad at me at practice one day. He had called a play in which I was supposed to pass the ball to Tim Brown, but Tim was covered and so I threw it to the open receiver, who caught it. But I still got in trouble because I did not follow Coach Holtz's instructions. Coach Holtz told me 'I don't care if Tim Brown is covered by three guys, throw it to him.' So the next play, I go out and throw the ball 60 yards straight up in the air, five yards in front of me. Then he put me on the scout squad. Ken Graham gets put in as the starter. Five minutes later, after practicing with Ken, Coach Holtz comes over to me and says, 'Son, I'm too old for this. I want you playing with me but you've got to follow my instructions.'" Tony politely responded, 'Yes sir, yes sir.'

"He was trying to prove a point with me, but I was too. I really thought I had thrown the ball to the right person. But in the end I won the battle when he brought me back in. Coach Holtz had the right idea in the way that he ran his practices. You practiced hard so that when it came to game time it was easy. It's repetition. If you prepare yourself during the week, then you are ready for game time. Games were fun. I never wanted them to end. We would still have plays left to run at the end of games. But you knew if you messed up during a game on Saturday you were going to get chewed out on Sunday. This was one of my biggest pet peeves with Coach Holtz. On a Monday he would have his secretary, Jan, call you at your dorm. She would say, 'Coach Holtz would like to have a meeting with you on Wednesday morning at 7 am.' I'd be sitting there thinking to myself, but I'm going to see him today AND tomorrow …why does he want to see me on Wednesday? Then you would sit there and rehash for the next two days, what did I do wrong? You are so nervous. You're nervous at practice. You walk into that meeting on Wednesday morning and you'd be so nervous that your hands would be sweating. Then he'd start with, 'I just want to see how you're doing.' And I'm thinking, damn, you should have asked me that at practice. You make me get up at 7 am and make me think for two days that I've done something wrong. This would happen maybe three or four times a year. He really had you on your toes."

In the end, all Tony did was perform like a giant in leading his team to a historic place in ND history.

Lessons from Tony's Notre Dame Value Stream of Life:

- Once you start something, always follow through and finish it.
- Treat others the way you want to be treated.
- Don't ever be afraid to ask for help.

Lisa Kelly

Tony Rice

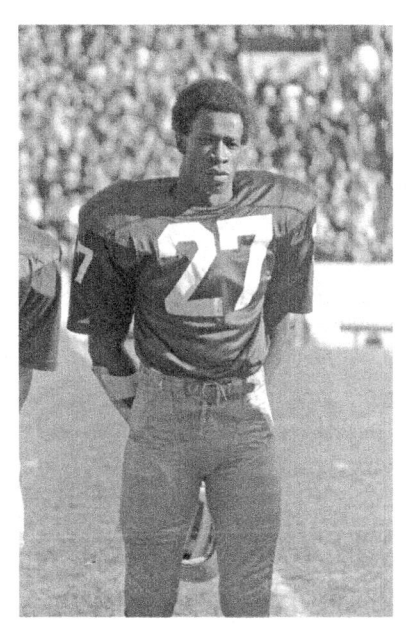

Notre Dame vs. Air Force, 1973. Mike Townsend (#27) on field before the game. (Photo courtesy of Notre Dame Archives.)

CHAPTER TWENTY FIVE

The Pharmaceutical Salesman
Mike Townsend

Mike Townsend, like his teammate Luther Bradley, was a towering 6'3" 183-pound cornerback at Notre Dame. In 1973 Mike and Luther combined for one of the most formidable defensive backfields in college football history. These were big speedy DBs with twitch muscles you seldom see. It takes guys like these to anchor an undefeated team such as the 1973 National Champions from Notre Dame.

"Mike T," as his teammates called him, has a personality and heart bigger than his physical size, speed and god-given athletic skills. He works today for Amylin Pharmaceuticals (www.bms.com). "We are actively marketing a new product right now for Type 2 diabetes that is a time-released medicine that is taken once a week in comparison to daily or twice daily usage. The administration of the dosages are far easier because the patient goes from administering it daily or twice

daily to once a week. This enhances the compliance level of the patient because they can choose a designated time for administering it weekly. We just launched the product last year and now we are moving it into international markets. Both my mother and my sister have type 2 diabetes and so it's a blessing that I am involved in something that enhances quality of life." When teammates speak of Mike there is one thing you will always hear: He was a great person, teammate and mentor to everyone, especially supportive of the young guys on the team. Mike and his brother Willie, a wide receiver and also a member of the 73 championship team, definitely took up space when they walked into a room. In fact the story of these brothers will go down in Notre Dame history. Mike now resides in Hamilton, Ohio, with his wife Kimberley and together they raised five children; two daughters and three sons.

When the Townsend brothers arrived at Notre Dame, neither one of them planned on playing basketball. Football was the sport they each had decided to play. But the story of how they were discovered by Notre Dame basketball head coach Digger Phelps is a great one. "At Notre Dame they have intramural sports teams. My brother and I and a few of the guys from the football team decided to play on the intramural basketball team for our dorm, Fisher Hall, to help us stay in shape during the offseason. It started off as a great way to stay in shape and we ended up being really good. The Fisher Hall team was efficient in putting points on the score board and many games we ended up with winning margins of up to 30 to 50 points. Eventually teams started to not even show up. We would wait for 40 minutes and then declare the game a forfeit. Because of our big wins we started to get a following amongst our fellow students."

"The next year, my sophomore year, was Digger's first year as Notre Dame's head coach. The previous coach had not recruited very well, and there were several key players who were injured, so Digger was basically looking for warm bodies to fill spots. He held open tryouts but they were during the football season and my brother and I didn't really pay it any attention. Digger still had two open spots when some of the students told him that he needed to look at the Townsend brothers from the football team. So Digger went to Coach Parseghian and asked for his permission to speak with Willie and me, and Ara agreed. At the next practice one of the basketball managers asked my brother and me if we can come early to football practice the next day because Coach Phelps wants to speak with us about joining the basketball team. We weren't exactly sure what to say, but I told my brother it was up to him, and he said, 'yeah sure.'"

"The next day we come to practice early and go see Coach Phelps. He says to us, 'I've already talked to Coach Parseghian and he said that I can come talk to you guys about coming to try out for the basketball team but there are some stipulations if you guys decided to move forward.

One. You can't play any basketball or attend any practices until football is totally over.

Two. If your grades drop below a 2.0 you have to drop basketball.

Three. You came here to play football and so football has to come first.

Four. If he decides this isn't working, he can pull you off the basketball team at any time.'

"I looked at my brother and said, once again, it's up to you. And he looked at me and said, 'yeah, we'll do it.' It was unique to be brothers and to play two big time sports at a school such as Notre Dame. My brother thought that since we had played both sports in high school that it would be no big deal, but there is a serious jump between the high school level and the college level, especially with the schedule that Notre Dame played. What Digger really needed were guys who could be physical on the court and he knew that as football players we would be able to rough house some other teams a bit and it would be no big deal for us. We went the next day to try out for the team."

"Word had gotten out that Willie and I were trying out for the basketball team and a crowd was forming at the ACC (Joyce Athletic & Convocation Center) to watch. When Digger got wind of this he changed the location of our practice to one of the basement gyms in the ACC. He had a manager meet us in the locker room and escort us to this private gym. We warmed up and this was the first time Coach Phelps had even seen us play, and he could already see that we could walk and chew gum at the same time. We did about 35 minutes of practice with the team so that he could see if we had any talent and he was quite impressed. Then he took his starting six, told us to pick four more guys and we were going to scrimmage. We had no idea who these guys were, let alone if they were any good. So we picked a guard, a forward, and the really tall guy and gave it our best shot. After about 35 minutes of scrimmaging we beat the starting squad by 30 points. We just blew by them. The tall guy we picked, his 'normal' shot was from the three-point line. Wow. Digger loves to tell the story of how he 'found' us. When Austin Carr was introduced into the ring of honor, he was telling our story! Digger is a special, special person to Notre Dame. His dream was to coach at Notre Dame, and he brought a special flair to being a coach at Notre Dame. He was a walking fashion show with perfectly tailored suits and his trademark carnation in his lapel."

Mike was originally sold on playing football at Purdue. He came home from track practice one day to find the Notre Dame coaches sitting in his family's dining room, ready to make him an offer that he simply could not refuse. He went on to have an outstanding career at Notre Dame including a 10 interception season in 1972 (a single season record that he has held for over 40 years and still stands today, while the game of football has changed drastically to a more aggressive mode of offensive prowess and less defensive skill prevailing), consensus All-American honors in 1973, named team captain his senior year and playing under Ara Parseghian on the 1973 national championship team.

When one sibling wants something in the absolute worst way, the other sibling usually wants the absolute opposite. But not so for the Townsend brothers, or at least not so fast. "I had two older brothers, the oldest who was attending college at Southwest Louisiana, and my brother who was only one year older than me, Willie, was playing football for the University of Notre Dame. Notre Dame had always been his dream since we were young kids. ND was pretty much the only team who was on TV all the time, and when they started recruiting Willie it was pretty much a done deal for him. He was also recruited by many other big-time schools, but Notre Dame truly was his dream. I remember seeing Woody Hayes from Ohio State in our dining room recruiting my brother, as well as coaches from Purdue and Colorado. The whole recruiting process left quite an impression on me. But when my brother decided to go to Notre Dame, I decided I wanted to go anywhere BUT Notre Dame. I was tired of being underneath his wing and wanted to set out on my own."

Mike was mostly recruited by Big Ten schools. Ohio State, Michigan and Purdue were actively pursuing him, along with Notre Dame and a school from the south (he couldn't remember if it was Georgia or Florida). In order to narrow down his choices he decided to look at each school from the standpoint of what he wanted to do when he left school. "I met this gentleman when I was in high school who told me about computers and that really piqued my curiosity. I decided from my conversation with him that I wanted to study computer science. Of all of the different schools that were looking at me, Purdue had the best computer science program. Notre Dame didn't even offer a degree in computer science. That simple fact made me move further towards Purdue. After my five visits I had it narrowed down to Purdue and Michigan. I ran it by my high school coaches and they helped me make my final decision on Purdue. It really did seem like a good decision for me. Especially when you added in that it was close to home so my parents could come watch me play, and with my brother at Notre Dame they could see both of us play on the same field once a year when ND and Purdue faced each other. Plus they were offering me a nice scholarship."

In the latter part of the spring Mike went to his high school coaches and told them that he had selected Purdue. He had not even told his parents at that point. His coach called the coaches at Purdue and they UPSed the papers to his parents' house for him to sign. "The papers arrived the next day while I was at track practice, and when I got home there sat a coach from Notre Dame in our dining room with my parents, along with the papers from Purdue on the table. He was just sitting there talking to my mother. He looks at me and says, 'Michael, how are you doing?' and I'm thinking to myself, what is HE doing here? He continues, 'I hear you want to go to Purdue.' How did he know that? The only person I had told was my high school coach, not even my parents! And then he continues on with all of the reasons why I didn't want to go to Purdue. I explained to him that the biggest reason behind my decision to attend Purdue was their computer science degree and he said, 'If I can get that changed, will you change your mind?' And of course I told him (as I'm laughing out loud) that I would consider Notre Dame at that point. Did he just really offer to add a degree program just to get me to come play football for him? By the end of the week Notre Dame had added a degree program in computer science."

A week later Purdue started calling, wondering where Mike's paperwork was and his high school coaches told them that he was still in the decision process. "When the Notre Dame coaches called back and told me that they were adding a computer science program at ND, I left the final decision up to my girlfriend. She asked me what the pluses were for each school and we sat down and made a list. As soon as she found out that there were no girls at Notre Dame, she all of the sudden was positive that Notre Dame was the perfect school for me." And that's how he made his final decision to go to Notre Dame!

When you grow up playing sports with your brothers and are in constant competition with them, you share a special bond. The bond Mike had with his brother Willie was especially close because they played the same sports - football and basketball. They both went to Notre Dame with the anticipation of playing football, but Mike's primary focus was to study computer science. He was looking forward to competing against other highly skilled players and seeing how his skill level matched up. "What made our situation even more special was the fact that we not only both played football at Notre Dame, but we both played on a national championship team together and we both played basketball for Digger Phelps for two years. That is quite a combination. My brother hurt his arm and ended up sitting out a year and so we ended up graduating the same year. That really was a blessing for us, to get another year together."

"Attitude is a little thing that makes a big difference." - Winston Churchill

Long before they were crowned national champions, that Fighting Irish squad knew they had something worth watching. "We knew before that season, during fall camp, that our team was special. I knew even then that we were going to do better than the year before, and that if we beat everyone that we played that year we would be in the running for a national title. We knew we were good enough to play on a level to compete for a national championship. Coach Parseghian realized how good we were as well. In games where the talent did not seem as strong as it should be, he'd make it an individual play-by-play challenge, to help us get better and better. He realized we were young men who were being molded into men who would go out into the world to become professionals in our various fields. He was developing us to be more than just football players."

That is what Coach Parseghian did best: he knew how to bring you to your greatest potential. "My senior year we had 110 players on the team and only 22 players started. But he had a way of making every player feel like they were a starter. He was best at taking what skill you brought to the table and maximizing it. He knew how to get you to the highest level. I thought that my football strength was as a wide receiver but Ara saw something different in me. At the beginning of my sophomore year Coach Parseghian approached me and said, 'We're going to take you out of offense and put you on defense.' And I stood there and thought, what?? I had played some defense in high school but not much. Most of the accolades that I achieved in high school were on offense. This is what he told me next. 'I put my best players on defense, because if the other team doesn't score, I don't lose.' And that right there sold me on defense. He knew how to put you where you would best help the team. Since college, I have coached junior high, high school and semi pro, and I understand now how coaches can see that a player would better fit in another position. Those are the best coaches, who see where the players need to be in order to maximize their skills."

When you think about Mike, you most likely remember the Tony Dorsett tackle from the Pitt game in 1973. "Tony Dorsett was averaging 210 rushing yards per game, and our defense was only allowing teams 165 total yards of offense. Total yards. So we were very excited to take on the challenge of Pitt and Tony Dorsett and Coach Parseghian made sure we were ready. It was a unique game. When we got there, Coach Parseghian told us that if we won the coin toss that we wanted to defer. Why would we want to defer? Well, Coach Parseghian was diligent on doing his pre-game research, and like any other game that is exactly what he had done. He had checked out the weather forecast and deferring was just the thing to do. We won the coin toss and deferred and at that moment the skies were clear. We set up, kicked off to Pitt and the clouds and snow started to move in. The snow got so bad that Pitt could hardly see. They had to rely completely on their running game and they were unable to put it in the end zone. When Pitt kicked the ball back to us the skies had just started to clear. We marched right down the field and scored a touchdown, no problem. And then by the time Pitt got the ball back the snow had returned. It did this all game long. What a genius Coach Parseghian was, and a pretty good weatherman as well!"

"We knew that Tony Dorsett was good. And we knew if we could just contain him it would be fantastic. He ended up with 200 yards rushing in that game, but he did not score one touchdown. He did all his work between the 20's. It was a special talent for me to be able to not only catch him that game but to make the big tackle. A tackle that happened after a 50-plus yard chase down the field as Tony headed towards their end zone for what was assumed would be a touchdown. I was so proud to have been part of what stopped him that day." That tackle was a memorable one that still sticks out in Mike's mind today.

Often times the memories that a college athlete holds most dear are not the most obvious, hit you in the face moments, but the subtle along the journey ones. "Of course you want to say the national championship is your favorite moment because it will be forever in your mind, but the Southern Cal game was pretty memorable as well because that game catapulted us into the national title spotlight. We were moving up in the rankings but not as fast as we would have liked. Beating USC at home epitomized the talent we had and the quality of play we had both on offense and defense, from the seniors all the way down to the freshman. That game meant so much from a national ranking standpoint and from a historical background as well. We had lost to USC so badly the year before, and here we were facing USC a year later in a game that everyone was calling 'the game.' Now everyone else knew how good we really were. We knew it, but now the world knew it."

"The practices during that week were quite intense. By Thursday, practice is shortened compared to the beginning of the week practices, and on Friday you just do a walk-through. Thursday we came out to practice and it had rained that day. We had just gotten new field turf that year and all of the sudden we decided to see who can surf the furthest on the turf. So we start sliding. The first couple of guys go 10 or 15 yards and we're having fun and laughing. Then Mike McBride comes out and slides for 45 yards on his chest and we all went crazy. The coaches come out and start yelling, 'What's going on out here? We're playing Southern Cal in two days and you guys are surfing on the darn turf!' At that moment we realized that the game wasn't 'that' important, but what was important was the group of us as a Notre Dame family. We chose our destiny. Now let's have some fun. Let's make sure we are ready for the game. And let's play on Saturday. When you find yourself playing Alabama and Bear Bryant for the national title game, that is unbelievable. It was the first time we beat Alabama and it was on a national championship stage. We were an 18 point underdog, no way were we supposed to be there. Beating them by one point we proved that we absolutely were supposed to be there. But that USC game was tremendous as well."

After an outstanding career at Notre Dame playing football and basketball with his brother, it was time for Mike to move forward to the next chapter of his life. Draft day was quickly approaching, and he had a choice to make: to play in the NFL or the WFL. "The Vikings were the NFL team that I wanted to play for. It was a very special honor to be drafted by the Vikings. Coach Bud Grant was well-known and they had great players and great fans. By this time I already had an agent and he was talking with Minnesota on my behalf. At the same time, the WFL was blooming and the Jacksonville Sharks were interested in drafting me as the number one pick in their draft. The owner of the Jacksonville Sharks was a huge Notre Dame fan. A subway alum with all kinds of Notre Dame memorabilia in his office. He was telling me, if you come here we'll take very good care of you and you'll get to play in Florida, which was a big selling point for me as compared to playing in Minnesota."

Minnesota or Florida?

Minnesota or Florida?

"I picked Florida. Had I gone to Minnesota I would have gone to a Super Bowl just one year after winning a national title at Notre Dame. That is my one regret of deciding to play in Florida. We had spent so much time trying to figure out what my worth was in the NFL compared to what my worth was in the WFL. My agent thought the WFL was really solid. The cities that the WFL teams were located in seemed relatively feasible from the standpoint of football. It was a new league and it was still under development, but I did my best to weigh the odds. I received more money up front by selecting the WFL and then from there it would be based on how the team did that year. So I took the chance and went to Jacksonville. The team did not do well, and the next year I got picked up by a team in Memphis. And then the following year I was with the Vikings. It did not work out exactly as I had planned, but it was the choice that I made. I played one year for the Vikings after my time in the WFL, and then one year with the NY Giants."

> *"A good coach will make his players see what they can be rather than what they are."* Ara Parseghian

"Coach Parseghian's philosophy of coaching and how he treated us not only prepared us for game day but also prepared us for life after football. He made sure we were prepared for life regardless of whether we ended up playing in the NFL or not. He told us, 'you came here on a scholarship, utilize it for your future career.' I knew I had other skills besides football. The fact that I went to Notre Dame and played football just enhanced those skills. I walked out of there with a diploma and a degree from Notre Dame and it was not like I was short. My hands were full. At that point it was just a matter of finding the right career."

Initially Mike went into sales, but any time he went on a sales call everyone always wanted to talk about football first. "Then they'd let you get back to the product that you were there to sell in the first place. But if you got to know them first by talking about Notre Dame and playing professional football, you'd almost always sell the product that you were selling. It was an easy icebreaker that helped me transition into sales. My first job was with IBM. Then I worked for Phillip Morris for a while. I was selling cigarettes even though I was an athlete and had never smoked in my life. I did a lot of research on smokers and tobacco and that allowed me to be successful in cigarette sales. Then I came back to Ohio working for Ford Motor Company before settling into Big Pharma."

"When I look back at my life I owe so much to my Notre Dame teammates and the ND family as a whole, but especially Coach Parseghian. You hear so much about the different styles of coaches, but our coach was nothing short of a great leader and competitor. Even today, Coach is his same competitive self." This past year, Mike was back at Notre Dame for the Michigan game and was on the sideline with Coach Parseghian. "He was taking the flag out to the military servicemen who were raising the flag. He had six former players, myself included, standing there with him. He looked at us and said, 'Are you guys ready to play?' He's forever competitive and forever a true gentleman. A great man and a great person to know. I could not have asked for a better father figure when I was at Notre Dame. He kept my brother and me headed down the right road."

Mike Townsend and his wife Kimberley

Lessons from Mike's Notre Dame Value Stream of Life:

- Put your education before athletics. Playing sports will teach you many things including determination, working as a team and how to be resilient in times of adversity, but your education will carry you throughout your lifetime.
- Going into anything prepared, whether it's a big game or an important business meeting, will set you up for success.
- Success will come to you if you not only have the faith but also the attitude that you can succeed. Having a positive attitude will take you much farther than you can ever imagine.

EPILOGUE

They've Only Just Begun

If history is an indication, they've only just begun. The question is what greatness will this University mold, shape and breed - a president, a supreme court justice, a corporate CEO, a Nobel prize winner, a scientific researcher; the potential is limitless and the children of these Saturday afternoon gladiators will also be shaped from this tremendous mold. The unique nature of this "mold" is that it has the ability to change and adapt to the future and to the challenges that life will present; yet the mold maintains its solidness and foundation.

The foundation is Notre Dame and the values it instills in all who enter its pristine gates and emerge with not only the best academic education, but also having experienced the thrill and education of life as a student-athlete at the greatest of universities.

Whether they achieve All-American status or toil as a walk on, never realizing that energy of playing in a game, each athlete who graduates today and tomorrow from Notre Dame will leave behind a legacy of being a student-athlete. What is most important is the excitement and pride we each have to discover how these student-athletes become men and what their mark on the world around them will be - how they will create families, how they will mold and shape their children and be impacted by their Notre Dame Value Stream experience. It is my honor to be able to tell stories of so many and I look forward to sharing the journeys and stories that are currently unfolding.

Lisa Kelly, "Biggest Fan of the Big East Conference" (Photographer: Scott Neer)

About the Author

Lisa had no choice but to love Notre Dame football. Ever since she can remember, Notre Dame football has been a part of her life. She learned her first colorful word at the tender age of three during the Notre Dame - USC game on a Thanksgiving weekend spent at her grandparents' house. She and her family made annual pilgrimages to Notre Dame to spend football weekends with her dad's college roommate and his family. Notre Dame football has always been an integral part of her life.

As a business major at Notre Dame, Lisa made sure she took advantage of three things in her four years. First, being a student of theology at the most renowned theologian institution in the world. Second, studying English to support her passion for effective communications no matter her career direction. Finally, and most importantly, leaving this great university with a degree in business with a specialty in marketing. Armed with these tools she engaged the world, continuing to use what she so aptly calls, the Notre Dame Value Stream.

Lisa began her professional career in the not-for-profit sector, working for the Better Business Bureau (BBB). She taught people how to be better-informed consumers and served as a dispute resolution arbitrator. She expanded her career horizons by branching further into her career field, working 13 years as a marketing professional in yellow page advertising. The fast paced environment of an agency setting and the creative outlet energized her career.

In 2007, she took a leap from the advertising world and accepted a job with a marketing and communications company, Katey Charles Communications. Their specialty was in web design and maintenance, and e-mail newsletter design and production. She knew little about HTML programming or copy writing, but knew that she could learn how to do anything. She spent two amazing years working for Katey Charles and learned so much about copy writing, web design and HTML programming. What she learned there was the stepping off point for where she is today.

When the economy took a downturn in 2009, Lisa, like so many others, was faced with a job loss. But such a loss with the right mental attitude turns into an opportunity. For Lisa, her loss turned into a marketing research position running in-house advertising, marketing and social media for a small company. She also took the lessons and skills she was learning and began her own blog. Blogging is hard work, taking patience and perseverance. Lisa's perseverance was the catalyst for a major life change before her.

In 2011, Lisa was contacted by an advertising agency on Twitter who was working on a contest sponsored by Volvo and the Big East Conference to determine the "Biggest Fan of the Big East Conference." She was selected along with 15 other alumni writers representing the 16 schools in the Big East Conference, to compete for the title of "Biggest Fan." Given that basketball is not really her forte, Lisa had to dig inward a bit for this contest. After eight writing assignments, a trip to New York City for media day, a trip to her alma mater for the Notre Dame - Syracuse match-up and endless self-promotion via social media, she rose to the top and was crowned the "Biggest Fan of the Big East Conference." In all honesty, she never expected to win this contest, but the more she thought about it, losing really is not in her vocabulary. If you're going to do something, give it your all and shoot for the top.

Shortly after the contest, Lisa realized she was constantly defending Our Lady's University. People were quick to find the shortcomings of Notre Dame and those associated with it, and she really wanted to do something that would showcase all of the positive things that emerge from Our Lady's University. And that is how this book took shape. Her first interview was with former tight end Oscar McBride. It was more like two friends catching up, but it was a wonderful walk down memory lane with Oscar and a discovery of how Notre Dame helped shape him into the man he is today. She realized that this was the beginning of something special. One interview lead to another. As she completed each interview, it was clear that a theme was emerging. Even though Lisa and these former players all came to Notre Dame from vastly different backgrounds, they all had similar experiences and each credited their time at Notre Dame and the Notre Dame Value Stream with playing a huge role in molding them into the people they are today.

In Lisa's words there are so many of these stories yet to be told and she hopes that you have enjoyed her journey through the lives of these Loyal Sons of Our Lady's University and the stories they tell. This book only touches the surface. She looks forward to continuing the journey and sharing all of the remarkable stories of Her Loyal Sons ... and maybe some of Her Loyal Daughters, too!

INDEX

Abraham, Clifton 137
Allen, Marcus 159, 160
Altria 16
Alvarez, Barry 48, 71, 107, 127

Banks, Braxton 126, 127
Barhorst, Warren 159
Baxter, Fred 112
Becton, Lee 108
Belden, Tony 151
Belichick, Bill 65
Bercich, Pete 104-110, 125
Bettis, Jerome 91, 107, 108, 113, 115, 120, 129, 141
Bledsoe, Drew 65, 115
Borders, Louis 185
Borders Bookstore 185
Bowden, Bobby 88
Bradley, Luther 4, 10, 76-84, 189
Bradshaw, Terry 97
Brady, Tom 65
Bremen Castings 105
Brooks, Reggie 108, 117-123
Brooks, Tony 108, 118
Brown, Bettye 37
Brown, Bobby 30-38
Brown, Cliff 78
Brown, Tim xiii, 18, 20, 24, 73, 127, 132, 155-161, 186, 187

Browner, Ross 78
Bruce, Aundray 159
Bryant, Bear 195
Bryant, Greg 50
Bryant, Junior 115
Bulac, Brian 150
Burns-Saraiva, Kristene 86
Burris, Jeff 56, 89, 113
Busch, Kyle 173
Bush, Reggie 167

Carter, Tommy 107, 113, 120
Cathedral Prep High School 94
Cerrato, Vinny 113
CFCares 23
Champions for Life 94
Childress, Brad 105
Churchill, Winston 193
Cocke Finkelstein 23
Coles, Laveranues 32
Conley, Leonard 128
Corrigan, Gene 18
Cosby, Bill 34
Covington, Ivory 32
Covington, John 113
Crosby, Susan vii
Croyle, Dave 7
Culver, Rodney 108

203

Davie, Bob 25, 26, 36, 49, 51, 102
Davis, Butch 31
Dawson, Lake 89
De La Salle High School 170, 174
DeCicco, Mike 3, 4, 5, 50
Delhomme, Jake 138
Devine, Dan 11, 81, 151, 152
Ditka, Mike 115
Dolan, Erin 100
Dolan, Pat 99-103
Dorsett, Tony 194, 195
Dowis, Michael Dee 185
Doyle, Chris 136
DuBose, Demetrius 91, 176
Duff, Vontez 164, 165
Dugan, Kevin 91
Dumas, Ray 183
Dunlap, Al 74

Earl, Glenn 164, 165, 167
Eastside High School 40, 41
Eck, Frank 74
Eck, Tom 72
Edwards, Marc 61-67, 89
Eifert, Tyler 121
Excessive Celebration 30, 31, 33, 34

Father Lange's Gym 95
Faust, Gerry 16, 18, 152, 158
Ferguson, Vagas 148-154
Fielder, Jay 138
Figaro, Cedric 159
Fight Song 102, 137, 138
Fit4Life Youth Foundation 86
Flannigan, Jim 89
Floyd, Michael 121
Fluencr 164, 167
Flutie, Doug 18
Foley, John 68-75, 184
Francisco, D'Juan 183
Franklin Township High School 102
Freeman, Matt vii
Frontiere, Georgia 129
Fry, Willie 78

Game Plan For Life 173
George, Eddie 62, 156
Getherall, Joey 35, 46-54
Gibbs, Joe 171, 172, 173
Gibson, Oliver 113
Gilbert, Lynne ii, vi
Glass, Bill 94
Gonzalez, Tony 90
Graham, Billy 83, 84
Graham, Ken 187
Graham, Tracy 56
Grant, Bud 196
Grant, Steve 39, 40
Green, Denny 105, 107
Green, Mark 126, 127, 183
Gruden, Jim 152

Haines, Kris 151, 152
Hamlin, Denny 173
Hasara, Tim 72
Hayes, Jay 136
Hayes, Woody 192
Hearst, Garrison 115
HerLoyalSons iv, vii
Hesburgh, Father Theodore 3, 4, 5, 19, 50
Hesiman Trophy 80, 95, 127, 132, 150, 155, 156, 160, 176, 185
Hill, Greg 78
Holden, Germaine 55-60
Hollenbeck, Bill 100
Holtz, Lou Everywhere!
Hope Unlimited 20
Howard, Dwight 27
Hughes, Dan 174

Ismail, Rocket 24, 88, 128

Jackson, Bo 159
Jackson, Jarious 35
Jackson, Jesse 34
Jacobs, Frank 136
Jarrell, Adrian 118, 137
Joe Gibbs Racing 171, 172, 173
Johnson, Anthony 108, 119
Johnson, Jimmy 42, 120, 124, 128
Johnson, Keyshawn 63
Jones, Jerry 177
Jordan, John 'Jay' 185
Jordan, Michael 20, 34
Joyce, Rev Edmond P 3, 4, 5, 50

Kelly, George 174
Kelly, Lisa 2, 200-202
Kennedy High School 39, 41
Kenseth, Matt 173
Kidd, Jason 27
Kiper, Mel 47
Kirkwood High School 15, 19, 20
Kirsch, Brandon 95
Knight, Bobby 52
Knight, Thomas 175
Kosar, Bernie 18
Krause, Edward Moose 4, 80, 135, 174

Lamping, Andrew vii
Lange, Father 95, 96
LAPD 46, 47, 53
Lamar High School 163
Latuda, Frank 72
Lawson, Rob 145
Leahy, Frank 134, 135, 136, 139
Leahy, James 134
Leahy, Pat 135, 136, 137
Leahy, Ryan 134-140
Levens, Dorsey 118
Lewis, Mo 65
Lincoln, Abraham 152
Linebacker in the Boardroom 7, 12

Lombardi, Vince 119
Los Angeles Police Department 46, 47
Lou's Lads 133, 139
Lundy Jr., Lamar 150
Lyght, Todd 129
Lynch, Dick 100, 102

Maiden, Alton 175
Malowitz, Lee 163
Manly, Bernard 136
Manning, Peyton 24
Maritz Travel Company 16
Masada Resource Group 23
Mauck, Carl 138
Mayes, Derrick 24, 86, 89, 175
McBride, Mike 195
McBride, Oscar vi, x, xi, xiii, 86-92, 113, 114, 201
McCoy, Mike xiii, 93-98
McDonald, Devon 39-45
McDonald, Ricardo 39, 40, 41
McDougal, Kevin 89
McGill, Karmeeleyah 114
McKay, John 79
McMahon, Tom 49
McNair, Ronald 34
Meyer, Urban 48, 49, 51, 52
Mike McCoy Ministries 94, 97
Miller, Alvin 15-21, 157
Minor, Kory 49
Mirer, Rick 120, 141-147
Mirer Family Foundation 142
Mirror Wine 141, 145, 146
Montana, Joe 151
Monte Vista Family Home 53
Moore, Elton 78
Moore, Joe 114, 136, 137, 138
Moore, Wally 96
Moorehead, Tyler vi
Murphy, John 96
Murphy, Pat 114

Musburger, Brent 159

NASCAR 27, 156, 170, 171, 172
Nelson, Lindsey 9
NoCoastBias iv, vii
Norman, Todd 137
Notre Dame Everywhere!
Notre Dame Family Everywhere!
Notre Dame Fight Song 102, 137, 138
Notre Dame Value Stream Everywhere!

Omega Psi Phi Fraternity 33, 34
Our Lady's University Everywhere!
Owens, Terrell 115

Pagna, Tom 96
Parseghian, Ara Everywhere!
Peterson, Anthony 115, 175
Phelps, Digger 190, 191, 193
Phillip Morris USA 16, 197
Play Like A Champion Today 52, 91, 94, 181
Playford, Larry 72
Powell, Colin 91
Power, Dr. Clark 88
Powlus, Ron 25, 63, 89
Proposition 48 69, 70, 71, 184

Randle, John 109
Ray, John 96
Relentless Wisdom: A Collection of Thoughts, Ideas, and Opinions 86
Rice, Jerry 115
Rice, Tony xv, 56, 71, 128, 131, 132, 181-188
Ricketts, Tom 135
Robinson, Jackie 173
Robinson, John 129
Rockne, Knute 101, 134

Rossum, Allen 22-29, 32, 51
Rudolph, Kyle 121
Rudy 164
Russ, Jim 108
Russell, Catherine vi
Russell, Marv vi, 4, 7-14, 78
Ryan, Buddy 90
Sanders, Barry 109
Sanders, 'Neon' Deion 112
Sanders, Norm vi
Sapp, Gerome 163-169
Schottenheimer, Marty 90
Schultheis, Bob 137
Sefcik, George 96
Sehorn, Jason 156
Sheddy, Tom 69
Shoults, Paul 96
Siegfried 121
Siegfried Family 121
Simon, Tim 78
Simpson, O.J. 95
Skyline High School 23
Smart Giving Cards 155, 156
Smith, Harrison 121
Smith, Irv 32, 57, 87, 88, 111-116, 120, 136
Smith, Nick 57, 88, 112
Snow, Jack 28
Sports World Ministries 39, 40, 41, 44
Spurrier, Steve 91, 171
St. Ritas High School 70
Stackhouse, Jerry 27
Stams, Frank 129
Stevens, Robby 69
Stokes, J.J. 115
Stroud, Cliff 175
Student-Athlete Everywhere!
Swann, Lynn 79

Tagliabue, Paul 115
Takazawa, Bob 72

Talbott, Robert 23
Taylor, Aaron 89, 119, 120, 137
Taylor, Bobby 27, 175
Tepper, Lou 174
Terrell, David 33
Terrell, Pat 124-133
Terrell Materials 125
Tice, Mike 105
TNNDN vii, 91
TNNDN Radio Network 91
Tobin, Vince 90
Townsend, Mike 189-198
Townsend, Willie 190, 191, 192, 193
Trust, Love, and Commitment 72

Usher 27

Vinatieri, Adam 65

Walker, Lee 174
Walsh, Steve 124, 128
Walters, Norby 18
Walton, Shane 164, 165
Wamphler, Jerry 96
Ward, Charlie 164, 176
Ward, Reggie 126, 127
Warner, Kurt 138
Warren, Earl 160
Washington, Katie 143
Watters, Ricky 88, 108, 119
West, Rod 41
Williams, Bob 100, 101
Williams, Brad 49
Williams, George 128
Williams, Vanessa 18
Witmer, John 108
Wooden, Shawn 32
Wynn, Renaldo 170-180

Yale 31
Yale Business School 31

Yonto, Joe 96
Young, Bryant 89, 113, 115, 175
Young, Steve 115
Youth For Christ 83

Zambrowski, Tony 94, 95
Zellars, Ray 89, 113
Zorich, Chris 88